Volume Nine

The Encyclopedia of

Photography

THE COMPLETE PHOTOGRAPHER:
The Comprehensive Guide and Reference for All Photographers

WILLARD D. MORGAN
General Editor

GREYSTONE PRESS/NEW YORK

Title Page Picture Credits:

Copal Company Limited

HANS BURST/*Zeiss Ikon Photo*

LOU BERNSTEIN

GEORGE L. HONEYCUTT/*Charlotte Observer and News*

The editors wish to express their appreciation for permission to use the color photographs in this volume to the following photographers and organizations:

GIULIO BRIANI / *Rollei-Werke*
L. FRIEDEL / *Leica Photo*
NORMAN ROTHSCHILD
HY PESKIN / *Sports Illustrated*

ERNST HAAS / *Magnum*

100 AVENUE OF THE AMERICAS

NEW YORK 13, NEW YORK

Cover and Book Designed by Harold Franklin

MANUFACTURED IN THE UNITED STATES OF AMERICA

Table of Contents — Volume Nine

FLOWER PHOTOGRAPHY

FREDERICK W. BREHM
Former Instructor, Photographic Technology, Rochester Institute of Technology, N. Y.

[Hints for lighting, background control, and flower arrangement are outlined here in an article which may serve to introduce you to a new and fascinating hobby.]

• *Also see: Botanical Photography; Copying and Close-up Photography; Garden Photography.*

FLOWER PHOTOGRAPHY CAN BE practiced in your backyard, in the woods, the fields, and in city parks. Wherever you live, there is a gamut of seasons, nearly every month producing interesting flower subjects. Every locality presents opportunities for flower studies.

The hobby of flower photography offers many different opportunities. For example, the garden enthusiast can photograph the evolution of various flowerings that occur from spring until fall. The study of individual varieties also holds many possibilities. The rose family, for instance, consists of many varieties, each one having distinctive characteristics. The application of color photography to roses alone will give a great degree of satisfaction to those who love both form and color.

Finally, nature lovers can find attractive material among the wild flowers, while the natural-science teacher who is interested in the biological nature of plant life can record structural detail and characteristics of growing things.

Today the world is picture-minded and the number of publications devoted to gardens and flower growing has greatly increased. The publishers of books, magazines, and catalogs are in the market for good flower pictures, both in black-and-white and in color. There are also opportunities for both the amateur and professional to write and illustrate descriptive articles that can be sold to trade and educational publications.

Figure 1. *Sidelighting was used to bring out the texture and shape of these wild roses.*

CHOOSING A SUBJECT

In early spring, the woodlands provide many photographic possibilities among the wild flowers, but the selection of those which are commonly known and easy to photograph should be considered first. It is comparatively easy to make some notations regarding the identity and history of each wild flower photographed. Simply carry a notebook. In time it will become a very valuable record. It is valuable practice to record, with each photograph made, the exposure as well as the botanical name of the flower. In public parks where flowers and shrubs are grown, the botanical name appears with the common name.

Intelligent planning is necessary for any venture. The successful photographer, in any branch of the business, visualizes a finished picture before beginning operations. To be more direct, the question arises, "What kind of picture do you intend to make?" Good pictures are not accidents but rather the result of careful planning. The four principal factors in flower photography are: lighting, composition or arrangement, film, and exposure. But before we go into these matters, a word or two about equipment.

CAMERAS AND LENSES

Since flowers are usually fairly small, it is necessary to have a camera which is capable of focusing quite close at short distances, and of framing the subject matter accurately at any distance. The ideal camera for this purpose, then, is the single-lens reflex, since it focuses directly through the taking lens with the image seen actual size on the groundglass. The better makes have available a great many useful accessories such as extension tubes or supplementary lenses for close-up work and built-in flash synchronization.

For the larger 2¼ format, there are the Hasselblad and Bronica cameras. For even larger film format, the Optika offers a variety of film sizes in the one unit, up to a 2¼ × 3¼ maximum. Those who wish to work with still larger film sizes will have to search the second-hand market for such cameras as the old revolving-back Auto Graflex, which was available in 3¼ × 4¼ and 4 × 5 sizes, and had a double-extension bellows.

Other types of cameras can of course be used, but not so easily. Simple 35 mm and roll-film cameras can be used with supplementary lenses and focal frames, but they are limited in the variety of work they can do. As an introduction to flower photography, you may want to use any camera you have. Afterward, you will find the single-lens reflex the best and most convenient.

LIGHTING

In all graphic illustration, the representation of form on a plane or flat surface is produced by an arrangement of light and dark. The appearance of the finished picture depends largely upon the way it is lighted. The procedure is not as difficult as it may seem. The subject must be considered in its relation to the light source, which in outdoor photography is the sun.

The angle of light is all-important and is determined by the position of the sun in the sky. What effect does the angle of light have upon the finished picture? When the sun is near the horizon, its rays are at a low angle and produce a side-light (Figure 1).

Sidelighting gives the effect of roundness or relief to vertical subjects. When the sun is directly overhead, it produces what is known as toplight (Figure 2), the effect of which is to cast shadows downward, which may or may not destroy the roundness that is required for good modeling.

Black-and-white pictures can be best taken in early morning before the sun has risen too high. The same angle of light can be secured in late afternoon, but in the early morning flowers are at their best.

A photograph taken when the sun is not shining brightly will appear without pronounced highlights or deep shadows. This type of lighting is useful in color photography and in the study of plant life where leaf formation, flower texture, and detail of plant structure are desired. As a rule, flat lighting is not so pleasing for black-and-white pictures as bright lighting, although there are exceptions.

Figures 3 and 4 are examples of satisfactory flat lighting in natural arrangements. If these pictures had been made in bright sunlight, the flowers would have appeared as a white mass without detail. The morning of a bright, hazy day is ideal for pictures of this kind. Regardless of the light intensities on a cloudy day, the direction of light is important and should be considered. Dramatic lighting in the arrangement of light and dark areas produces an attractive picture.

PHOTOGRAPHING CUT FLOWERS

It is good practice to experiment with cut flowers before trying to take outdoor pictures. When the light is coming from a low angle, place a flower upon a support, move around it, and note how the shadows change as you change your position. In general you will find that when the direction of light comes from over the shoulder, a satisfactory modeling will result.

It must be remembered that experience in reading light effects is the real foundation of successful photography. There is no definite rule as to the exact position of the flower with reference to the direction of the light. Begin by experimenting with simple lighting first. By observing the good flower pictures to be found in catalogs and garden publications, you will soon recognize the principles of lighting. Imitating these good examples will help you to develop a style of your own.

When making photographs of cut flowers, you have the advantage of placing them wherever it is convenient to operate. The experience gained in this preliminary practice will be helpful in later work. Place the surface upon which you intend to arrange the flowers outside where the light is unobstructed. Select a flower and determine the composition or pose that is most satisfactory to you. You will suddenly realize, when making portraits of flowers, that they have personality and expression. The pose may consist of a full front, a partial side view, or a close-up of only a portion of the blossom. A complete front view, as a rule, is not too satisfactory unless a detailed study is to be made of the flower structure. A partial side view has more pictorial possibilities.

The close-up study of a flower that does not include the entire blossom should not be attempted until the photographer has acquired a feeling for good composition. In addition to the position of the flower itself, its stem, leaves, and buds must be considered in regard to the composition. How much or how little to include is largely a question of balance, which must be determined before the picture is made.

Left: Figure 2. *Toplighting, in this instance, gives translucence to the petals and casts most of the swamp rose-mallow's leaves into shadow.*

Right: Figure 3. *An example of flat lighting on a bright, hazy day; the size and modeling of petals are pleasing. This photograph of the double peony was taken in the flower's natural setting.* (Photo: Minor White)

Figure 4. *It was necessary to select flat lighting for this view of a garden path in order to secure detail in the small, light-colored flowers.*

Arrange your flower so that the light gives the correct modeling, then make the exposure.

BACKGROUNDS

The background plays an important part in the over-all composition; its color, texture, distance from the subject, and the angle from which the light strikes it, all influence the effect of the picture. Usually white, gray, or black material will be best. These tones can be secured in both cardboard and woven fabric. If fabrics are selected they should be plain, without figures or interwoven designs.

Fabric backgrounds should be kept on rollers or carboard tubes about two inches in diameter to avoid wrinkles. They should never be folded. When used, they should be stretched smoothly upon a wooden framework or other support and fastened in place with thumbtacks.

Usually light-colored flowers are photographed with a dark ground, and dark-colored flowers with a light ground, the choice depending somewhat upon the purpose of the picture. Dead-black backgrounds help to dramatize well-lighted flower arrangements.

ARRANGEMENT

When the light comes from a comparatively low angle, the background frame can be so placed that the light strikes the edge but not the surface. A stepladder is a convenient support upon which to place the covered frame, since it can easily be turned to meet the change in the direction of light. The subject should be some distance from the background to avoid the feeling of being crowded. A white background may cause reflections that are objectionable if the subject is too close. As a rule, no reflections are required from the background as the subject should be in the sunlight.

If the flower is to be shown without a base, any method of support will do. Care must be exercised to see that the supporting device does not appear in the picture.

When a complete tabletop is meant to be shown, its cover or drape must be adjusted carefully to avoid wrinkles. The table color should be of a darker tone than the subject photographed, and unless desired, it should have no reflective surface.

POSING CUT FLOWERS

When flowers are posed in a vase that is not transparent, the vase can be filled with mud to hold the flower in the position wanted. Flowers with long stems are difficult to hold in position and require some time to arrange. Plastic or modeling clay also is a good medium for holding flowers. A number of flowers can be arranged in any formation desired, by placing each

Clusters of flowers, such as these daisies, can be photographed easily by using a single-lens reflex or rangefinder camera with a focal frame.

one in a separate ball of plastic or in pin holders.

When you use plastic or any other method to hold flowers in position out of water, you must work quickly, particularly with flowers that droop soon after they are cut. Every preparation should be made before the final posing. Sometimes the set-up is made with inferior flowers similar to those selected for the picture. The pose is arranged and studied, backgrounds are chosen, and the camera set up and roughly focused. When all is ready, the actual flowers are posed and the exposure is made.

USING REFLECTORS

Reflectors can be used to advantage when photographing both cut flowers and growing plants. An ideal reflector can be made of a piece of white cardboard about 14×18 inches with tin foil fastened on one side. This combination gives reflectors with two different reflecting powers. They should be very carefully used because misplaced reflection will spoil an effect. The proper use of reflectors is largely a matter of experience and practice.

Make one exposure and, after a print has been finished, inspect it carefully to decide whether or not the effect of the reflector is too great or insufficient. It is important to keep exact records of precisely what has been done in each test with respect to subject distance, lens stop, shutter speed, light strength, and finally the position of the reflector and which side was used. In this way, it will be possible to make changes intelligently; without records, the experiment becomes sheer guesswork.

GROWING FLOWERS

When photographing growing flowers, the general principles of lighting and the time of day selected for photographing should follow the general outline given for cut flowers. As the growing flower cannot be moved, the picture must be taken when the light is coming from the right direction.

Sometimes it is possible to make a slight change in the position of the growing flower in regard to lighting, or to improve its composition. Be careful that the change in arrangement does not make it look unnatural. A few pieces of string, narrow adhesive tape, some long pins, spring clothespins, and slender sticks painted green will be found helpful in the arrangement of growing flowers. Sometimes a very fine blossom may have unsuitable supporting foliage. The flower can be cut and fastened on a satisfactory support and, if carefully done, the change will not be noticeable.

When flowers are close to the ground, or when the foliage is a dark and compact growth, a reflector can be used to improve the lighting. It should be held close to the ground and the light reflected onto the darkest areas.

One of the difficulties in photographing growing plants is the presence of highlights or sun spots in the background which are not observed by the untrained eye until after the picture is taken. In order to avoid them, carefully observe the image on the groundglass; sometimes by turning the camera slightly they will disappear. It is also helpful to carry a large piece of black fabric which can be placed over objects in the background. There are times, in photographing shrubs, when the ground will be littered with fallen blossoms that will cause a very spotty appearance. By placing the black fabric on the ground, this undesirable effect can be avoided.

Success in flower photography depends upon observation, planning, and execution. A record of exposure time, light conditions, time of day, and other notes should be made when you take the picture. With this reference available, corrections can be made if it is necessary to take another photograph.

FILMS

For black-and-white photography, the most satisfactory material is a medium- to slow-speed panchromatic film. High speed is seldom necessary in this work, and the finer grain and better image sharpness of the slower films will be valuable if big enlargements are to be made.

Most flowers will be photographed in color. For 35 mm cameras, there is Kodachrome II, which has ample speed, exceedingly fine grain, and high resolution. Its color rendition is somewhat on the snappy side, though softer than the older Kodachrome. Kodachrome X has still higher speed. For those who desire softer rendition, Anscochrome will probably be preferred. These films all produce color slides for projection, though prints can be made from the transparencies.

If prints are the aim, Kodacolor film will be the best choice. It produces negatives which are used to make enlarged color prints. The brilliance and contrast of the image depends, to some extent, on exposure and processing. If the user is not doing his own processing, he may find it wise to try several different processors until he gets the results he desires. It is well to remember that transparencies also can be made from Kodacolor negatives, if projection slides are needed. These slides will have slightly more contrast than those made on color transparency film, but the difference probably will not be noticeable.

For larger cameras, Ektachrome roll and sheet films are available, and Anscochrome also is available in larger rolls and sheets. Kodacolor

Capturing both flowers and insects in natural settings is easier if flashbulb or electronic flash is used with sunlight. The haziness of the out-of-focus background compliments the subject.

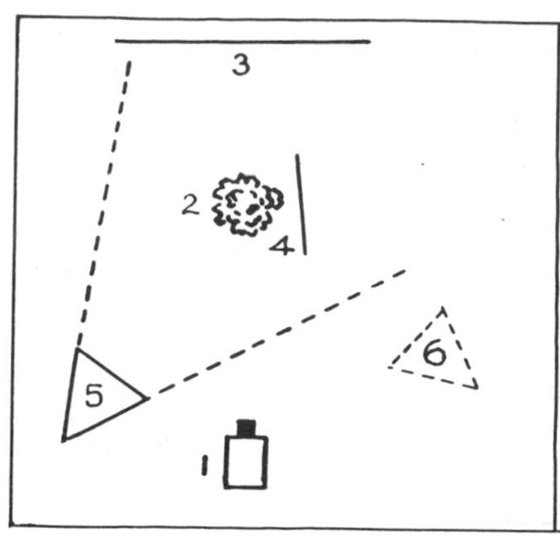

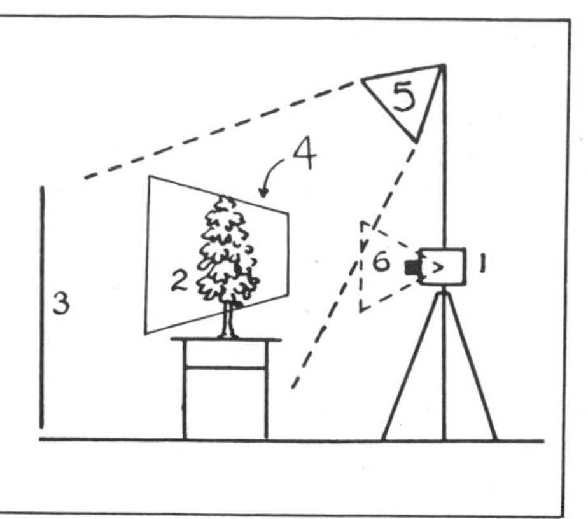

Above: Figure 5. *Indoor-lighting scheme showing side elevation (right) and floor plan (left) of a typical color set-up. 1—camera; 2—subject; 3—background; 4—reflector; 5—number 1 photoflood; 6—60-watt frosted bulb.*

Above: Figure 7. *The composition of this group of day lilies could be improved.*

film is available in larger rolls, and the similar Ektacolor film in sheets. The latter film is not universal in type as is the roll film; instead there is a "Type S" (short exposure) balanced for daylight or electronic flash, and a "Type L" (long exposure) balanced for tungsten light.

EXPOSURE

Because most flower photography is done close-up, exposure is critical and a good meter essential. The incident-light meter is preferred for this work. It is important in close-up work to take the added extension of the lens into account, or underexposure will result. A calculator for this purpose is supplied as part of the Kodak Master Photoguide.

With black-and-white film, improved rendition can usually be obtained with a light-yellow (K-2) or light-green (X-1) filter. These will improve the usual excessively dark rendition of green leaves and will prevent deep red flowers from appearing black in the final print. Heavier filters such as the orange (15) and red (A, No. 25) are seldom needed and should be used with caution. It would be wise to make a special "flower-filter test chart" using flowers as test objects.

For such a test collect a number of flowers of the following colors: red, blue, yellow, and white, with additional green foliage. It will be helpful to have a light and dark tone in each color. For example, a red and a pink rose, a light- and dark-blue delphinium.

Arrange the flowers in a fan shape so that one flower will not cast a shadow on another. They should be placed in a vase containing water and modeling clay, or wire can be used to keep them in position.

Make the test in early morning sunlight or on a bright hazy day. Follow the directions previously given for general lighting. Use a black background and have the direction of light coming from over your shoulder, a little to one side.

A low shooting position enabled the photographer to emphasize the rhododendrons in the foreground in contrast to the majestic peak on the northwest face of Mt. Hood, Oregon. (Photo: Irving B. Lincoln)

Figure 6. *With the addition of leaves, the composition of day lilies has been improved.*

The test can best be made by using a light meter in the manner directed by the manufacturer.

1) Make one exposure, without a filter, on each type of film you expect to use; 2) make one exposure with each filter, using the filter factor recommended for the particular film; 3) record carefully the exposure, filter, and filter factor used.

It is a good idea, while the set-up is still intact, to make a Kodacolor shot of the same group of flowers. After the black-and-white and color films are developed, mount prints of all the tests on a notebook page with the color print, so that you can see at a glance the colors of the flowers and how they reproduced in black-and-white through each of the selected filters.

Filters are seldom required with color films. However, there are conversion filters for the use of tungsten-type film in daylight. Also, there is a skylight filter, which is especially valuable when working on cloudy days or in the shade; the skylight filter reduces the over-all blue or purple cast which otherwise results under these conditions.

The same general rules apply to color photography of flowers, except that the lighting must be flatter than for black-and-white material. Black-and-white film has a much greater contrast range and will register detail in shadows, while color film will not. Proper direction of light and judicious use of reflectors will overcome this difficulty. The use of a good exposure meter is essential.

ARTIFICIAL LIGHT

To photograph flowers successfully in color and by artificial light, lights particularly adapted to the use of color film for indoor work are required. Regardless of the equipment used, the general lighting effect should correspond to outdoor conditions. The set-up should be well illuminated from front, sides, and top, in addition to spotlights for accentuating highlights.

In the set-up in Figure 5, the function of the 60-watt bulb is to project some light on the shadow side of the arrangement so that the detail in the shadows will not be lost. Just how much contrast there should be between the highlights and the shadows is largely a matter of taste. The general effect of lighting should be studied before the exposure is made. By moving both the photoflood and the modeling light, a wide variation of contrasts can be secured. Texture should be visible in the brightest highlight and detail in the deepest shadow.

Black and dark-gray backgrounds are well suited for this work. Generally speaking, light should not be reflected by the background. Note the position of backgrounds in the diagram.

Instead of incandescent lights, flashlamps or small electronic-flash

Right: Figure 8. *Plastic or florist's clay may be used to arrange cut flowers if the base is not to appear in the picture.*

A simple way to measure the proper distance from the lens to the flower is with a string which has knots indicating correct distances for sharp focus.

units can be used. The latter also will often be found useful in photographing outdoors in dark or shady places where additional light is needed. Since electronic-flash units have color quality practically the same as daylight, they will balance well for fill-in light on daylight-type color film. When used as a primary light source, speed of an electronic-flash unit is helpful whenever a flower is flexible or moving in the breeze.

COMPOSITION

The arrangement of flowers to be photographed requires a somewhat different method of posing than when they are arranged for decorative purposes only. This is especially true when the flowers are to be photographed in color. The primary object is to make an arrangement so that deep shadows do not exist. Just how deep a shadow can be without losing the detail of leaves and supporting stems depends on film, exposure, and development, and can be known only by experience. Follow the advice given previously regarding lighting and the keeping of records and prints for reference.

A common mistake is to include too many flowers in the arrangement. The greater the number of flowers, the more difficult it is to arrange them to avoid deep shadows. The real beauty of individual specimens can be more readily appreciated when the number in the arrangement is limited. Remember that flowers shown in a picture produce an entirely different sensation than when they are seen in the garden. For this reason we should think of flowers in terms of portraiture rather than *en masse*.

Symmetry and balance are two factors that enter into all pleasing composition. Symmetry is described as a harmonious relation of parts. True symmetry is the arrangement of parts with geometrical exactness, but in the arrangement of flowers there should be a freedom of placement that embodies the general idea of symmetry without resorting to mechanical accuracy.

For example, in Figure 6 the three blossoms are symmetrically arranged and yet the spacing is somewhat irregular. The general outline of composition represents a vertical triangle. In the lower left hand corner of Figure 7 there is a blank space which gives the impression of imbalance. In Figure 6 a leaf has been placed in a natural position to fill the blank space and supply the necessary balance.

Avoid straight verticals as much as possible, particularly in the center of the arrangement. Straight-stemmed flowers may be curved by applying slight pressure; the iris in Figure 8 illustrates this point. The slightly curved leaf at the left side is graceful and balances the arrangement. By combining naturally curved branches and leaves with flowers having straight stems, a more satisfactory arrangement will be made.

FLUOROGRAPHY

In normal X-ray photography (radiography), the X-rays or Roentgen rays pass through the object being examined and strike the special X-ray photographic emulsion directly. This means of photographing body or machinery structures is perhaps most familiar to persons who have had their teeth X-rayed. (See *Radiography.*) Fluorography, on the other hand, uses a regular camera to photograph the visible image of the X-ray as it is seen on a fluorescent viewing screen.

Fluorography is chiefly concerned with photographing the fluorescent image (set up by X-rays) of medical or industrial subjects. However, it also applies to the photography of the television receiving screen and the photography of cathode-ray oscillograph patterns. Scientists have been interested in photographing the fluorescent-screen image since 1896, at which time a means of making indirect radiographic motion pictures was described.

With fluorography, the use of 35 mm film is possible, whereas in regular X-ray photography where no optical system is used, the film has to be life-size or slightly larger. The large radiograms are more detailed and therefore better suited to minute diagnosis, while fluorograms are valuable for diagnosis which requires less detail, such as mass pulmonary examinations.

The substantial savings involved in the use of 35 mm film has made possible free or nominal-cost chest X-ray service. Using the 14×17 film otherwise needed for a chest X-ray would make the cost of such a project prohibitive.

A number of special films are available for fluorographic work. Depending on the type of fluorescent screen used, the film may be either entirely blue-sensitive, or blue- and green-sensitive. Kodak supplies its Photoflure film in both sensitivities. In general, the exposure required for the green-sensitive film and a green-fluorescent screen will be about half that required for a blue screen and blue-sensitive film.

To prevent fogging, X-rays must be prevented from passing beyond the fluorescent screen. This is done with commercial equipment by covering the fluorescent screen with a sheet of lead glass on the camera side. In this way light passes freely through the glass, while the X-rays are stopped.

Motion pictures of the fluorescent screen, showing the X-ray of a living person with parts in motion, have obvious educational and clinical value. However, the short exposures required by a movie camera running at 16 or 24 frames per second mean that an exceedingly powerful X-ray source is required, with a resultant danger to the patient from radiation exposure. Attempts to reduce this danger have resulted in the design of such special high-speed lenses as the Kodak Fluro-Ektar, *f*/0.7, and others. Kodak supplies a high-speed green-sensitive film to be used with this lens; it is known as Kodak Cineflure film and is available in 16 mm and 35 mm.

Another approach is to use electronic means to brighten the screen image to be photographed. This involves using an electronic-image tube, such as the image-orthicon, and viewing the image through a closed television circuit. With this method the film is exposed from the receiver screen of the television system. Since the image-orthicon is far more sensitive than the fastest film available, it reduces the X-ray dosage considerably. Other methods suggested include the use of a light amplifier and the combination of a photoconductor with an electroluminescent layer.

Another approach to the reduction of exposure is to make some arrangement to shut off the X-ray tube during the shutter-closed part of the movie-camera cycle. A special 35 mm Cine-Fluorographic camera developed by Photomechanisms, Inc., is designed to do just that. This camera has a switching device connected to the X-ray equipment so that the tube is triggered only when the camera shutter is open. The system has the practical effect of cutting the X-ray emission precisely in half.

The photographer should by now need no warning as to the danger inherent in working with X-ray equipment. All such equipment must be well shielded at all times to prevent radiation from reaching the camera operator or his subject. Random tests on actual patients must never be performed, and some sort of "dummy" should be placed in the patient's position while setting up or checking exposure.

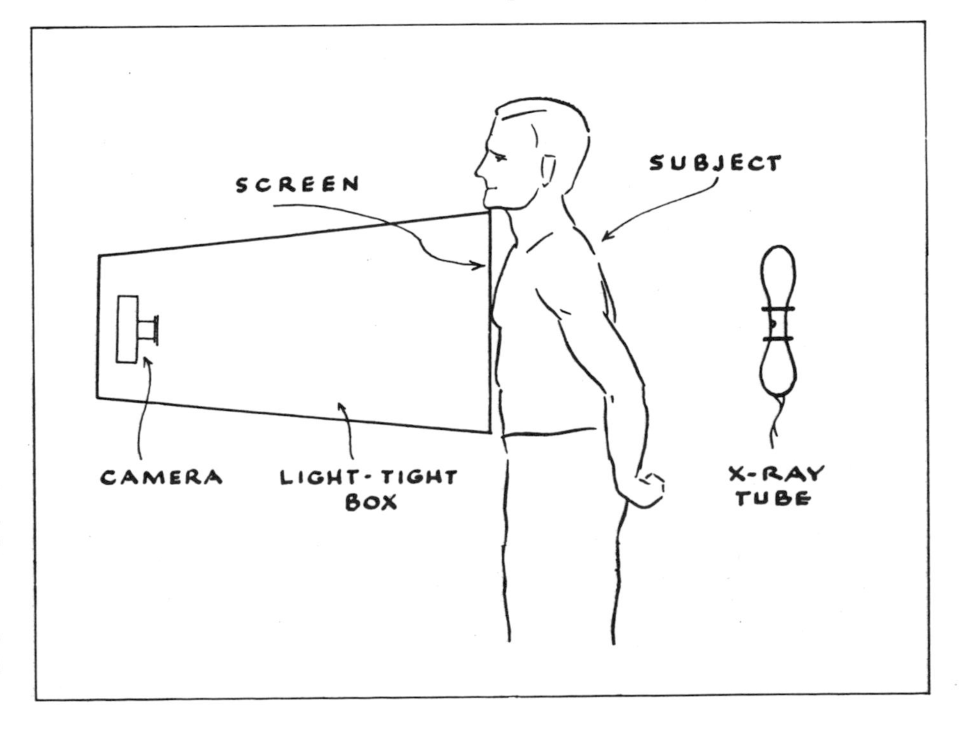

This diagram shows the general position of the camera, subject, screen, and X-ray tube. (Lloyd E. Varden / Journal of Laboratory and Clinical Medicine)

F-NUMBER SYSTEM

E. L. JONES
Writer, Editor, Former Publisher of "Aeronautics"

[To many novice photographers the *f*-number system is a mystery. Here is a clear and thorough explanation of the system and the relationship between one *f*-number and another.]

• *Also see: Exposure; Lenses.*

HOW MUCH FASTER IS *f*/2.5 THAN *f*/4.5? To what new shutter speed must one change from $^1/_{100}$ of a second to allow for a 2.4× filter? Or, to what larger stop must one change for the same filter, without changing shutter speed?

The answers seem obvious when worked out, but mathematical processes at the moment of exposure are confusing and time consuming for the beginner. Too few are familiar with the difference made by a stop or two. Here is an attempt to aid the bewildered photographer and also to clarify material for the more advanced worker.

F-NUMBER DEFINED

The *f*-number indicates the dimensional relationship of the diameter of the lens (or stop or aperture) to its distance from the film when focused at infinity (focal length). Put another way, the *f*-number (relative aperture) =

$$\frac{\text{f (focal length)}}{\text{d (diameter)}}$$

A one-inch diameter lens (stop) one inch from the film (when focused at infinity) would be *f*/1. The same at two inches would be *f*/2; at three inches, *f*/3, and so on. The diameter of any lens (aperture or stop) divided into the distance from the film (focal length) furnishes the *f*-number, as given in the formula above.

These *f*-numbers are obtained when the focus is at infinity, of course. If a tube is inserted, moving the lens further away, as when photographing an object close-up, then the focal length changes according to the foregoing formula and a larger stop is indicated. (See article on *Extension Tubes and Bellows.)*

AREAS COMPARED

The lower the *f*-number, the greater the diameter of the lens or stop, and conversely. The area of the lens decreases rapidly with the increase in the numerical value of the *f*-number. For instance, the light reaching the film through a one-inch lens at two inches is but one fourth that of the same lens at the one-inch distance; at four inches it is but $^1/_{16}$ that at one inch. Increasing the distance between film and lens gives the same effect as decreasing the lens diameter of the camera for a given focal length.

By squaring any two *f*-numbers (multiplying each by itself) and dividing one into the other, one obtains a measure of their relative speeds (light-entrance ability). A one-inch diameter squared is one. A half-inch (.5 inch) stop squared is .25 inch or ¼ square inch. Obviously, at the same focal length, the one-inch diameter lens is four times faster than the half-inch lens.

The first vertical column of Table 1 shows the squares of the commonly used *f*-numbers given in the second column. The upper horizontal column also gives the squares of the same *f*-numbers arranged in the second horizontal line from the top. By dividing the square of one *f*-number into the square of another *f*-number, one immediately finds the relationships of their respective areas.

Example: *f*/1.9 is 5.61 times faster than *f*/4.5 because $1.9^2 = 3.61$, while $4.5^2 = 20.25$, and

$$\frac{20.25}{3.61} = 5.61$$

VARYING THE SPEED

To obtain proper exposure, the light meter is consulted. It shows various combinations of shutter speeds and of apertures or stops for the same correct exposure, according to the film being used. One selects his stop and shutter speed,

Figure 1. *This table may be used to find the relative value of two* f-*numbers. Given one shutter speed, to find the equivalent exposure for any filter factor, for instance, find the indicated unfiltered stop in the second vertical column of* f-*numbers. Follow across horizontally to the right to the nearest figure to the filter factor. The* f-*number at the top of that column is the new and correct aperture with the filter. Example: Assume* f/11 *is the indicated stop, and the filter factor is 5. Find* f/11 *in the second vertical column and follow the line until 5.97 and 3.8 are found (the nearest figures to the factor of 5). Following these to the top* f-*numbers, we find* f/4.5 *and* f/5.6. *The new stop is about halfway between, or* f/5.

Squares of F-Numbers →		1.69	1.96	2.25	3.61	4	6.25	12.25	16	20.25	31.36	39.69	64	121	256	484	1024	2025
F-Numbers → Squares ↓	F-Numbers ↓	1.3	1.4	1.5	1.9	2	2.5	3.5	4	4.5	5.6	6.3	8	11	16	22	32	45
1.96	1.4	1.16	1															
2.25	1.5	1.33	1.14	1														
3.61	1.9	2.13	1.84	1.6	1													
4	2	2.36	2.04	1.77	1.11	1												
6.25	2.5	3.70	3.19	2.77	1.73	1.56	1											
12.25	3.5	7.25	6.25	5.44	3.4	3.06	1.96	1										
16	4	9.46	8.15	7.1	4.44	4	2.56	1.3	1									
20.25	4.5	12	10.3	9	5.61	5.06	3.24	1.65	1.26	1								
31.36	5.6	18.5	15.9	13.93	8.7	7.84	5	2.56	1.96	1.54	1							
39.69	6.3	23.4	20.1	17.6	10.9	9.92	6.35	3.24	2.48	1.96	1.26	1						
64	8	38	32.6	28.4	17.7	16	10.2	5.22	4	3.16	2	1.6	1					
121	11	71.6	61.7	53.8	33.5	30	19.3	9.87	7.56	5.97	3.8	3	1.89	1				
256	16	151	130	114	71	64	41	21	16	13	8	6.4	4	2.1	1			
484	22	286	246	215	134	121	77	39	30	24	15	12	7.5	4	1.89	1		
1024	32	606	522	450	283	256	163	83	64	50	32	25	16	9	4	2	1	
2025	45	1198	1033	900	561	506	324	165	126	100	64	50	32	17	8	4	2	1

say $^1/_{50}$. Then, what would be the new shutter speed for the same aperture with a 2.3× filter (having a factor of 2.3)? By simple arithmetic it is 2.3/50 of a second. Dividing 2.3 into 50 we have 22. The nearest speed to $^1/_{22}$ on most cameras is $^1/_{25}$.

Suppose the speed originally was $^1/_{100}$ of a second and the filter factor seven. The new time with the filter is $^7/_{100}$ of a second. Seven into 100 goes 14 times, so the nearest to $^1/_{14}$ of a second will be the new exposure time.

VARYING THE APERTURE

If we are photographing moving objects, we must determine a minimum shutter speed, perhaps $^1/_{100}$ of a second. We can vary the aperture and obtain the same increase in light value accomplished otherwise by slowing the shutter speed.

Customary advice is to use "one stop larger" or "two stops larger," and so on. A stop larger, it must be remembered, is one with a smaller number. On some lenses the maximum aperture is not, however, a full stop larger than the next marked *f*/stop; *f*/3.5, for instance, lies between *f*/4 and *f*/2.8 and represents only about one half stop increase in exposure over *f*/4. Likewise, *f*/1.8 is only about one third of a stop faster than *f*/2, the next larger stop after *f*/2 being *f*/1.4.

FILTER FACTORS

Using the table in Figure 1, which gives filter factors, one might take a reading or estimate the normal exposure at, say, *f*/11 for some certain shutter speed, determined by the speed of the object perhaps, and considering the light condition. We find *f*/11 in the second vertical column. The filter factor is, say, seven. Following horizontally along to the right from the *f*/11 in the second vertical column, we find that *f*/4 will give 7.56 times the light

$$\left(\frac{11^2}{4^2} = 7.56\right)$$

and that *f*/4.5 will admit 5.97 times the light. The proper aperture for this filter lies between *f*/4 and *f*/4.5. This method may be followed for all filter factors.

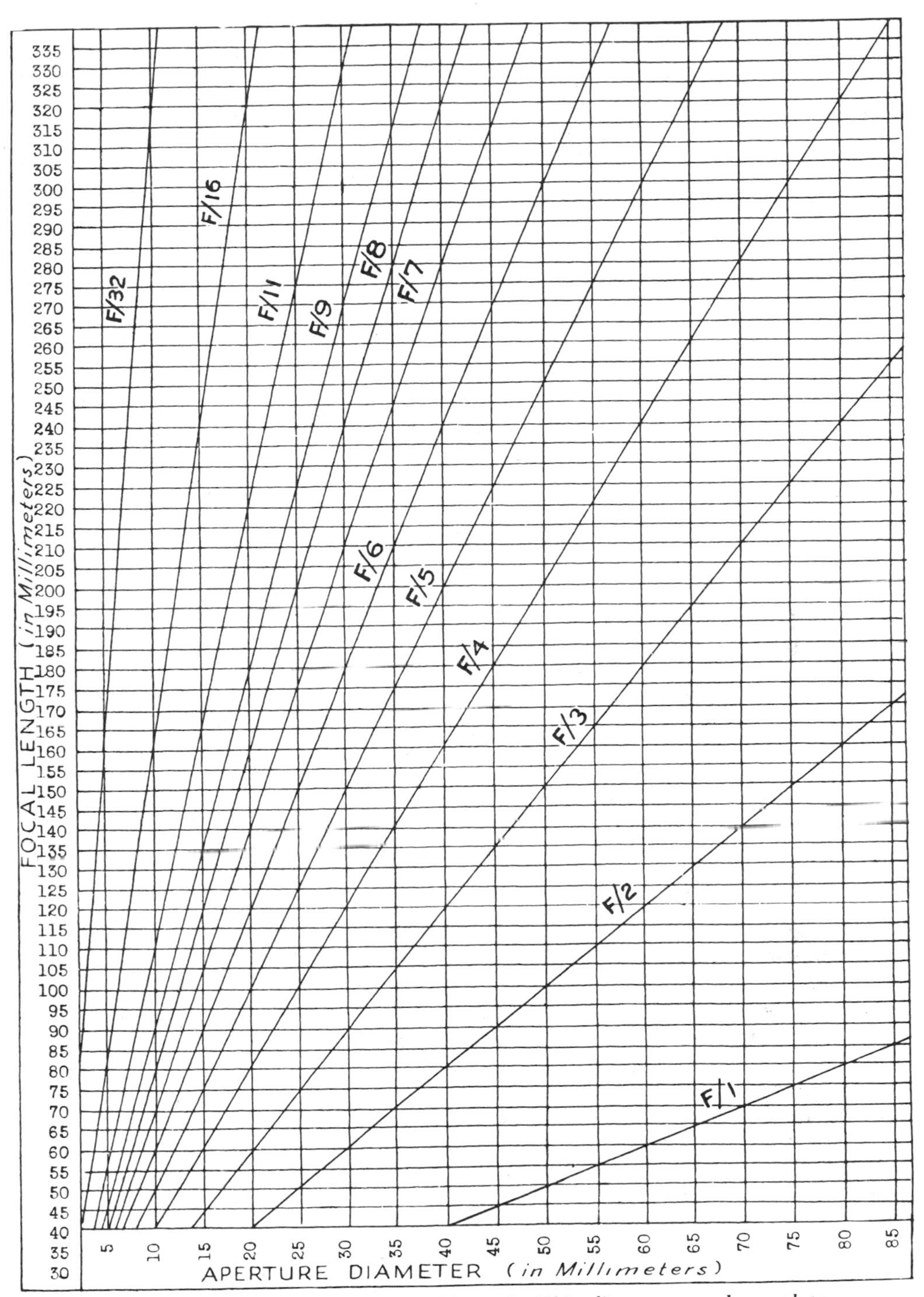

Figure 2. *This diagram may be used to compute the new* f-number *when employing the bellows extension or tube.*

EMULSION SPEEDS

Although emulsion speeds are usually found by setting the meter's calculator dial, the system that is used with filter factors also applies to them. Sometimes we are working with two cameras, one loaded with black-and-white, the other with color film, and we wish to determine the exposure for both with a single meter setting.

Suppose we are using a 35 mm camera loaded with Kodachrome II film having an ASA rating of 25, and a sheet-film camera loaded with Super Panchro Press Type B film rated at ASA 250. We can see at a glance that the black-and-white film is ten times faster then the color film. Assuming we are using the same shutter speed on both cameras, the table will show, for example, that if the large camera is set to *f*/11, the 35 mm camera requires a setting at *f*/3.5 to give correct exposure on the slower color film.

EFFECTIVE APERTURE

As the amateur progresses, he may want to use tubes or bellows for close-ups. Immediately the focal distance is changed, and what was $f/4$ may now be $f/5$ and more, according to the length of the tube inserted or the additional extension of the bellows. The new focal length must be measured, and the new f-number determined according to the formula given previously, so that correct exposure may be made under the changed condition. Or, the graph (Figure 1) may be used with equal facility for calculating the new f-values.

Figure 2 will be found useful in obtaining the new f-number for any new focal length. For example, take a three-inch lens (75mm), fully open at $f/3$. If the horizontal line running from 75mm in the left-hand vertical column is followed across, it will hit the curve for $f/3$ at exactly the intersection of the 25mm-diameter vertical line. The horizontal lines represent focal lengths and the vertical lines represent aperture diameters in millimeters. Inches and fractions or decimals could be used as well.

Suppose this same $f/3$ lens of 75mm normal focal length is mounted at the end of an extension tube, or the bellows is equally extended until the new focal distance is 100mm. To find the new f-number, it is necessary to read up the 25mm vertical line only from the bottom to the intersection with the 100mm line. There the $f/4$ curve is met and $f/4$ is the new f-value. (100 divided by $25 = f/4$.) The same procedure may be followed for any other lens.

The reader may make his own chart applying to his own camera and lenses—enlarging the scale, if desired, for greater legibility. Any graph paper may be used. Along the bottom at regular intervals mark units of diameters up to the diameter of the largest lens in stock. Up the left side mark similar units of focal length up to the maximum possible bellows extension or over-all tube length. Draw vertical and horizontal lines through all these points.

From zero, in the lower left-hand corner, draw a "curve" (line) for each lens to the intersection of the vertical and horizontal lines representing the normal diameter and focal length of each lens respectively. Then mark these curves according to the lens speed indicated on the lens or calculated.

Additional curves should then be drawn from zero to all intersections of vertical lines representing actual diameters of the lenses on hand, with all horizontal lines representing the new focal lengths given each lens by bellows extension or by tubes. Dividing these known diameters on the bottom scale will give the f-number for each of these additional curves.

□

FOCAL LENGTH

The two main factors when considering the characteristics of a lens are its focal length and relative aperture. The first governs its image size, the second, its speed. Thus a lens is usually referred to in this manner: 107mm Kodak Ektar $f/3.7$. The figures indicate the focal length, followed by the maker, the type of lens, and its maximum relative aperture.

For normal photography the focal length of a lens should be about equal to the diagonal of the film size in use. For a given film size, the longer the focal length, the greater the magnification. Thus, a four-inch lens will form an image twice as large as the same object's image taken at the same distance by a two-inch lens. In close-ups the increase in magnification is not directly proportional to the focal length, however.

Today the focal lengths of most lenses are marked on the barrel or rim, or the information can be obtained from the manufacturer. However, it is often necessary to know the exact focal length of a lens, or of lens combinations. This information is essential, for instance, in determining the f-number, hyperfocal distance, or depth of field of a lens at a certain diaphragm opening.

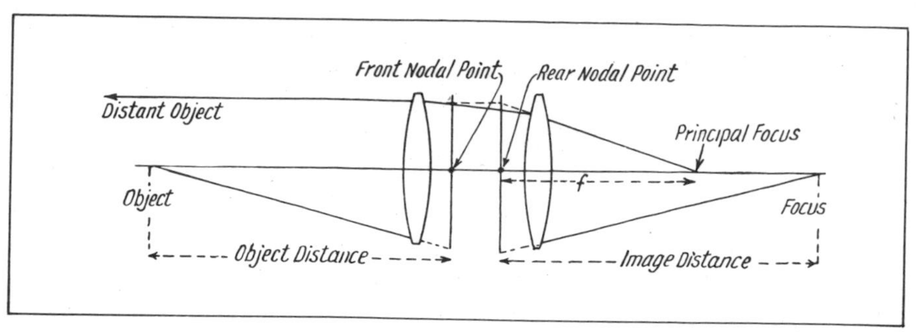

Figure 1. *The focal length (f) is shown as the distance between the principal focus and the rear nodal point or node of emergence.*

FOCAL LENGTH DEFINED

The focal length of a lens has often been broadly defined as the distance from lens to film when the lens is focused at infinity. Properly speaking, the definition is much more precise than that.

The focus of a lens is the point on the optical axis behind the lens at which a sharp image point is formed of an object point before the lens on the optical axis. The principal focus is this point when the object is at a great distance or infinity. With a thin and simple lens, the principal focal length is the distance from the principal focus to the center of the lens. But with any other lens the point of measurement is not the center, but what is known as the node or nodal point of emergence.

There are two nodal points—the node of admission and the node of emergence. A single ray which strikes a lens obliquely is bent or refracted, but emerges in a line parallel to the line followed at the point of entry. If these two parallel lines are continued to the lens axis, they meet at the nodal points—the node of emergence being nearer the image.

The principal focal length of a lens is therefore finally defined as the distance along the lens axis between the point of principal focus and the node of emergence. (Figure 1.)

Each lens has a front and a rear focal length since light can pass through the lens in either direction.

If these lengths are measured in strict accordance with the definition given above (from the respective nodal points), they have equal values and, therefore, this length is called "the equivalent focal length of the lens."

The equivalent focal length may differ considerably from the actual distance between the rear surface of the lens and the principal focus, because it depends upon the location of the nodal points in regard to front and rear surfaces of the lens. In a telephoto lens, the nodal points lie in front of the lens so that the equivalent focal length is much longer than the distance from the lens to the film. In most ordinary lenses, however, the nodal point of emergence lies between the front and rear surface.

MEASURING FOCAL LENGTH

For a simple, thin lens, or for a lens whose nodal points are known, the following formula can be used:

$$\frac{1}{u}+\frac{1}{v}=\frac{1}{f}$$

u = distance from object to lens (measured to node of admission on complex lenses)

v = distance from lens to image (measured from node of emergence on complex lenses)

f = focal length

When the object is at infinity, v = f in a simple lens. In most cases, however, lenses are of a complex structure and the nodal points are not usually known. In this case, focus a foot rule on the groundglass and measure the image (if there is no groundglass, expose a negative and measure the image). Then move the camera closer and focus (or expose) again, measuring the image and also the exact object distance. Then:

$$f=\frac{v_2-v_1}{r_2-r_1}$$

v_1 = smaller object distance

v_2 = larger object distance

r_1 = ratio of reduction at v_1

r_2 = ratio of reduction at v_2

For example, a 12-inch ruler is placed upright in a certain position and photographed. Its position is carefully marked, and the image size is measured and found to be ½ inch. The ratio of reduction (r_2) is $12/(\frac{1}{2})=24$. Now we move the ruler closer to the lens, say 36 inches nearer. This, then, gives us the distance $v_2-v_1=36$ inches. The ruler is again photographed, and its image this time is $1^1/_3$ inches. The ratio of reduction (r_1) is $12/(1^1/_3)=9$. Now from the formula above:

$$f=\frac{36}{24-9}=\frac{36}{15}=2.4 \text{ inches.}$$

A simple geometrical method of measuring the focal length is to stand the camera on a piece of paper and turn it until the image of a very distant object is at one edge of the groundglass. Draw a pencil line, A, along the base of the camera (or perpendicular to the film plane at that point). Rotate the camera until the same object is at the other edge and mark the line B. Then extend the lines until they intersect at C, making a triangle with the groundglass plane D. The line *f* will then be the focal length. (Figure 2.)

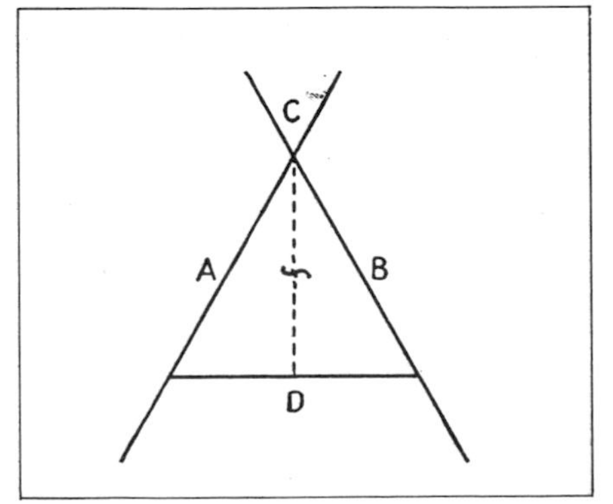

Figure 2. *The geometrical method of measuring the focal length, sometimes known as Grubb's method.*

For cameras with which a 1:1 reduction is possible, to find the focal length focus with groundglass on a distant object and mark the lens or pointer position on the focusing bed. Focus at a near object to get a sharp image the same size as the object (1:1) and mark the pointer again. The distance between the two marks is the focal length.

Also see: Depth of Field and Hyperfocal Distance; F-number (f-stop) System; Lenses and Their Characteristics; Lens Optics and Types.

With the twin-lens reflex, the focusing mechanisms of both lenses are connected together for simultaneous focus.

FOCUSING

There are two basic ways of focusing. One is to change the distance between film and lens; the other is to adjust the focal length of the lens itself.

In the first method, some means is provided for moving either the lens or the film, depending on the construction of the camera and the focal length of the lens. Large cameras generally have long focal-length lenses that require considerable movement in focusing. This movement is accommodated by a collapsible light-tight bellows which expands or contracts as the lens moves along its track. To further facilitate focusing with the view camera, both the lens board and the film back are movable in most of the larger models.

With the 35 mm camera the lens is mounted inside a threaded metal tube; the necessary in-and-out movement for focusing is provided by rotating the lens within the limits of the mount. The Stereo-Realist camera is one special case where neither bellows nor lens threads are used. Instead, the internal film carrier is moved to and from the lens for focusing.

The second method of focusing, changing the focal length of the lens itself, is used in many roll-film cameras. The lens is designed so that moving its front element away from the rear one changes the focal length sufficiently for focusing. Such a lens must be specially designed to maintain its corrections at all lens-element separations. This method cannot be applied to those lens designs in which the interelement spacing is an essential part of the correction formula.

GROUNDGLASS FOCUSING

A basic method of focusing, and one that was used for many years, consisted of substituting a screen of finely ground glass for the film. First the image was visually focused on the screen; then the screen was removed and replaced by the film or plate holder and the exposure made.

Naturally this was a slow working procedure. The first improvement came with the reflex camera, in which the groundglass was placed at the top of the camera, and the image reflected to it by a mirror which swung out of the way when the shutter was tripped.

A variation, to avoid the loss of the visual image at the instant of exposure, is found in the twin-lens reflex. The twin-lens reflex is something like two identical cameras, one on top of the other, with the upper camera used for focusing and viewing and the lower one for taking the picture. The focusing mechanisms of both lenses are connected; the two lenses are usually mounted on one lens board so that they focus simultaneously.

The modern single-lens reflexes now provide these basic improvements over the earlier types:

1. The lens diaphragm on most newer models has a presetting device which permits the diaphragm to remain wide open for focusing. The diaphragm is automatically stopped down to the previously selected aperture just before the exposure is made.

2. The blocking-out of the image at the moment of exposure is overcome in the newer cameras by an "instant-return mirror," which snaps out of the way just long enough for the exposure, returning immediately afterward to the viewing position.

3. The early reflex cameras had to be used at a low position, with the image viewed by the photographer looking down into the hood. In addition, the mirror which reflected the image to the groundglass reversed the picture left to right. Both difficulties have been overcome by the development of the "pentaprism" hood. This hood reflects the image straight back to the eye, so the camera can be used at eye level with the image appearing in its normal position.

RANGEFINDER FOCUSING

The mirror rangefinder, which measures distances by tilting one mirror until the image seen in it coincides with the image in a stationary mirror, is far from new. It has had military use for many years. As a photographic instrument, it was supplied as an accessory with the first Leica (Model A). Here the distance was first measured with the rangefinder; then the lens-focusing scale was set to the measured distance.

In the later Model D Leica, the rangefinder was built into the camera body and connected directly to the lens-focusing mount so that when the images in the rangefinder coincided, the lens was correctly set for that subject distance.

By ingenious lens-barrel design, the Leica was able to accept lenses of different focal lengths up to 135mm. Correct focusing for different focal lengths has been achieved by compound threading of the lens-focusing mounts, so that the back edge of the mount, which operated the rangefinder, moves at the same rate regardless of the total movement of the lens itself. In the longer-focus lenses, this system was not used. Instead the back edge of the lens barrel itself was cut to a spiral shape. This accomplished the correct rangefinder movement which had to be much less than the actual movement of the lens barrel.

Modern single-lens reflexes provide an instant-return mirror that springs back to position immediately after the exposure is made with only a momentary blackout of the image.

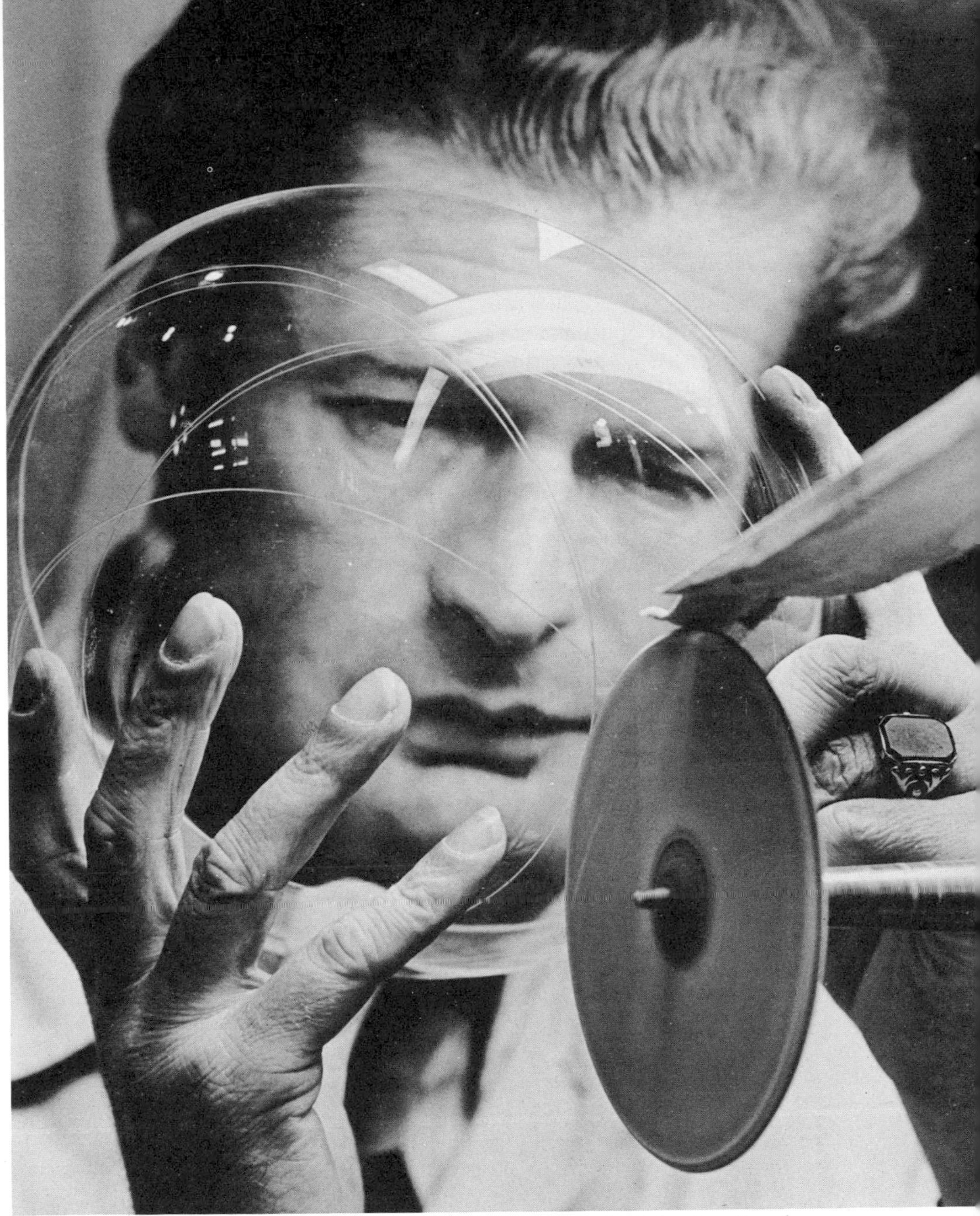

Precise focusing to fit the subject matter can enhance the pictorial qualities of almost any photo. The sharply focused hands and equipment frame the concentrating face of this craftsman. If the face were also in sharp focus, the photo would appear overcrowded with images. The photo was taken with a Leica III F, 135mm Hektor f/4.5 lens, exposed one half of a second at f/8. (Photo: Herman Laitenberger)

Some of the newer single-lens reflexes provide rangefinder focusing by a different system. This system consists of two prisms cemented to the groundglass with their sloping surfaces facing in opposite directions. With this device, the image will appear split unless it is in focus.

SCALE FOCUSING

Simple cameras, especially those with lenses of small aperture, are often provided with no means of focusing except a scale which is a pointer moving over a range of distances. The photographer must either measure or estimate the distance from the lens to the subject and then set the pointer at that distance.

The success of the method, particularly with simple movie cameras, is attributable to the fact that most lenses, especially those of short focal length or small aperture, have ample depth of field to cover minor errors in focusing.

Professional motion-picture photographers often prefer to focus by direct measurement when the image appears quite sharp over a large range. Here, to assure maximum sharpness, the camera assistant measures the distance from camera to subject and sets the lens scale accordingly; the groundglass in the camera is used only for composition.

One problem when using focusing scales is knowing the points from which to measure. The expression "lens-to-subject" is vague—it may mean from the front of the lens or it may mean from the diaphragm plane. Current standards call for calibrating lens-focusing scales in the distance from film plane to subject. Many cameras have a mark at the exact position of the film plane, and it is to be assumed that the focusing scale is calibrated accordingly. Sometimes the focusing scale is marked "from film" or "feet from film" to indicate that it is calibrated from the film plane and not from the lens itself.

FOCUSING ATTACHMENTS

Special attachments are sometimes used for focusing. The Leica formerly supplied a device, with the code name NOOKY, which had a small extension for focusing at closer-than-normal ranges. It also had an auxiliary prism to be placed in front of the rangefinder windows and viewfinder, so that the rangefinder operated correctly at the closer distance, and the viewfinder was corrected for parallax. The new Dual-Range Summicron lens works on the same principle for its close range.

A number of afocal attachments are available to transform normal lenses into wide-angle or telephoto lenses. In all cases these attachments are really small telescopes of zero focus. They do not change the focal length of the camera lens; instead they vary the magnification of the image, which produces the same effect. However, they are usually afocal only at infinity.

Because these attachments completely upset the focusing scale of the lens at close ranges, they usually have an auxiliary focusing table from which the correct focus may be derived.

FOG

JOHN N. HARMAN, JR.

[One of a negative's or print's most serious defects is fog, whether it appears as a blatant streak or a light veil. Analyzed here are light fog, chemical fog, and fog from such other causes as X-rays and static electricity. The photographer is told how to detect and prevent defects due to fog.]

• *Also see: Defects in Negatives and Prints.*

This print from a film-pack negative illustrates one type of fog resulting from careless insertion of the pack-adapter slide while the camera is in bright light. Fog of this sort is frequently less intense and more localized. Similar effects may result from uneven withdrawal of film-pack tabs.

FOG, IN THE PHOTOGRAPHIC SENSE, can be described as unintentional exposure of a photographic emulsion to light or some other activating agent so that parts of the sensitive layer, unrelated to the desired image, are rendered developable. The visible evidence of fog is an easily recognizable deposit of silver which may vary in density from light gray to heavy black, depending upon the extent of the fogging action. These silver deposits, which appear in the developed negative or print, are sometimes restricted to isolated areas, but in other instances they are evenly distributed in an unbroken veil of gray. The appearance and distribution of fog is related to its method of formation and will usually indicate the cause.

Photographers are prone to accept a small amount of fog as a natural condition of sensitized photographic materials and to become alarmed only when strong evidences of local or general fog are visible. A fog density of 0.2, for example, is seldom serious enough to cause difficulty. There is no reason for tolerating greater amounts of fog, for an understanding of the possible causes of fog, coupled with an analysis of the working conditions, will in most cases quickly indicate the source of trouble.

Local fog is readily noticed by its spots or streaks, but general fog, particularly when it causes only a slight degrading of highlights or over-all flatness, often escapes casual inspection.

Frequently the shadow portions of negatives are robbed of detail and flattened in their tonal separations by chemical fog due to overdevelopment. Although appearing as a general veil of silver deposited throughout the negative, chemical fog is more pronounced in thinner sections of the negative than in denser parts where the release of bromide during development has a restraining effect upon fog densities. Such negatives are incapable of producing good prints, even by elaborate printing procedures, for the presence of more fog in shadow densities than in highlight densities makes it virtually impossible to obtain satisfactory contrast.

There are many factors and conditions which can contribute to the occurrence of fog: light fog resulting from the direct action of light; chemical fog formed by improper development or by reaction or contact with some chemical or fogging agent; fog from other miscellaneous causes, such as pressure marks, static, X-rays, deterioration, and similar conditions.

CAMERA DEFECTS

One of the common sources of light fog is light leakage in the camera. Tiny pinholes in the bellows, imperfect joints between bellows and frame, and sometimes inadequate covering of the lens by the shutter in its closed position admit unwanted light to the photographic emulsion. Such fog normally occurs only within the picture area of the negative, while the margins remain clear.

When the openings admitting light are small and in a suitable position, they can act as lenses, leaving sharply defined registrations on the film of any point-light sources in the field of view. If the fogging action has occurred while the camera was stationary, the heavier fog deposits may appear as points or as straight lines. If fogging happened during camera movement, wavy lines may result.

Sheet-film holders or film-pack adapters get rough treatment from some photographers and, with age, have a tendency to leak light. For instance, there is a narrow rib along the handle end of the holder which fits a groove in the camera back for trapping light. If the rib is chipped, there is a good chance of a light leak at this point.

When the film-holder slide is pulled out for an exposure, the slot through which it enters is automatically closed by a light trap. This usually consists of a series of springs covered with velvet, but sometimes is a thin strip of rubber or plastic. It is important, when reinserting the slide after an exposure, to push it straight in. If the corner of the holder is first inserted into the slot, it will open the light trap and light will leak in and fog the film.

Film packs are, at best, only moderately light-tight and should be put into the adapter in relatively subdued light. In addition, care should be taken never to press on the front of the pack, either before or after use. The pressure pushes back the safety cover and light leaks around its edges. Film packs should be handled as little as possible and only by the edges.

Occasionally fog is produced by light leaking past a loose, broken, or torn inspection window in the back of a roll-film camera. The transparent material in such windows must be in perfect condition or sufficient light may pass through it and, scattered by internal reflection, reach the film surface. This type of fog is usually indicated by a local patch of dense silver, occurring in each negative in a position corresponding to the location of the viewing window.

CARELESS LOADING

Care must be taken in loading roll films into hand cameras to prevent excessive amounts of the protective paper leader from being unwound. Conducting the operation in dim light, and maintaining a firm grip on the film spool until it is in place with the leader threaded into the take-up spool, will usually prevent fogging the end of the film. When fog due to careless loading occurs, the first few exposures of the film are usually masked with a general deposit of silver, which also obliterates the margins; the other end of the film is unaffected.

Similar fog which appears on the opposite end of a roll of film can be traced to careless handling of the film after exposure. Recommended practice requires removing the film spool from the camera in dim light, sealing the tightly wound roll with care, and wrapping it in foil paper or other suitable material, or restoring it to its original film carton before handling in bright light. The photographer who does not observe these instructions may notice edge fog near the end of the developed film. Edge fog appears as a dense deposit of silver along one or both edges of the film band, and frequently spills over into the picture area.

In severe cases, when the protective paper trailer has been loosely wound on the exposed roll of film, the light causing the edge fog penetrates far enough to be reflected by the printed numerals and markings on the protective paper backing. This condition is immediately apparent when dots or numbers are visible in the negatives and prints.

FOG FROM LENSES

Another problem frequently classed as fog arises when light rays that would otherwise be directed by the lens to form part of the image are scattered. This haphazard projection of light may constitute only a small percentage of the light passing through the lens, but it nevertheless can seriously detract from the brilllance and quality of the image. Usual causes of this difficulty are dirt or moisture on the lens, wrong adjustment of the lens elements, and to a small extent internal reflection of a portion of the light on the inner surfaces of a multiple lens. Fog produced by these conditions may be minimized by keeping lenses clean and in good condition.

Light flare produced when sun or other strong sources of light strike the lens also can cause localized silver densities on the developed film which are sometimes considered as fog. The obvious remedy in such cases is to employ a lens shade during exposure. Lens flare has been considerably reduced by the coating of lenses during manufacture.

Sometimes over-all fogging of a picture occurs as a result of light flare through what appears to be an excellent, properly coated lens. Careful inspection usually will show the cause. Some of the black paint may have chipped off the inside of the lens barrel, leaving bright metal spots which can reflect light. Or some lenses, having thick components with deep curves, have the outer rim of some elements beveled backward to reduce the thickness of the required mounting ring. This beveled-glass surface is always painted black in manufacture, but the paint sometimes chips off and causes reflections.

The remedy in both cases is a trip to a competent lens mechanic who has proper dull lacquers. The wrong kind of paint, such as com-

White markings of this sort in prints are the visible evidence of fog caused by chemical dust coming into contact with the negative prior to or during development. The spots may be more difficult to identify when partly masked by an image.

mon black enamel, is useless.

DARKROOM ILLUMINATION

A very common cause of light fog is inadequate light sealing of darkrooms. Often the silver deposit found on developed negatives can be traced to some small, unsuspected but effective light leak in the walls, joints, doors, or ventilation system of a photographic workroom. A partly covered piece of sensitized material exposed in the darkroom will, when it is developed, indicate the presence of any actinic light by a density difference between covered and uncovered parts of the sample.

Safelights that are too bright or of an improper color for the particular photographic material are also a common cause of light fog. If testing indicates this to be the trouble, it may be necessary to replace the safelight filter, or to use the safelight at a greater distance from the film or with a less brilliant lamp. In some instances the fogging action is caused not by the filter, lamp, or position of the safelight, but by the presence of small openings near joints or fastenings of the filter holder which allow passage of "unsafe" light.

As far as high-speed panchromatic films are concerned, no safelight is really safe. The surest protection against fog is to handle all such films in total darkness.

CHEMICAL FOG

It is easiest to differentiate chemical fog from light fog by describing the former as the placing of silver-halide grains in a developable condition by chemical means rather than by the direct action of light. There are a number of types of fog which fall into this classification. One of the most common types is due to the use of a developing solution unsuited to the film or paper employed, or development for too long a time or at too high a temperature.

An incorrectly prepared developer, particularly one in which there is excess alkali or insufficient potassium bromide to restrain the developing action, can cause severe fogging. Only gross excesses in time or temperature of development will ordinarily produce fog, but variation in the amount of fog can be expected according to the individual characteristics of a particular emulsion. When chemical fog results, it can usually be controlled by a ten-percent increase in the bromide of the developing solution.

Another type of chemical fog, which occurs most frequently in tray-developed sheet films and drum-developed movie films, is caused by contact of the developer-soaked emulsion with the air. It is called aerial fog. This effect does not occur with all developers, but those which have a high concentration of alkali and low bromide are usually susceptible. The addition of a very small amount of a desensitizer, such as Pinakryptol Green, will usually prevent aerial fog.

It is important to realize that certain modern high-speed films have a fog level considerably higher than normal. If after all other remedies have been tried, there is still a high fog level with films rated 650 ASA and higher, it may be a characteristic of the film.

DICHROIC FOG

Dichroic fog, so called because it appears as one color when viewed by reflected light and as another by transmitted light, is also chemical in nature, being formed by the combined action of a developing agent and a silver-halide solvent. The method of formation results in silver particles that are colloidal in size. They are usually yellowish-green when viewed by reflected light and purplish-pink by transmitted light.

Developers contaminated with hypo or containing ammonium salts or other silver-halide solvents can, under prolonged development, produce dichroic fog in the shadow portions of the negative.

Dichroic fog was common in the early days of photography when pyro-ammonia was a popular developer. The recent introduction of rapid-fixing baths containing ammonium thiosulfate has caused a rediscovery of this form of fogging. It can occur as a result of transferring a film directly from the developer to the rapid fix without intermediate rinsing. It also can occur as a result of excessive use and exhaustion of an ammonium-hypo bath. Fixing baths which have lost their acidity, permitting the activity of the developer to be carried over on the negatives, are also a potential source of trouble.

Adherence of two unfixed films because of lack of agitation can form dichroic fog, as can exposure of the emulsion to bright light before fixation is complete. Dichroic fog occurring during fixation can be completely prevented by rinsing developed films and prints in a short stop bath of dilute acetic acid prior to fixation. In some instances, dichroic fog can be removed by bathing the emulsion negative in a solution containing two grams of thiocarbamide and one gram of citric acid in one liter of water.

STORAGE TROUBLES

Storage near fogging agents can be an annoying cause of chemical fog. Sulfides are especially damaging in this respect, and sensitized materials should be stored well away from possible sources of hydrogen sulfide, such as sewer gas and the vapors arising from sulfide toning solutions. Solutions of hydrogen peroxide also are dangerous and should be isolated. Many resinous woods, varnishes, and aromatic compounds, particularly turpentine, can cause fog on photographic emulsions. Some metals, notably zinc, magnesium, and aluminium, also have been reported as sources of direct fog through oxidation. Other metals, such as bronze, brass, copper, tin, and solder can cause intense chemical fog if present in the developing solution as part of the developing equipment.

Another type of fog occurs when developer is stored in tanks and used with continuous replenishment for months. A growth of bacteria in such tanks often occurs, resulting in an accumulation of sulfides in the developer which can cause very serious fogging. This happens most frequently in the large wooden tanks used in old-fashioned motion-picture film processing, but can occur in any kind of tank. The cure is to empty the tank, scrub it out

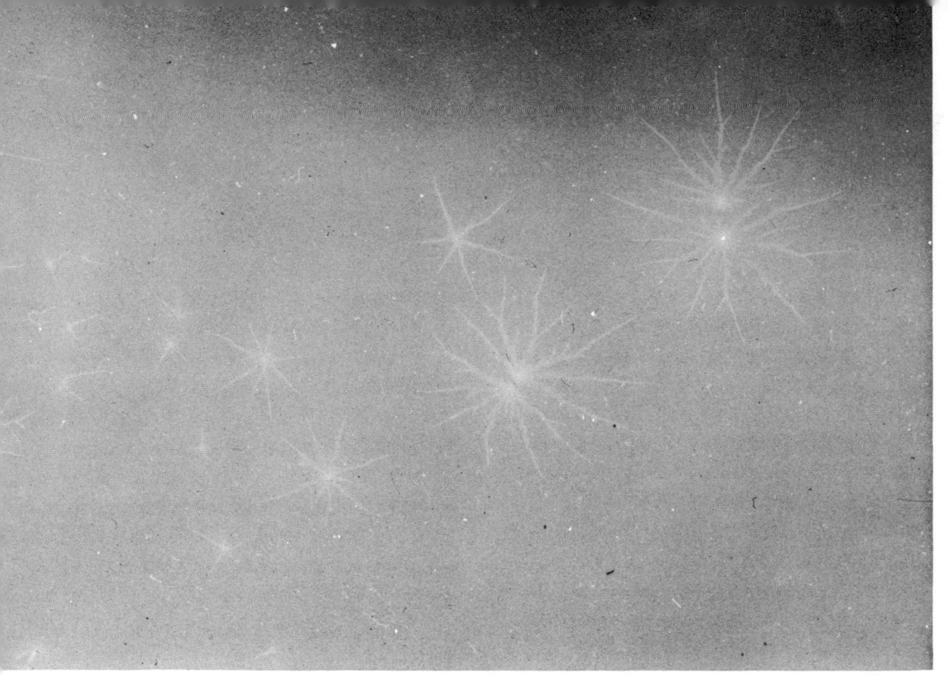

Static markings similar to this and sometimes more branched in appearance can result from an electrical discharge at or near the film surface. Friction from rapid film movement and very dry atmospheric conditions favor the formation of static.

thoroughly with a chlorine bleaching solution (strong Clorox, or a strong solution of sodium hypochlorite), then rinse it with clean water and refill.

Temporary salvage of a developer tank which is causing slight fog due to bacterial attack is treatment with lead acetate. This precipitates the sulfur as lead sulfide, which is insoluble and therefore harmless. Such "first aid" will often clear up the situation for a time, but the tank should be emptied at the earliest opportunity and thoroughly cleaned.

Chemical dust present in the air, especially that of developing agents, is a potential cause of fog-spotted photographs through contact of the dust with film or paper. This type of fog most often occurs when chemicals are stored and developers prepared in rooms used for storage and handling of sensitized materials. The obvious correction is separation of the two operations.

Repackaging of sensitized materials should be done only with paper known to be photographically inactive, for most writing and wrapping papers retain small amounts of chemicals used in their manufacture which often fog, and in some cases desensitize, silver-halide emulsions. Many dyestuffs also show a fogging effect on sensitized materials; so colored-paper stock or printed matter should be kept away from undeveloped films and papers.

OTHER SOURCES OF FOG

An infrequent yet important type of fog is that produced by unintentional exposure of sensitized materials to radioactive materials. In hospitals and doctors' offices, this is a likely source of trouble, and can be eliminated only by adequate protection of the storage space with lead or by storage of the sensitized material in a more remote location.

One unsuspected cause of X-ray fogging comes from the use of X-ray equipment to examine travelers' luggage at certain customs checkpoints, usually in Europe. Travelers should never pack film, exposed or unexposed, in their luggage; it should be kept in a separate package so that it will not be X-rayed.

Discharges of static electricity occurring in the handling of photographic film produce a distinctive type of fog mark having a branched, tree-like appearance. This so-called "static fog" is usually produced only in exceedingly dry weather and then most frequently at low temperatures. Winding or unwinding of a roll of film, movement of film through a camera, and drawing of film from the front to back of a film pack build up an electrical charge on the film which, under favorable conditions, dissipates harmlessly. Under unfavorable conditions, it discharges as a spark which is recorded on the film. Some films are made with antistatic coatings to minimize this tendency, which is most frequently found in aerial and motion-picture photography. The effect can also be observed when working with roll films if the adhesive tab attaching the paper leader to the film is briskly pulled away from the film.

Photographic emulsions also may be fogged before development by pressure exerted in handling. Such pressure marks result when the emulsion surface is scored or abraded. With very sensitive emulsions which do not have a protective top coating of clear gelatin applied during manufacture, abrasion marks may result when the photographer's hand or finger carelessly brushes across the surface of the emulsion. Moon- or crescent-shaped "kink" marks occur when films are buckled severely.

A related error is frequently made by negligent workers with moist or soiled hands, when contact of the emulsion surface with the operator's hands results in fingerprints that are photographically recorded and developed as part of the image.

A final source of fog is deterioration. When sensitized materials are kept beyond the expiration date indicated by the manufacturer, and when storage conditions are excessively hot or moist, a definite fogging action may set in. This type of fog is usually most dense near the border of the film or paper. It may be eliminated by the addition of potassium bromide or benzotriazole to the developer; however, outdated materials frequently have other shortcomings.

COLOR FOG

All the sources of light fog mentioned above apply to color film as well. The result is usually a flare as in black-and-white film. Such fog will appear as a green stripe or smudge on negative film and have a similar pattern in orange on color-reversal film.

Over-all fogs of various types also occur on color film. However, one must not mistake the over-all orange cast of a Kodacolor negative for fog. This orange is actually a color-correcting layer or layers, and is a normal part of the negative.

Color films are subject to one serious type of fog due to contamination of color developer by bleaching solutions. The result is usually an over-all pink or magenta stain which cannot be removed.

Over-all green fog on transparencies may be due to the use of a green safelight while developing; this would be a pink fog on a color negative. Other types of colored fog can usually be traced by the fog color to the type of light which caused them—the same color in the case of transparencies, a complementary color in the case of negatives.

AVOIDING AND DETECTING FOG

When fog does occur, there should be a general check-up of the technique being employed. Possible sources of light fog should be investigated and the nature of storage conditions and chances for development fog examined. It frequently happens that two or more types of fog are present simultaneously.

Causes and Prevention of Fog

APPEARANCE	POSSIBLE CAUSE	PREVENTION
Picture area fogged, but margins clear.	Camera leaks light.	Check camera and film holder for light leaks.
Patches of fog, densest near corners and edge, but margins clear.	Film holder, pack adapter, or locking device on camera leaks light.	Check film holders and adapters for tightness.
General fog, extending through both picture area and margins.	Unsafe darkroom illumination; improper development; storage near fogging agents.	Check safety of darkroom light; check developer, developing time, and temperature; check storage conditions.
Fog at all edges of film lessening gradually toward center.	Deterioration; improper storage.	Check expiration date of film; check storage conditions.
Dense fog at edges of roll film, mostly in margins.	Camera loaded or unloaded in bright light. Film not protected adequately after removal.	Load and unload in subdued light; wrap film after removal.
Numbers and dots show on negatives.	Film loosely wound and removed from camera or handled in bright light.	Wind exposed film tightly and keep away from bright light.
Branched, tree-like markings.	Static discharge.	Advance film through camera slowly; unroll for development slowly, especially in dry weather.
Fog patches yellowish by reflected light, pink by transmitted light.	Dichroic fog.	Use acid short stop; use fresh developer; don't splash hypo; use fresh fixer.
Small, isolated black markings.	Chemical dust.	Conduct chemical mixing away from loading and developing rooms.
Narrow, sometimes crescent-shaped marks.	Pressure or abrasion.	Handle film by edges; do not buckle.

FOOD PHOTOGRAPHY

ALBERT GOMMI
Advertising and Editorial Photographer, Specialist in Food and Still-Life Illustrations, New City

[Pictures of food in preparation or set on a table abound in advertisements, recipe books, and the editorial sections of women's magazines. An experienced photographer of foods here describes his equipment and technique, and explains the creation of setting, composition, and arrangement, and the commercial aspects of food photography.]

• *Also see: Commercial Photography.*

ANYONE SKIMMING THROUGH A "home" magazine today cannot fail to realize how much the use of food photography has grown in the past decade. Today many advertisements and many editorials are illustrated with magnificent examples of the food photographer's art. Of these, a large number are original in concept and execution; practically all of them are technically excellent.

At one time a good food picture merely depicted a prepared dish or a food product with accuracy and detail, usually in a formal and correct table setting. Today's best food pictures go far beyond that. They capture a mood, set the stage, involve the viewer, and create a feeling and an atmophere about the food that makes it far more appetizing and appealing than a mere straightforward picture ever could.

This has been the great change in approach to food work, and it is actually part of the over-all changes that have revolutionized editorial and advertising photography in the past ten or fifteen years. Now that technical perfection is taken for granted—due to the vastly improved films, advanced techniques, and superb equipment available—the creative photographer is free to go

Right: *In black-and-white work, the choice of background is important for proper contrast and separation. A finely developed sense of composition and design is also essential.*

Good food photographs depict a mood, set the stage, involve the viewer, and create a feeling and an atmosphere about the food that makes it more appetizing and appealing.

beyond a literal rendition of his subject.

Not long ago photographers hoped that their subject would "stay put" for the several minutes needed to expose a set of separation plates through tri-color filters, and then hoped that the carbro print would be good when seen three days later. Now photographers expose on a sheet of fast color film and see the finished color picture in less than two hours. Today's commercial photographers can be truly creative, free of most of the cumbersome technical burdens that used to make every color assignment a formidable task. And with this freedom comes the absolute realism and "believability" that only photography can achieve.

For the graphic presentation of food, no other medium can compete with color photography in giving new glamour and taste appeal to an all-too-familiar subject. In the constant striving to create new, more appealing, and more persuasive graphics, today's art directors are relying more and more on the camera's ability to create fresh, new imagery within the framework of complete "realism." Nowhere is this more apparent than in the food field.

This greatly increased demand has given rise to a group of photographers whose specialty is food. They have developed, by long experience and constant practice, a highly refined approach to their subjects, and have become "specialists" in the true sense of the word. In the past, these specialists were found only in New York and Chicago. Today they are more numerous and dispersed geographically. In recent years the West Coast has developed a small but highly competent group of food specialists whose work is often outstanding.

All of these people share their involvement in one particular branch of the photographic field. Most of them also share a great interest in food itself—its preparation, its lore, its history. Many are fine cooks and food experts outside of the studio. They are highly creative and artistic people who have, by imagination and skill, changed the photographic presentation of food from the literal "food shot" of 20 years ago to some of the most exciting photographs seen today.

TYPES OF FOOD PHOTOGRAPHY

Food photographs can be divided into certain basic classifications, depending upon the purpose of the picture and its ultimate use.

Editorial: Pictures used to illustrate articles on food in the editorial pages of various publications. Free of commercial requirements and limitations, these pictures offer the greatest creative scope to the photographer and magazine art director. Hence they are often the "trend setters," and much that is new and fresh will be found first in this area.

Advertising: Pictures used to illustrate advertisements for various food products. Sometimes following a preconceived and carefully planned layout, and sometimes "created" before the camera, these pictures constitute probably the most difficult and exacting form of food photography. They must fulfill the requirements of good advertising in selling a product, and still be interesting and beautiful enough to stop the eye and stir the interest of the reader.

Point-of-sale: Pictures used in displays in stores, supermarkets, etc., to help sell a product at the "point-of-sale." The requirements of these pictures are similar to those of advertising, but the pictures are usually simpler and bolder in concept since they are used essentially as posters.

Booklet: Pictures used to illustrate a recipe pamphlet, cookbook, instruction leaflet, etc. These are fairly simple pictures of finished dishes to illustrate a recipe.

Process or "how-to": These are food pictures showing the steps in making a recipe or using a food product. Simplicity and clarity are the prime requirements here.

Package: Pictures used on the actual food package, such as a picture of a cake on a cake-mix box. A high degree of technical skill and a knowledge of the packaging field are required for this work.

Outdoor billboard or poster: These pictures will be tremendously enlarged, sometimes on a billboard exceeding more than 30 feet in length. They require very careful planning to allow for such enlargement—extreme sharpness, simplicity of design, and attention to small details are necessary.

Publicity: These are pictures that will be sent to the food editors of various publications. Usually accompanied by a recipe, they show the various uses of a food product. They must be planned to reproduce well even on newspaper stock, and are therefore kept clean-cut and simple, having as much contrast as possible.

MAKING A FOOD PHOTOGRAPH

Most food pictures are the result of the combined efforts of a group of specialists working together. Preliminary discussion between the art director, photographer, home economist, and stylist serves to determine how the food will be prepared, what dishes and props will be used, what background feeling or mood is to be achieved, and many other details.

The home economist now needs time to test her recipes, the stylist to gather together a suitable choice of props. A second brief conference after the props have been collected and the recipes devised is sometimes helpful, and if basic changes must be made they are determined at this point.

Finally, at the appointed time, the actual picture-taking begins. Sometimes it requires only an hour or two, sometimes an entire day of intensive effort, depending on the complexity of the problem and the number of variations or different approaches that the photographer and art director may decide to try. In many cases, such as in pouring liquid products or sauces onto a food, many exposures are taken, since to a certain extent a perfect-looking "pour" depends on a bit of luck. If these "pours" are done on or into a prepared dish of food, the food must be set up again after each exposure. It is easy, therefore, to use the better part of a day for the successful completion of a "simple" picture of a cream sauce pouring over chicken croquettes.

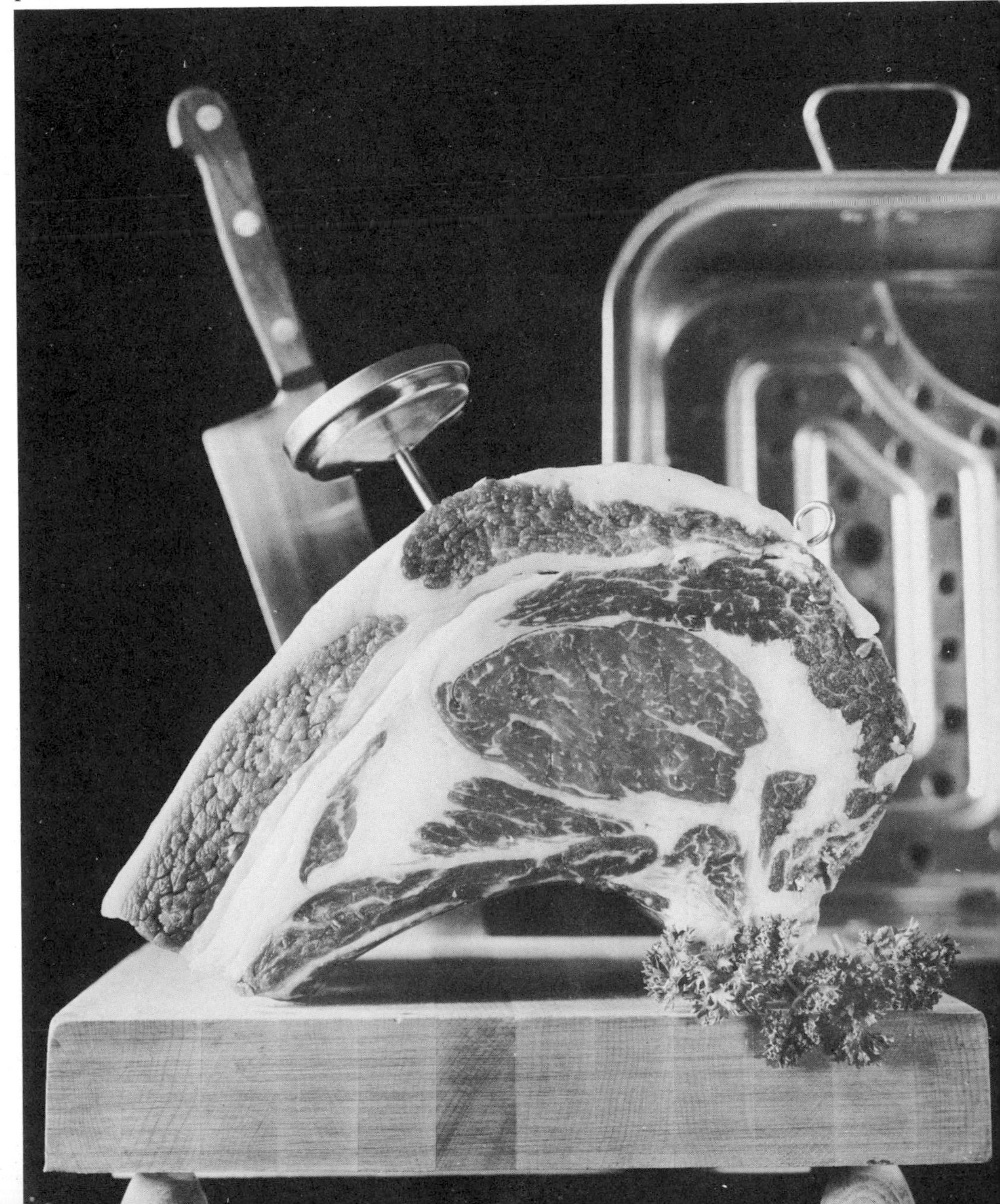

Some foods require a hard direct light to produce sharp and strong textures. Dark shadows are usually filled in with a soft frontlight or a reflecting white surface.

In most really good food pictures, especially where cooked foods or "recipes" are shown, a combination of patience and skill on the part of both photographer and home economist produces an outstanding bit of "appetite appeal." All too often this does not happen until many hours and many sheets of film have been used. Persistence, extreme patience, and careful attention to every detail are "musts" in good food work—perhaps more than in any other branch of photography.

THE FOOD STUDIO

The studio that specializes in food work possesses certain basic characteristics of layout and equipment which set it apart. It is usually rather small, since huge sets are not required. It has, of course, an efficient, carefully planned, and well equipped kitchen. This kitchen differs somewhat from the "homemaker's dream kitchen," since it is often the work center from which must flow a whole series of elaborate dishes in less time than the average housewife would need to prepare a simple dinner.

It requires far more work surface than a home kitchen. If at all possible it should be a "double" kitchen—that is, have two sinks, two refrigerators, two stoves, and so on. At least one large freezer is a necessity. All this extra capacity is always welcome, and often imperative when large "spreads" are being prepared. The entire work area should be well lit and adequately stocked with all the necessary "tools" for food preparation. A staff maid is often employed to keep the kitchen clean and to help the home economists with their work.

The kitchen actually can be in the studio area or adjacent to it. It is very inconvenient and inefficient when situated at any distance from the camera area; locating it in a narrow hall or on another floor invites really serious problems.

A very useful item of special equipment is a traveling serving cart, sturdily built and on rubber wheels. This cart can be wheeled right up to the set-up table, and, like a surgeon's tray, keeps everything needed at hand during the last few moments of preparation.

Sometimes the better part of a day may be taken up in assembling all the elements of the food picture. The final arrangement must look appetizing. For this effect much depends upon the composition and lighting techniques employed.

Another area vital to the efficient food studio is the prop room with its prop bench. Some studios keep an extensive stock of dishes, silverware, tablecloths, and glassware on hand. They must be stored properly on racks so that they can be seen and selected quickly. The props which are not a part of the permanent collection are usually rented or borrowed; provision must be made for their unwrapping and rewrapping with minimum breakage.

Adjacent to the camera area, or in the prop room itself, a large table is usually reserved for laying out the props to be considered for the job at hand. Dishes are placed on cloths to judge color combination, and arrangements are "roughed out" for study.

Proper air conditioning is important in the camera and kitchen area since many foods, such as icing on cakes, gelatin molds, and candy, cannot take much heat.

Like other types of studios, the food studio needs its workshop. While the workshop does not need the capacity and size to build large and elaborate sets, it should be equipped well enough to handle the numerous odd jobs that come along constantly. Very often paint spraying is required, and a well ventilated area near a window should be provided for this work.

The darkroom and finishing areas of the food studio do not differ in any respect from the norm, and should be set up to handle the volume of work anticipated.

CAMERA AND TECHNIQUE

For the usual food work in a studio, the 8 × 10 view camera is the most convenient, flexible, and practical instrument to use. First of all, exact arrangement is important in almost all food pictures. The photographer must be able to see the slightest changes in relationship among essentially very small objects. This is very difficult on a small groundglass and almost impossible through a viewfinder. Secondly, there is a real need for the swings and tilts that the flexible view camera provides.

Thirdly, a wide range of focal lengths is needed—from a 20-inch lens to avoid distortion of the edge dishes on a large spread, to the shortest wide-angle lens that will cover the film to make half a walnut look much bigger than it really is. Finally, an image is needed that is large enough to allow the photographer to judge, before the enlargements are made, the appearance of the food in the smallest dish in a two-page spread containing, say, a six course meal.

LENSES

A good set of quality lenses is most important, since the selection of the proper focal length can change the entire "look" of a picture. When distortion must be avoided, a 14-inch or longer lens should be used on an 8 × 10; however, many problems call for a much shorter lens, and focal lengths down to five or six inches are often employed. It is interesting to go through a group of food ads in the magazines and see how many were done with very short lenses. When properly used, the short lens can give tremendous impact and drama to food subjects, and often helps to produce the reader "involvement" in the picture that is so often sought.

All of these lenses should be in "synch" shutters, so that they may be used with strobe lights when needed. The soft-focus, or portrait, lens can be very successfully used in food work to create a dreamy mood or a special effect, and many very beautiful "portraits" of food have been done with it. However, it must be used with taste and discrimination, for a bad soft-focus picture can be worse than a bad sharp picture.

LIGHTING

Lighting and composition are the really personal variables that each photographer uses to develop a style of his own. Beyond the basic rules and common sense of good lighting, and the requirements of reproduction, lighting offers an infinite field of variation and exploration.

Photographers must learn how to light by experience and arrive at a solution of how the subject should be lit through personal interpretation. Formulas, therefore, are to be avoided, since they stifle creative effort. However, like the rules of drawing and painting, they should be learned thoroughly before they can be set aside.

In general, the lightings most generally used in food work can be classified in a few main categories listed below. How these lightings are used and the degree of subtlety and sensitivity employed often mark the work of the best people in the field.

Direct light. Direct or hard raw light is produced by a spotlight, an open bulb in a reflector, or direct sunlight. Often used from somewhat behind and above the food subject, direct light produces very sharp and strong textures, and can be harsh in effect. The resulting dark shadows are usually "filled in" with a soft frontlight or a reflecting white surface.

Diffused light. Diffused or "soft" light is usually produced by either one source of a "bank" of lights through a diffuser of spun glass or plastic, or the light from the sky (not sunlight), as in the case of a north skylight. Diffused light is most pleasant on many food subjects, and produces good textures and "roundness" without being excessively harsh.

Bounce light. Bounce or indirect light is light which first hits a reflecting surface, like a white wall, then reflects or "bounces" back onto the subject. Producing extremely broad soft highlights and soft-edged shadows, bounce light can be effectively used in food work if it is understood and controlled properly. When used indiscriminately, bounce light on food can result in a flat, washed-out appearance, lacking depth, texture, and brilliance.

Any of these types of light can be produced by strobe units as well as by incandescent lights; strobe is used, of course, when there is motion involved in the subject, such as in pouring liquids, melting ice cream, or falling soufflés.

Some photographers have adapted strobe lights as their only light source, since their convenience, speed, lack of heat, and constancy of output, both in intensity and color temperature, make them an almost ideal light to work with. However, others feel that they can achieve greater control with subjects which do not move by using incandescent lights, especially in the tiny areas sometimes so important in food work. Much depends on the individual's approach, and each photographer must find out for himself what lights suit him best.

SPECIAL EQUIPMENT

In any case, the food specialist adapts some of his lights to special purposes, whether they are strobe, incandescent or both. Very often a tiny area must be hit with light that can be controlled precisely, and "snoods" or funnels are needed to narrow down even the smallest light. "Midgets," the tiny spotlights so handy in all still-life work, are almost a necessity in food work as are a variety of clamps, arms, pivots, ball joints, etc., to hold small things in various positions. The food specialist also equips himself with at least one "set-up" or camera table which is adjustable in height, easy to clean, and to which background cloths may be pinned.

COLOR PROBLEMS IN FOOD

Food, by its very nature, demands complete color fidelity in photography. Most foods are well known to the average viewer, who will instantly detect any deviation of color. In the case of food products themselves, very accurate color is demanded by the client, and again the food photographer is required to stay within the narrowest bounds of color accuracy.

For all practical purposes, there are basically two professional methods available today to achieve quality color pictures. One is the direct positive-transparency process, as represented by Ektachrome and Anscochrome film, and the other is the color-negative process, represented by Ektacolor or Kodacolor negative film. Both are capable of excellent results, and their choice is determined by the ultimate use of the picture and the photographer's personal preference.

The color-negative process is being used more and more, since it produces a negative from which a positive color print of almost any size, a positive transparency, or an excellent black-and-white print can

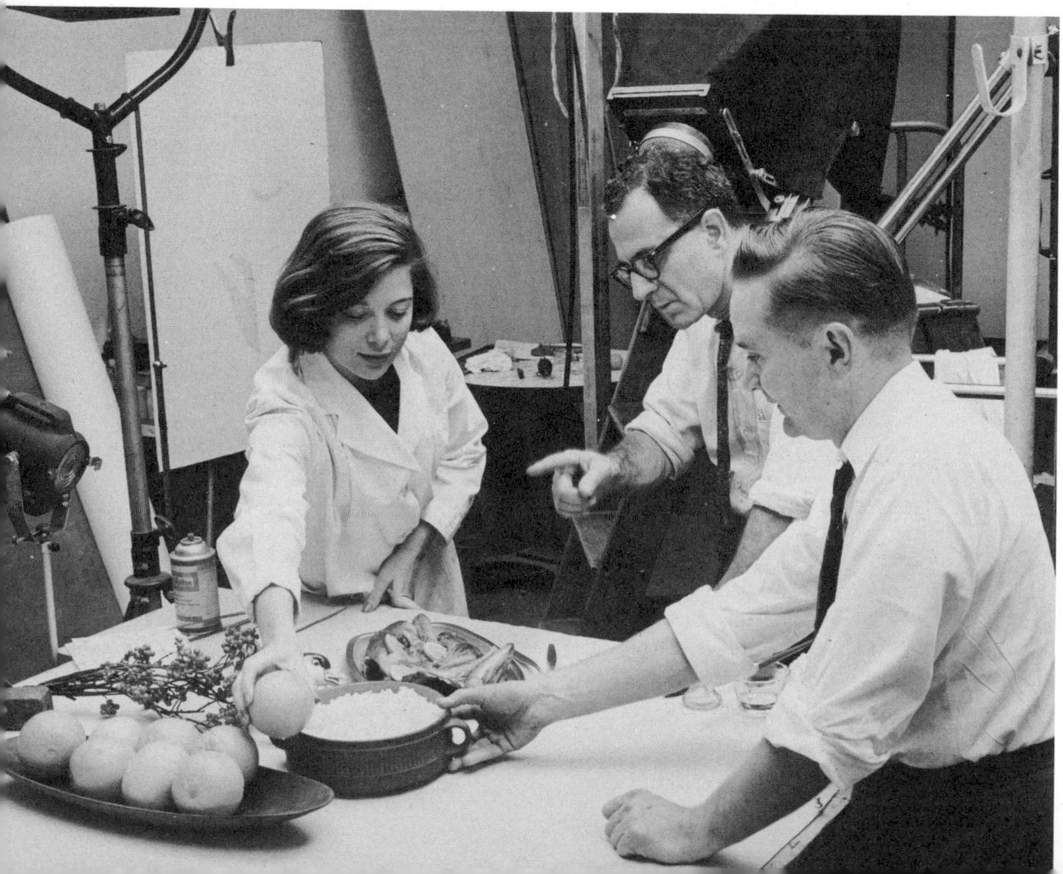

Important food pictures usually require a staff of workers, operating under the direction of the photographer.

be made. After use, the negative is returned to the file, where it is safe until needed for more prints or any other requirement. These advantages are considerable, and it is now apparent that this process ultimately will be the method most generally used for color work.

Many food studios have adapted techniques to insure constant color accuracy. One such technique is to test thoroughly a given emulsion number, and then to buy a large quantity of this number, usually several months' supply. The film is stored in a deep freeze to maintain complete color stability. Before this supply is exhausted, a new emulsion number is tested and adjusted for different filtration, so that it is ready for "switch-over" when the old emulsion is finished. Frequent testing is also carried out along the way, especially before a critical assignment, to be sure that none of the factors, including processing, has changed. Corrective filters are constantly used to adjust color to a fine point of accuracy and to compensate for any "drifting" in processing.

Light sources must also be checked frequently, to be sure they are at correct color temperature. Constant vigilance and frequent testing are daily routines if the color standards that good food work demands are to be maintained.

Aside from film and lights, the photographer can, within certain limits, control the color of the subject itself. Here, experience and judgment are required. For instance, a dark green vegetable such as broccoli or spinach will tend to photograph an unpleasant, almost black color. If the lightest of the batch is chosen, and if the home economist can make it a little lighter and greener in cooking, a much better color rendition will result.

There are many ways of complementing the natural appearance of food, just as good "make-up" complements the appearance of a model. This is not "faking," which is never employed in good food work; it is simply the result of selection, care, and good kitchen techniques which brings out the natural beauty already present in food. Consultation and cooperation between photographer and home economist are needed throughout the process to insure the best possible food picture.

Here strong sidelighting brings out the texture of the roast.

In some rare cases, color is deliberately forced into a picture by the use of "extra" filtration. For example, a picture of a basket of tomatoes is being made, and the fruit being used is a bit short of the rich red desired by the client. A slight additional red, such as a .05R or .10 filter, may be tried. Again, experience and testing will tell the story.

The best answer to color problems in food work is to get the right food and prepare it properly. One of the basic needs of a food studio is a knowledge of places where the finest and freshest food can be obtained. Out-of-season fruits and vegetables are often air-expressed great distances for a specific picture, and even the simplest problem needs careful and time-consuming shopping in the local markets.

BLACK-AND-WHITE PROBLEMS

Many photographers maintain that a really good black-and-white photograph is much more difficult to do than a color picture. This is particularly true of food where most of the appeal of the subject is in its color.

To achieve contrast and "separation," the photographer must choose his dishes and background with great care, and if at all possible he should try to control the actual food in preparation. Secondly, his lighting can achieve excitement by bringing out form and texture, without the "crutch" of all that beautiful, appetizing color. Great care must be taken that two strongly contrasting colors, such as pink icing on a yellow cake, don't appear in the final print as almost identical gray tones. At times the use of filters to darken one color and lighten another is indicated, but it is always more desirable to set up the food properly for black-and-white so that it has its own inherent contrasting values.

Another danger lies in the opposite direction, when the contrast in the subject itself exceeds the printable range of the film—for example, a pure snow-white sauce on a square of almost black devil's-food cake. Sometimes the old technique of over-exposure and under-development will do the trick, but if not the home economist must make the cake lighter and/or the sauce darker, to bring them into range.

These problems are not peculiar to food photography alone, but they seem to come up more often here. Actually, a sound knowledge of good black-and-white procedure will solve most of the technical problems, but injecting interest and appeal into a colorless food subject must be achieved by the imagination and ability of the man behind the camera.

COMPOSITION AND ARRANGEMENT

Someone once said that the designer's responsibility is to find new ways to say old things. This applies very specifically to the food photographer as well. Practically all of his subjects are "old" and all-too-familiar. He must find new ways of presenting them, new ways to express graphically their deliciousness, their wholesomeness, or whatever attribute he may wish to emphasize.

A new Paris gown on a beautiful model will be of interest to a woman viewer even when badly photographed. But an apple pie is an apple pie, and how do we make it exciting? Here, perhaps, is the very heart of the food specialist's skill—his ability to impart interest, drama, and excitement to the most commonplace of subjects, and yet keep within the bounds of reality and "believability."

Composition, or arrangement—arrangement is a better term for our purpose, for we cannot "compose" as completely as the painter—is probably the single most important element in food work. As in all still lifes, the relationship of forms to one another and the interplay of objects and their background become paramount. This is even truer in food, where the objects that can logically be used are comparatively limited in scope. The photographer "designs" by this choice of objects, by his lighting to some extent, but mainly by "arrangement."

A finely developed sense of composition and design, combined with that intangible quality of good taste —an infallible sense of what is right in accessories and settings; an abiding interest in food itself; infinite patience in dealing with "little things" that always go wrong; and the sound technical base that allows him to put the picture on film the way he wants it to be are the attributes a good food photographer must have.

Ideally the kitchen should be in the studio area where the photographer can supervise the preparations for a new food scene. The kitchen should be designed for fast production of the dishes, and this usually calls for two stoves, two sinks, and two refrigerators.

GIULIO BRIANI / *The Color of a Dream*

L. FRIEDEL / *Meditation*

Next page: HY PESKIN / *Saturday's Children*

NORMAN ROTHSCHILD / *Sixty-four*

FOREIGN TRAVEL PHOTOGRAPHY

PHILLIP ANDREWS
Travel Writer, Photographer, Correspondent; Executive Editor, Travel Press Syndicate

[Traveling and photography are synonymous terms for many persons. We all like to record a new experience with our cameras. To make travel photography more rewarding, the author presents a wealth of information. Planning the trip, equipment to take, customs regulations, subject selection, exposures, processing, and all-weather photography are just a few of the subjects covered.]

• *Also see: Action Photography; Architectural Photography; Architectural Photography with the Small Camera; Candid Photography; Cycling and the Camera; Flight Photography; Sports Photography; Tropical Photography.*

The flight which begins picture-taking travels can produce prints or slides which later will set the locale and prepare an audience for the vicarious pleasures of the trip. This Boeing 707 jetliner was heading across the Pacific. (Photo: Byron Wingett / Boeing)

ANYONE WHO TAKES GOOD PICTURES at home should be able to take good pictures when he travels abroad. Processing laboratories report, however, that pictures taken by U. S. citizens outside the country are generally below the technical standards of those made in more familiar surroundings. Moreover, there is a wide disparity in the quality of pictures taken by overseas travelers—even of identical subjects under similar conditions.

Discounting the number of people who rarely use their cameras except on vacation trips and whose photographic experience is rather limited, the results indicate that foreign-travel photography does present certain special problems and considerations.

SUBJECT SELECTION

The matter of subject selection often presents a dilemma. There are the alternatives of shooting at virtually everything that comes within camera range, thus running short of film when more interesting subjects come into view, or hesitating, in the interests of film conservation, and so missing opportunities which are not likely to recur.

There is also the problem of local regulations. The traveler may, for example, decide to spend a valuable day of his itinerary in making interior pictures at Windsor Castle in England, the Vatican Museum or St. Peter's Cathedral in Rome, only to discover after he has arrived on the scene that such photography is not permitted. Having learned his lesson, he will forego the Louvre Museum in Paris—to find out after he has left the city that he could have added the *Winged Victory, Mona Lisa,* and other Louvre masterpieces to his color-slide or print collection by paying a fee of five francs, or about one dollar.

The traveling photographer should make sure beforehand that he will be in the right place at the right time—otherwise he may arrive late at a bullfight to find that he has not only missed the colorful opening ceremonies, but that the sun is setting beyond the arena and the ring is in shadow. Or, he may learn too late that the Paris flea market is

Paris appears in a seldom-seen mood in this photo which utilizes the overcast day to produce a striking effect of Seine and city. (Photo: French Embassy)

deserted every day except Sunday.

Exposure problems may range from the stained-glass windows of a dimly lighted cathedral to night views of illuminated châteaux along the Loire River in France; from the starch-white streets and houses of the Greek Island, Mykonos, to the extreme tonal and color contrasts of a Mexican market place.

VARIETY OF SUBJECTS

A single day and evening abroad may present the photographer with a greater variety of subjects than he would encounter at home in a lifetime—snow-clad mountains, unique structures (such as the Eiffel Tower or the leaning tower of Pisa), a Gothic cathedral (exterior and interior), small children in native costumes, night scenes of a large city, a brilliant seascape, and a nightclub floor show. Each requires a different treatment, and it is a rare cameraman who can draw upon his experience for the answer.

The questions inherent in the perplexing variety of subjects, situations, and conditions are compounded by the abundance of equipment involved. Decisions about what should be taken and what should be left at home are subject to such considerations as excess baggage charges when traveling by air, varying availability of accessories and film abroad, mobility, and customs regulations.

As the photographer is constantly on the move, equipment may be subjected to climatic extremes of heat, cold, and humidity, and require protection against damage. There remains the problem of what to do with the exposed film. It should be processed as soon as possible after exposure, and the photographer must determine whether this is feasible en route or, if it is returned to the United States, how it should be mailed.

Despite the differences between photography at home and abroad, it is a rare American who does not carry at least one camera when he ventures outside the country. The purpose of this article is to encourage proper preparation, so the traveler may approach a variety of subjects and situations with the same confidence which he displays when taking pictures within walking distance of his own darkroom.

PLANNING THE TRIP

Travel abroad, without proper planning, can be full of difficulties and disappointments even without the added element of photography. Just as the photographer consults an expert before purchasing an expensive piece of equipment, he will also be well advised to discuss his travel plans with an authority —his local travel agent. When all details of the itinerary have been arranged in advance with the travel agent's help, the photographer is free to concentrate on the primary reasons for the trip—to enjoy himself and take pictures.

"Special-interest" tours, some of which are designed expressly for photographers, include many features and attractions which would be difficult, if not impossible, for the

The traveling photographer must decide whether to attempt a "grab" shot of appealing personalities or whether to ask their permission for a photograph. This posed portrait study allowed time for careful framing and exact focusing to bring out the details desired. (Photo: Zeiss Ikon)

individual traveler to arrange. Most package tours allow ample free time for indulging individual interests. As the majority of Americans abroad carry cameras with the avowed intention of using them at every opportunity, tour conductors will not only stop at scenic points but, with their intimate knowledge of the region, may suggest subjects which are not apparent to the casual tourist.

The traveler may choose from many special-interest tours which have been organized for architects, interior designers, farmers, students, skiers, skin-divers, and almost every other conceivable kind of group, providing the touring cameraman with an opportunity to concentrate on his favorite camera subject.

Another advantage of group travel is that other members of the tour may be used as models, stand-ins, assistants, and even photographers, when the traveler himself wants to get into an occasional picture.

ESSENTIAL DOCUMENTS

In recent years, travel in the free world has become a relatively simple matter for U. S. citizens, but there are still some formalities required where the travel agent can be of considerable assistance. It cannot be assumed that he will attend to these details automatically, however, so it is advisable to inquire about obtaining passports, visas, and inoculation certificates.

Passports are required for all foreign countries except Canada, Mexico, Bermuda, the Bahamas, and the West Indies. (Puerto Rico and the Virgin Islands are U. S. territory.)

PASSPORTS

A passport may be obtained by applying to the Passport Office, U. S. Department of State, 1717 H. Street, NW, Washington 25, D.C., or at passport offices in New York, Boston, Chicago, New Orleans, San Francisco, or Los Angeles. Passports also are issued by nearly 4000 federal, state, and county courts. The fee for a new passport is $10; it is valid for three years unless a shorter period is specified.

You must apply for a passport in person. Applicants need proof of citizenship (birth or baptismal certificate, naturalization papers); a witness, other than a relative, who has known the applicant for at least two years; two identical photographs, full face, between two and one half and three inches square, on thin paper, with flat lighting, either black-and-white or color.

HOW TO TRAVEL

In making travel arrangements, the first decision will be whether to make the overseas portion of the trip by sea or air. Ship travel is pleasant, but practical only if ample time is available.

Cruises offer excellent photographic fare, depending upon the number and variety of ports of call, and on the amount of time permitted ashore. They are particularly popular with movie makers, as they tend to follow a logical story line. Cruises also enable the traveler to take along as much equipment and film as he desires—the amount and

When the photographer slows down to a walk, as on this muddy forest road, he may come up with some unusual shots. (Photo: Zeiss Ikon)

The candid approach to travel photos reveals attitudes and dress which would be carefully, and artificially, arranged by the subjects if they were allowed time to pose. (Photo: Zeiss Ikon)

weight of baggage is almost unlimited, and customs formalities en route are virtually nonexistent for cruise passengers.

In crossing the Atlantic by ship, the time of year may have a bearing on whether the northern or southern routes are chosen for the east- or westbound crossings. Late in the year, going by the northern route and returning on the South Atlantic will provide the maximum number of sunlit days. The reverse procedure is recommended for the late winter and early spring, as it enables the traveler-photographer to follow the sun northward on his trip through Europe.

Air travel is of course faster, but it has one disadvantage for the photographer: excess baggage (over 44 pounds on economy flights and over 66 pounds on first class) is charged at a percentage of the applicable fare per kilo (2.2 pounds). This places limitations on the amount of photographic equipment which may be carried (although each passenger is permitted to carry one camera free of additional charge).

Multi-stopover plans, available on

Tourists with an eye for humor may produce photos which are a change of pace from the usual travel shots. The matron with camera turns her back on the sea to photograph Positano, on the south Italian coast. The bikini-clad girl is oblivious to the scenery and thinks only of the sun. (Photo: Michael E. Bry)

all major international airlines, permit stops at numerous places en route at no additional charge. A New York-Rome round trip, for example, allows unlimited stops (within the validity of the ticket) in such widely separated cities as London, Glasgow, Edinburgh, Paris, Zurich; Frankfurt, Hamburg, Hanover, Stuttgart, Copenhagen, and Milan. One airline offers 27 stops on a round-trip ticket between New York and Athens. Since the travel agent cannot be expected to suggest all the possibilities, the photographer-traveler should make inquiries concerning multi-stopovers and other bonuses and cost-saving plans.

GETTING AROUND

In general the slowest means of transportation will offer the most intimate and unusual opportunities for photography. Hiking and cycling are both feasible and rewarding in settled areas, but more time than film will be consumed in regions where towns and cities are widely separated.

Traveling by car allows maximum flexibility in pace; travel agents can arrange for you to rent or purchase a car abroad. Car-rental costs can be greatly reduced if two or more people travel together, but a compact car can become quite crowded with four passengers plus baggage and photographic equipment.

A state driver's license is either sufficient in itself or can be the basis for obtaining necessary documents to drive a car in most foreign countries. When passport photos are made, it is a good idea to print at least four additional copies for possible use on foreign driver's licenses and for other purposes, such as visas.

Motorcoach travel, particularly in Europe, is not only comfortable and economical, but presents an infinite variety of photographic potentialities.

The possibility of travel by waterways within certain countries should also be investigated. A boat trip up the Amazon in South America leads through country that is practically inaccessible by any other means. Boats and barges operate on the canals and rivers of Britain. A cruise along the Rhine or Danube Rivers provides the only angle from which to equal some of the great classics of travel photography, since castles and other buildings face these rivers.

PICTURE PLANNING

Experienced travelers say that a trip abroad, like Caesar's Gaul, is divided into three parts: contemplation or preparation; realization; recollection or reminiscence.

In addition to guide books, read a history book, even a brief one, covering the countries you will visit. One reason for advance picture planning is that the foreign-bound photographer is confronted by an embarrassment of riches. The wealth of photographic potentialities, coupled with the need for conserving film, frequently forces a hasty decision on whether to take a picture now or wait for a better shot later in the trip. The seasoned traveler, returning to places previously visited, naturally has less difficulty in making a selection than does one for whom each day's sights are a continual surprise. The first-time visitor, however, can compensate for this by advance study of countries—their history, geography, customs, annual events, architecture, and other subjects having a direct bearing on pictorial potentialities.

A calendar of coming events, available from the official tourist bureaus of the countries to be visited, will enable the photographer to be in the right place at the right time. These bureaus, addresses of which can be obtained from any travel agent, furnish information only and do not make travel arrangements.

Illustrated travel books provide a more visual basis for picture planning in advance. Highly recommended for travelers to certain areas are Eastman Kodak "Vacation" publications which are obtainable at most photographic dealers. These books are colorfully illustrated and give general and specific information on picture-taking techniques and areas.

Magazines such as *Holiday,*

People and their surroundings combine to show more about an area than if each were photographed separately. When he has returned home the photographer may, through his prints or slides, see more details of the places he visited than he saw when actually there. A notebook in which to jot down information will add to the value of the photographs. This one was taken at Ein Kerem, situated among groves of fruit trees and cypresses on the edge of Jerusalem in Israel. It was the birthplace of John the Baptist.

National Geographic, and *Travel* (back copies of which can be examined in many public libraries) will provide a visual prelude to a camera trip abroad. Standard guide books are a valuable source of information.

CAMERAS, ACCESSORIES, FILM

The next step for the photographer-traveler is the preparation of his equipment. What should he take, what should he leave at home? The answers which follow are intended for the amateur who would like to take the best possible pictures on his trip without limiting his enjoyment of traveling.

For the tourist to whom photography is incidental, a simple camera capable of taking snapshots under a limited range of "normal" conditions, plus a flash attachment for informal interiors, will be sufficient for most situations. Many intermediate and advanced amateurs, however, have developed a near-professional approach to photography and have come to rely on a variety of cameras and lenses, each delegated to a particular type of subject or situation. This practice is not feasible in foreign-travel photography for a number of reasons:

1. Most countries limit the amount of equipment which can be imported "for personal use," free of duty. Two cameras of different sizes or types (one still and one movie camera, for example, or one 35 mm and one 2¼ × 2¼ reflex) are usually the maximum allowed per person. A photographer traveling with a companion not interested in taking pictures can double the amount of his equipment. It should also be noted that regulations, although specific and sometimes stringent in wording, reflect the letter of the law, and a reasonable amount of additional equipment can be brought

Right: *This is the type of photo that makes photographers want to travel. The castle of Neuschwanstein at Fuessen, Germany, seems to float in the air.* (Photo: Pan American)

Children are good photographic subjects in any language. These Welsh youngsters were dressed in 18th-century costume for a local holiday. (Photo: British Travel Assn.)

Monuments are a favorite subject of travelers, but too many can become a repetition of buildings to the viewer. Sometimes a photo of part of a structure can express its feeling better than an over-all shot, as this interpretation of the ruins of Whitby Abbey in Yorkshire, England. (Photo: Michael E. Bry)

into most countries without difficulty. Similar restrictions and tolerances apply to accessories and film.

2. In traveling by air, the amount of photographic equipment which can be carried free of excess baggage charges is an important consideration.

3. Too much equipment impedes mobility. Overloaded gadget bags become increasingly heavy when carried day after day.

4. An excessive amount of equipment will give the traveler a professional look, which will not only impede his progress through customs but may attract the scrutiny of police and other officials after he has entered the country.

CAMERAS

Small roll-film, 6×6 or 6×9 cm and 35 mm cameras are ideal for foreign-travel photography. As for interchangeable lenses, it may be advisable to leave the medium (50mm) lens behind and take a medium wide-angle (35mm) lens and a medium long-focus (86 or 90mm) lens in its place.

If more than one camera is taken, lenses, filters, and other accessories which are interchangeable between the two will reduce weight and bulk and attract less attention in passing through customs.

A Polaroid Land camera makes an ideal second instrument for several reasons. First, it provides prints immediately that can be sent to friends and relatives at home. Second, natives of foreign countries can sometimes be induced to pose if presented with pictures of themselves made possible by Polaroid's quick development. In some primitive areas, the photographer will be considered something of a magican. Finally, prints can be used to test exposure, check on compositional elements, and determine black-and-white tonal values of color patterns in a subject.

Subminiatures are convenient for obtaining candid shots and for use by those who do not want to miss exceptional picture opportunities but prefer not to be identified as tourists.

If a movie camera is taken, the cost of the trip and the results achieved will justify the additional expenditure for a turret or zoom-lens model. A pistol grip will not add materially to the weight or bulk and, where a tripod is not feasible, will help to steady the picture.

ACCESSORIES

Lens hood. This is helpful not only to shield the lens in bright sunlight, but also to protect the lens from accidental damage and from the elements.

Filters. They require relatively little space and, since almost every conceivable filter situation may be encountered, a fairly complete assortment should be taken along for black-and-white work. For color, a sky filter is virtually essential. It should be used only when necessary, as it will contribute an undesirable warm tone to pictures taken under normal conditions.

Exposure meter. It should be considered basic equipment, due to the wide range of unfamiliar and unusual light conditions which will be encountered.

Tripod. This will help immeasurably in making smooth-appearing movies. The very small models, when telescoped to their minimum length, can also be used as a carrying handle in much the same manner as a pistol grip.

The interiors of churches, castles, and other buildings of interest are so large that, for still photography, flash is ineffective except when used for close-ups and details. Tripods are not permitted in many buildings and are technically barred (although they may be used with discretion or by official permission) on the streets of some cities—Paris and London, for example. If a tripod is included in your kit, it should be a model that can be reduced to the smallest possible size when not in use. Rubber tips should cover or replace the spikes so that the tripod will not damage bare floors.

Camera clamp. This is a good substitute for the tripod, as it can be affixed to a bench, table, chair, or other stationary object—excluding, of course, fine furniture in churches, museums, and other public buildings.

STROBE AND FLASH

Although there will be few opportunities for use of strobe or flash, those that do arise will add balance and contrast to a travel-photo collection by providing a change of pace from the usual scenic and exterior views. Lighting equipment is particularly recommended for the ship traveler, as he will have ample time and opportunity to use it on board.

In addition to its use for interiors, such as wine cellars, cheese caves, workshops, restaurants, trains, planes, and other small and medium-sized interiors, a supplementary light source can be very helpful when the sun is exceptionally strong. For example, close-ups of people and objects against a brilliant background can be brought into a more pleasing balance by means of the additional light for shadow fill.

American-type flashbulbs are not easily available in some foreign countries. Small-sized bulbs will be adequate for most occasions. Batteries may be purchased in most countries, but a fresh set should be installed before leaving.

MISCELLANEOUS ITEMS

A changing bag can be improvised by using a coat or jacket, but as the bag is easy to pack and adds little weight, it may be taken along for emergencies.

A roll of cellophane tape, gummed stickers for labeling purposes, and a pair of small scissors are among the miscellaneous items which may prove to be useful.

If time permits, a local photographic excursion of several days will aid in the choice of equipment. All equipment should be thoroughly tested, especially if it is new.

PACKING AND CARE OF EQUIPMENT

The camera should be kept close at hand, together with filter, expo-

The traveler may try to catch the mood of a time and country in a photograph. Some photos from a trip will have meaning only to the photographer, others will be understood in the same way by many viewers. A Spanish woman crosses the deserted bullfight ring in Ronda, Spain. (Photo: Michael E. Bry)

The close-up candid shot is a favorite of all. But a leisurely look at an occasional vertical view gives the photographer's audience a change, as in this photo taken along the Seine in the Parisian spring. (Photo: Michael E. Bry)

sure meter, and a spare roll of film.

Flight and gadget bags are usually weighed. Therefore, if the traveler is in danger of exceeding his weight limitation, a telephoto lens or other heavy piece of equipment can be carried in the passenger's topcoat pocket.

By making his camera as much a personal accessory as his hat, watch, or wallet, the traveler will be prepared for photo opportunities at all times. Moreover he will be less likely to leave it behind in a public place. When dining, the camera should never be hung over the back of a chair or on an unguarded coat rack.

When traveling the strap should be let out and the camera carried over the shoulder, with a second or "anchor" strap to keep it from swinging loosely when hiking, cycling, motor scootering, or horseback riding or when engaging in any similar activity which may jar the camera.

In picture-taking situations, the strap can be shortened and the camera carried at chest level. By reinforcing the strap with thin, strong wire, the chances of its being cut and of the camera being stolen are minimized.

When traveling by car, the camera should never be placed in the glove compartment, on the ledges above the instrument panel, or behind the back seat. When it is not being carried, the best place for it is on the floor in the rear, on the side away from the exhaust pipe. If the camera is left in the car, even for short periods, it should be covered to protect it against the sun's heat and to avoid tempting potential thieves.

Always guard against the possibility of theft. Cameras and photographic equipment in general are easily disposed of and difficult to trace. They should be kept in a safe place when not in use. Cameras left in a hotel room should be kept in locked luggage. Expensive equipment can be left with the manager or cashier for safekeeping.

CAMERA CARE

Elementary rules of camera care should not only be observed but intensified when traveling abroad, since equipment is more likely to be damaged because of greater use and handling. Moreover, time and circumstances may not permit the necessary repairs.

When the camera or other equipment is carried in luggage, it should be packed near the top and wrapped in a towel, a sweater, or other garment to prevent jarring.

The camera should be protected from dirt and grime. Lens tissue and a soft sable brush should be taken along and used frequently to keep the camera clean.

In the salt air of the shore or the sea, the camera should be kept in a tightly closed container or plastic bag to protect it from sand and spray.

If the camera is dropped into salt water, it should be taken to a technician for an immediate thorough cleaning. If this is not possible, the camera should be soaked in fresh water—admittedly a drastic measure, but one which will minimize corrosion.

In rainy weather, the camera should be kept under a coat, or otherwise protected, when not in use. A lens cap will keep rain or snow from the lens; a lens shade will help protect it in use.

FILM PROTECTION

Film should also be given special care when traveling. Leading brands of still-camera film are available with "tropical" packing; the roll is hermetically sealed in a moisture-barrier package—a metal can with a neoprene gasket for 35 mm color film or sealed metal foil for roll film.

Where the climate is hot and humid, the air contains a high percentage of moisture. Remember that it takes film less than an hour to come to equilibrium with the prevailing atmospheric conditions. Thus, when the exposed film is replaced in its original metal container and the cap screwed on, the moisture which it has absorbed will be sealed in, resulting in accelerated deterioration and possible loss of maximum density.

To better preserve exposed 35 mm film, pry out the gasket from the inside of the metal-container lid and do not screw the lid on tightly. This will allow the film to "breathe" and help lessen the moisture content.

CUSTOMS REGULATIONS

Regulations governing the importation of photographic equipment for personal use vary from country to country. In general, two cameras of different types, plus a "reasonable" quantity of film and accessories, will be admitted without difficulty.

If the traveler is carrying more than the permissible amount of equipment or film, he may be required to pay duty or post a bond as a guarantee that the items in question will not be sold or otherwise disposed of while the visitor is in the country. An alternative is to place equipment which will not be used and some film in bond at the point of entry, reclaiming it at the time of departure. The disadvantage here is that the visitor must leave from the same point at which he entered the country.

Whenever any payments are made to an official, either as a deposit or duty, or when any items are left in bond, a formal, legible receipt should be requested and kept with other valuable documents.

If the traveler is asked to pay duty on an excessive amount of film, he may suggest to the customs officer that such film as he does not intend to use within the country be officially sealed. As it is not feasible to have each roll treated in this manner, all surplus film should be placed in a package which cannot be opened without breaking the seal. If only one roll from the package is used, however, all of the film will be subject to duty when leaving the country. If a few additional rolls are required, it may be more economical to purchase extra film for use until the next border is reached.

Most foreign countries are accustomed to camera-carrying American tourists, and any reasonable amount of equipment and film is usually passed without any problems or delays. Many U. S. citizens returning from abroad are surprised to find that our own customs authorities are more thorough than any they had encountered in other countries.

At present the duty-free allowance for returning residents is limited to $100. In order to conserve this allowance for goods purchased abroad, and to avoid having a duty levied on foreign-made products which were purchased in the United States, it is advisable to have a bill of sale, a copy of an insurance policy, or a notarized statement listing all items of photographic equipment and supplies taken out of the country.

Any foreign-made equipment should be registered on form number 44SS to be obtained from U. S. customs authorities at the American departure point. This form must be kept, as it may be requested when re-entering the United States. There is no charge for this service.

If photographic equipment is purchased abroad, the fact that it has been used en route does not make it exempt from duty, the amount of which is generally 15 to 20 percent of its wholesale value.

Apart from customs regulations, there are certain other restrictions designed to protect commercial importers of merchandise. Only one European-purchased Leica, for example, with one attached lens, may be brought in by each returning citizen. For customs purposes, however, no distinction is made as to the age of the traveler. Thus an infant is technically entitled to his own Leica and lens as well as a $100 duty exemption.

If movie film (8 or 16 mm, black-and-white or color) manufactured outside the United States is returned to this country for processing, duty will be levied, paid by the company, and charged to the account of the owner. Film of U. S. manufacture should not be returned in foreign-film cartons, as it will be subject to duty.

In general, it is recommended that film purchased abroad be processed in the country of manufacture. Payment of duty is avoided, and the photographer can check on the results of his picture taking. Special censorship and customs regulations apply to exposed films in certain countries where no processing facilities for some types of U. S. film are available. In certain cases, film cannot be sent or taken from one country to another for processing.

Specific information concerning processing facilities and customs regulations on film may be obtained from: Sales Service Division, Eastman Kodak Company, Rochester 4, N. Y.; Ansco Export Department, 435 Hudson Street, New York 14, N. Y.

BUDGETING FILM

Subject to customs regulations, weight, bulk, and other considerations, the foreign-bound traveler will do well to budget his film as he does his time and money.

Requirements will vary according to interests and opportunities, but the average photographer uses one 20-exposure roll per day for 35 mm cameras. With a 35 mm camera, 36-exposure rolls are preferable for two reasons: fewer film changes are required; and customs officials are inclined to count the number of rolls and to disregard the number of potential pictures represented.

If a collection of color slides is the objective, the traveler should stock up on such films as Kodachrome II, Kodak Ektachrome, or Anscochrome. For limited light conditions on very dark days, or when photographing large interiors, a few rolls of Kodak High Speed Ektachrome or Super Anscochrome may be required for high shutter speeds or maximum depth of field. Color prints, as well as slides, can be made from these films.

Color prints are more economical, however, if a color-negative film such as Kodacolor is used. Two-by-two-inch transparencies can also be made from Kodacolor negatives.

Black-and-white film for still cameras is obtainable almost everywhere, as are processing facilities. When good local service is available and the travel schedule permits, it is suggested that an occasional roll be developed and examined to check exposures and picture quality.

PROCESSING PROCEDURES

Only reputable dealers or laboratories should be patronized. Small, off-trail stores and studios may have limited facilities and are inclined to use chemicals to the point of exhaustion.

Despite the availability of black-and-white film, characteristics will vary according to brand and type,

The curiosity of the traveler will open many aspects of photography to him. A polite request to view the workroom of a small shop selling wood carvings resulted in this photo in northern Italy. (Photo: Michael E. Bry)

The juxtaposition of new and old will bring the camera to the eye of the perceptive photographer. A shepherd tends his flock along the centuries-old Via Appia Antica, only minutes from the center of Rome. (Photo: Michael E. Bry)

so the traveler should carry a substantial supply of a type with which he is familiar.

Film prices abroad, particularly in popular tourist areas, are usually somewhat higher than in the United States. As the price of Kodachrome II in foreign countries includes the cost of processing, the original purchase price will be considerably higher than in the United States, where it is sold without processing charges included.

For convenience in mailing Kodachrome II to the states for processing, Kodak Prepaid Processing Mailers may be purchased from photographic dealers. Kodachrome purchased abroad (with processing charges included in the price) will be processed without additional cost by any Kodak laboratory. Non-Kodak laboratories will charge for processing, whether or not such costs were included in the original purchase price.

At least one week should be allowed for color film to be returned when it is mailed to a laboratory within the country being visited. Additional time will be required if the film is mailed from one country to another for processing. The return address should be one at which the traveler expects to remain for a considerable length of time. Registered air mail is recommended for sending film to the United States for processing.

Duty will be assessed on films intended for commercial use. Film for other use should be plainly marked: "Exposed film for processing. Pictures for personal use exclusively—not for any commercial purpose.

BEGINNING THE TRIP

Picture-taking opportunities present themselves even before the traveler boards the ship, plane, train, motor coach, or car that takes him on his journey. An early arrival at the station, terminal, pier, or airport will not only allow ample time to see that all transportation details are in order, but may provide unusual photographic fare—especially at ship sailings.

When traveling by sea there will be an endless round of shipboard activities. Even if strobe or flash is not used at any other time during the trip, there will be enough opportunities aboard ship to justify taking the equipment. A supplementary light is essential for shooting ship shows and parties, and is also useful in deck scenes, to compensate for extreme contrasts created by intense light reflected by the water and by the bright exterior of the ship. The best time for exterior views is when masses of white clouds are present; clouds tend to cut down extreme contrasts by reflecting some light into the shadows.

PLANE PICTURES

The following suggestions for taking photos in flight are adapted from the book, *New Horizons World Guide,* prepared and published by Pan American World Airways.

While flying do not take movies or snapshots, in either color or black-and-white, when haze or smoke make it difficult to see the ground. A small amount of haze won't greatly affect photos; however, it is a good idea to use a haze filter.

To avoid reflection from the airplane window, hold the camera close to, but not touching, the window. Let your body cushion the camera from vibration. Take pictures from the shady side of the plane, if possible. This will usually be on the left side when flying east, the right side when flying west.

When taking aerial pictures, a shutter speed of at least $^{1}/_{100}$ of a second should be used for stills (32 frames per second for movies). Suggested exposures in flight are:

Still-camera settings in sunlight for Kodacolor or black-and-white film rated at a daylight speed of 50: landscape, $^{1}/_{100}$ at *f*/8 or $^{1}/_{200}$ at *f*/5.6; clouds (from above), $^{1}/_{100}$ at *f*/11-16 or $^{1}/_{200}$ at *f*/8-11.

Still-camera settings for Kodachrome II or Anscochrome at $^{1}/_{100}$ (for $^{1}/_{200}$ use next larger lens opening): below 2000 feet, bright sun, *f*/5.6-8; hazy sun, *f*/4-5.6; cloudy bright, *f*/2.8-4. From 2000 feet to 4000 feet, bright sun, *f*/8; hazy sun, *f*/5.6; cloudy bright, *f*/4. Above 4000 feet, bright sun, *f*/8-11; hazy sun, *f*/5.6-8; cloudy bright, clouds from above, *f*/11.

Movie-camera settings for Kodachrome II, Daylight Type 8 or 16 mm (16 frames per second; at 32 frames per second, use next larger lens opening): below 2000 feet, bright sun, *f*/11; hazy sun, *f*/8, cloudy bright, *f*/5.6; cloudy dull, *f*/4. From 2000 to 4000 feet, bright sun, *f*/11-16; hazy sun, *f*/8-11; cloudy bright, *f*/5.6-8; cloudy dull, *f*/4.5-6. From 4000 feet and up, bright sun, *f*/16; hazy sun, *f*/11; cloudy bright, clouds from above, *f*/16; cloudy dull, clouds from above, *f*/16.

Before taking photos from a plane, find out if photography is permitted. There are times when it is not, as when flying over restricted areas. The best vantage point is a window seat on the shaded side of the plane, well back of the wing.

Photographs taken at altitudes of less than 1000 feet are likely to be blurred. Panning in the direction of flight, that is, keeping the subject centered in the viewfinder, will help to compensate for the plane movement.

A pale yellow filter is suggested with black-and-white film. A sky filter should be used with color film, but not in early morning or late afternoon.

PICTURES FROM VEHICLES

Taking pictures from fast-moving surface vehicles—trains, cars, and buses—generally is not feasible. When the usual precautions against vibration are taken, however, there will probably be little evidence of movement if the object is a distant one, or if it is photographed directly ahead or to the rear. Panning also helps to minimize movement.

The motorist probably will want a photo of the car he is using, particularly if it is colorful or of distinctive foreign design. Generally, the car should be an incidental rather than a dominant part of the composition. When "posing" the car, it may best to show it entering the picture and pointing at the center of interest. Road signs bearing the names of places make good titling subjects for the movie enthusiast and help to orient slide collections and print displays.

Foreign motor-coach itineraries, particularly in Europe, are designed for tourist travel and incorporate points of photographic interest. The driver will stop for picture taking.

The wide scenic view is a standard for travel photographers, a favorite of armchair viewers. Mount Fujiyama, Japan. (Photo: Pan American)

REMINDERS AND SUGGESTIONS

Anyone who takes good pictures at home should be able to take good pictures when he travels abroad. If this theory is not always borne out by results, it may be attributed, in part, to the fact that fundamentals have been forgotten in the excite-

ment of the trip.

One of the more common faults of the amateur photographer abroad is his attempt to encompass a maximum amount of scenery within a single frame. With the movie maker, this tendency is evidenced by rapid panning in an effort to compress miles of landscape into a few square feet of screen. Wide-angle or panoramic shots are instrumental in establishing locale, but these wide-angle shots should be incidental to medium-range and close-up shots, and should be relatively fewer in number.

Another common fault is that the photographer often takes pictures from the angle or point of view that is most convenient for him, rather than from the angle that best suits the subject. By looking at a collection of travel slides, it is often easy to tell whether the photographer is tall or short, or whether he used an eye-level or waist-level viewfinder.

EXPOSURE PROBLEMS

Poorly exposed pictures, despite the wide latitude of modern film and the extensive use of exposure meters, are also quite characteristic of foreign-travel photography—un-

Keep the camera easily available for shots which will arise in an instant and be gone just as quickly. A priest crosses a street in front of a bus in Rome. (Photo: Esther Bubley / The Lamp, Standard Oil Co., N.J.)

doubtedly due to a wide range of unfamiliar subjects and light conditions.

Scenes in tropical and subtropical regions, for example, are likely to contain extreme contrasts of light and shadow. Frequently there is more "photographic" light than experience or the meter may indicate. White marble structures, such as the leaning tower of Pisa and the adjacent baptistry, or Grecian temples, reflect considerable light and are frequently overexposed.

Conversely, many of the buildings in London and castles along the Rhine are dark subjects that may require a stop more than would normally be indicated. To further complicate the situation, a wide range of exposures may be necessary for subjects within a limited area. The white cliffs of Dover, for example, reflect a considerable amount of light, even on overcast days, whereas nearby Dover Castle absorbs so much light that it is usually underexposed.

When in doubt as to the correct exposure for color, one may "bracket" the recommended exposure, i.e., one shot can be made at the indicated aperture, another at a half stop greater, and still another at a half stop smaller. When using black-and-white, take shots a full stop each way.

ALL-WEATHER PHOTOGRAPHY

Weather is of as much concern to the photographer as to the airplane pilot. Far from being a deterrent, changes in weather conditions should provide increased interest and variety to any record of foreign travel. The photographer can transform ordinary street scenes into pictorial gems by venturing out in the rain and mist. Wet pavements produce interesting foreground reflections, and dark skies provide contrast for architectural subjects. A plastic bag will help to keep the camera dry; a lens hood will protect the lens and will minimize the possibility of its being exposed to the direct rays of reflected light.

On misty days, compositions will be strengthened by the elimination of distracting details. The light is often stronger than it appears to be, and an additional shot at a half stop smaller than the indicated aperture may be advisable. In wet or humid weather, the lens should be checked against condensation prior to each shot.

Snow scenes, because of the dominant white, would seem to be unaffected, photographically, by weather conditions. Experience indicates, however, that snow requires a considerable amount of light in order to register its brilliance adequately on film. Pictures taken at right angles to the light source are generally most effective.

MORNING, NOON, AND NIGHT

Early morning is a good time to photograph street scenes. Crowds and traffic have not yet appeared to obstruct the view, and the sun is weak enough to permit shooting against it for some unusual backlighted compositions.

Sunsets are favored photographic fare for the tourist, and their variety throughout the world is infinite. Near the equator, sunsets are of extremely short duration and the photographer must act quickly. The bracketing of exposures is especially recommended for sunsets, as it is difficult to obtain an accurate meter reading. A difference in exposures may produce "different" sunsets on succeeding days, from the same shooting position.

A color-film record of a trip abroad cannot be considered quite complete without views of such nocturnal attractions as Piccadilly Circus—the London equivalent of Times Square—or the illuminated châteaux in the Loire River valley in France. Experts suggest that the best time for city night views is at dusk, when some daylight remains to limn the skyline, and building lights have just been turned on. This is a tripod-cable-release situation, and although some experimenting with exposures may be necessary, half a second exposure at $f/3.5$ should produce reasonably good results on standard color film. Illuminated night views can be effective with daylight-type color film, even without a compensating filter. As the danger of reflected light in the lens is perhaps even greater than during the day, a lens shade is recommended.

BEACHES, WATER, AND MOUNTAINS

Because a large number of Americans live and take pictures in areas where there are no mountains or ocean beaches, these subjects frequently present problems due to the photographer's lack of experience.

The tendency in beach scenes is to show a vast expanse of sand, water and sky. General views can be improved if the viewfinder is pointed along the shore, rather than across the beach toward the ocean. A high point of land will improve the composition, as will a figure, boat, piece of driftwood, or other object in the foreground.

Water, photographically speaking, is as variable from place to place as the land. To capture the distinctive blue of oceans or lakes on film follow these suggestions:

Choose as high a camera angle as possible. The higher the angle, the less color-degrading surface reflections from the "shiny" water will be reflected to the lens. It is this high angle of viewing which makes coastal waters appear extremely vivid from a plane but much more subdued from a boat. A beach-and-ocean scene will be more effective if taken from a cliff, the roof of a hotel, or from any other high position, rather than at sea level.

Frontlighting produces a better color than backlighting. With the sun shining toward the camera, the highly reflective surface of the water mirrors the sun's specular reflection, causing a loss of water coloration. The smoother the water, the more intense the color, due to fewer reflections.

Slight underexposure with Kodachrome II, Ektachrome, or equivalent film will help preserve blue water color. A less-than-normal exposure with these films will also improve the rendition of a white-sand beach, an extra-bright subject.

Mountains would seem to gain photographically by direct sunlight, but actually they photograph best in unsettled or cloudy weather. Early-morning or late-afternoon light will produce a more interesting variety of shapes, forms, and shadows than will light at midday. Colors are likely to be more varied in early spring or autumn than in midsummer.

Many photographers will instinctively tilt their cameras upward when confronted by a mountain.

The coast of British Columbia inspired this view of clouds, harsh land, and water framed in a ship's rigging. (Photo: British Columbia Government)

Tours arranged for a specific profession or interest can result in a series of fine photos on one subject. Children in this school in Paraguay concentrated in spite of the photographer, who used natural light. (Photo: UNESCO)

The intent is to emphasize its height, but the result is to flatten it out. Mountains are at their pictorial best when the camera is held level and when they are viewed from an opposite slope.

FLOWERS AND FOLIAGE

City dwellers are impressed with the quantity and variety of flowers and foliage seen on their travels abroad, and have an understandable inclination to bring back as much as can be crowded in their supply of film.

A general view of a Japanese cherry orchard in bloom or a vast field of tulips in Holland is difficult to resist, and a few such views can be impressive. But some film should be saved for close-ups, using flash or a reflector to lighten the shadows of a few flowers silhouetted against the sky, or using a supplementary lens to emphasize the color and design of a single bud or blossom. Fast shutter speeds are best in photographing flowers and foliage, as even a slight breeze will cause a blurred image.

Move in close to catch the details of life and work which make every minute of your trip different from what you saw daily at home. (Photo: Zeiss Ikon)

FESTIVALS AND SPORTING EVENTS

In most parts of the civilized world, people today dress very much alike, and traditional costumes are reserved for fairs, festivals and other special events. Itineraries planned to coincide with such celebrations as carnival time in Rio de Janeiro or the Queen's Birthday in Britain will provide spectacular subject matter. Religious processions and celebrations are impressive and colorful, but one should determine ahead of time under what circumstances photography is permitted.

Zone focusing can be effectively employed for fast shots of parades and festivals and for candid photos. Wide-angle lenses are best for this purpose, due to their relatively greater depth of field.

Cameras with eye-level viewfinders are convenient in crowds where it is necessary to shoot over the heads of other spectators. Twin reflexes can be held above the head, upside down, with the picture sighted from below.

It's virtually impossible to take a poor photo of Thai dancers. Each attitude is a carefully contrived pose; an impression of movement sometimes can be achieved by using slow shutter speeds and shooting just as the dancers move from one position to another. (Photo: Pan American)

Sporting events, which usually provide color and excitement, have the additional advantage of attracting a varied and colorfully attired group of people. (See *Action Photography* and *Sports Photography.)*

The bullfight, which can be seen in Portugal, France, Spain, and certain Latin American countries, is a special event outside the knowledge of most Americans. Bullfights take place in the late afternoon, and the spectator will have a choice of seats on either the sunny or shady side of the arena. The latter are more expensive but worth it for the photographer. As there may be some distance between the seat and the center of action, a long-focus lens is usually required.

INTERIORS

Although flash equipment may be useful for some interior shots, there will be many instances where it is either inadequate or not permitted.

The alternative is to use a tripod, or other fixed camera base such as a clamp, which will permit a time exposure. Exposures may vary from a split second to half a minute or more, but the following recommendations for daylight-type Kodachrome II, or its equivalent in speed, will provide a basis for reasonably accurate work.

For objects that appear to be well illuminated, such as paintings and sculpture in the Louvre or Prado museums, three seconds at $f/8$ should suffice. For a fairly dim room interior, with no skylight and few windows, 10 to 12 seconds at the same aperture may be required. Most churches and cathedrals are dimly lighted and have dark walls; they may require as much as 15 seconds at $f/5.6$.

Bracketing may be employed to assure correct exposures. If Kodachrome II or Anscochrome is used, one exposure should be made at half the indicated time and another at twice the normal time. A dimly lighted interior, for example, might be given 15, 30, and 60 seconds at $f/5.6$. As Kodacolor has wider latitude, additional exposures may be made at one third and three times the estimated exposure.

Where no tripod or clamp is available, the following procedure, adapted from Kodak's *Vacation Europe,* is suggested:

For the exposure range between $^1/_{25}$ and $^1/_5$ of a second, the photographer can sit on a chair and rest his elbows on a table or bench in front of him, or he can turn the chair around and rest the camera on its back. For longer exposures, the camera may be rested on a bench, chair seat, or mantelpiece.

If available furniture does not provide a sufficiently high viewpoint, there is always a solid wall against which to brace the camera. The technique is to stand as close to the wall as possible to frame and focus the picture. After the shutter is set, the camera should be held firmly against the wall with one hand; the photographer will then make the exposure with his other hand, preferably using a cable release.

A rubber fruit-jar ring may be used for a nonskid base. If the camera is to be aimed at an angle, a coin or two can be tucked between the camera and the wall.

In churches and cathedrals, particularly in Europe, windows are both a problem and a subject of particular photographic interest. Generally in photographing interiors, it is best to avoid windows in the composition, since proper exposure of the dark interiors will greatly overexpose the window and its surrounding areas.

Except for cameras equipped with fast lenses, stained-glass windows will necessitate a time exposure. Kodak, which has processed thousands of stained-glass-window slides and color prints for returning travelers, makes the following suggestions:

Try to fill the picture with the window, since the surrounding area will be rendered black, regardless of how much detail the eyes can perceive. Get as close as possible to the window without obtaining a distorted view. As the windows are usually at some distance from the viewer, a telephoto lens may be helpful.

Since some stained-glass windows are nearly transparent, while others are quite dense, there is no single exposure suitable for all. The average opalescent window, not illuminated by the direct rays of the sun, will require about one second at $f/5.6$ with conventional color film, $f/8$ with Kodacolor.

PEOPLE IN THE PICTURE

All views of such landmarks as the Eiffel Tower in Paris or Sugar Loaf Mountain in Rio de Janeiro are bound to resemble other views of the same subjects. But a close-up of a Portuguese fisherman mending his net, or of a Haitian woman balancing a huge basket of fruit on her head, represents the photographer's personal choice of subject, point of view, and interpretation.

The difference between one country and another is often marked less by its terrain than by its people. Although dress has become somewhat standardized throughout the world, traditional costumes and distinctive local dress are still to be found in villages and rural areas. Islands, even those which lie rather close to the mainland, are particularly rich in atmosphere and are relatively unaffected by modern influences.

In Holland (with the exception of Vollendam, where inhabitants wear traditional costumes as a lure for tourists), about the only place where characteristic Dutch dress can be found is the island of Maarken. Similar anachronisms may be seen on Italy's island of Sardinia; in Corsica, off the southern coast of France; in the Canary Islands, which belong to Spain; and in Britain's Channel Islands (Guernsey, Jersey, and Sark). A difference in atmosphere is also evident between islands of one group. The "Out Islands" of the Bahamas, for example, or the "Neighbor Islands" of Hawaii, have yet to acquire the veneer of New Providence and Oahu, where Nassau and Honolulu are situated.

Don't be in too much of a hurry to get off the ship which takes you to new places. Nearby may be the possibility of a fine photo, as this one taken with an Asahi Pentax, 58mm Takuma f/2 lens, 1/10 of a second at f/5.

The photographer in search of local color and unusual characters is less likely to find them on the fashionable streets and boulevards of a city than at such places as Les Halles (the great central market of Paris) early in the morning, or in a London pub in the late afternoon as workers stop off for their preprandial "pint."

CANDID METHODS

There are two ways in which to get pictures of people at work or at play. One is to shoot without their being aware of your presence or intention. The other is to ask permission.

In taking candid photographs, close-ups in particular, it is necessary to be as unobtrusive as possible. A battery of cameras and bulging gadget bags are bound to attract attention. A telephoto lens can be helpful, but it is rather bulky and difficult to conceal when mingling with people at close quarters.

Some successful candid photographers prefer a wide-angle lens, since it reduces the over-all dimensions of a 35 mm camera and, without the case, can be worn chest-high concealed by a coat or jacket until it is ready to use. Even then only the inconspicuous lens need be exposed to view. Another advantage of the wide-angle lens is that its depth of field permits zone focusing, and all the photographer need do is aim and shoot.

A right-angle viewfinder can be helpful, since people are more inclined to notice the direction in which the photographer is facing than the position of his lens. A reflex camera can be used to catch subjects off guard simply by pointing the lens in one direction while pretending to be interested in, and focusing upon, some other object. Members of certain religious sects and natives of some countries, it should be noted, are strongly averse to being photographed.

YOU ARE A GUEST

A reluctance to be photographed is not always based on superstition or religious belief. Some subjects may be self-conscious; others may regard photography as an invasion of their privacy. Under such circumstances the photographer should bear in mind that he is the foreigner and a guest of the country he happens to be visiting.

To obtain the cooperation of subjects, it may be necessary to take one or two portrait shots, with the promise of forwarding a print to the model. A Polaroid Land camera, which provides a black-and-white print in ten seconds, can be extremely helpful in gaining cooperation. If the subject is inclined to look directly at the camera, a few head-on shots may be taken as a gesture of the photographer's good will. Once the model's confidence has been obtained, he may be asked to continue with whatever he was doing.

Pantomime is usually adequate, but a few phrases in the language of the country may be helpful. An English-speaking acquaintance, or perhaps the hotel concierge, may help with the pronunciation; or the phrases may be copied down on a piece of paper and shown to the "model" at the appropriate time. The following phrases are suggested by *The Men's Guide to Europe,* edited by Eugene Fodor, published by David McKay Company, New York:

English

1. I would like to take your picture.
2. Please don't look at the camera.
3. Thank you very much.

Danish

1. Mä jeg tage et billede af Dem?
2. Vaer sa venlig ikke at kigge pa apparatet.
3. Mange tak.

Dutch

1. Mag ik een foto van U nemen?
2. Kijk niet in de camera, als 't U blieft.
3. Hartelijk dank.

French

1. Je voudrais vous photographier.
2. Ne regardez pas l'appareil s'il vous plait.
3. Merci beaucoup.

German

1. Ich möchte Sie gerne photographieren.
2. Bitte schauen Sie nicht in die Kamera.
3. Ich danke Ihnen sehr.

Italian

1. Vorrei farle una fotografia.
2. Non guardi l'apparecchio, per favore.
3. Grazie infinite.

Norwegian

1. Far jeg lov til a ta et bilde av Dem?
2. Se ikke pa kameraet er De snill.
3. Takk skal De ha.

Portuguese

1. Eu gostaria de tirar una fotografia sua.
2. Por favor, nao alhe para a camera.
3. Muito obrigado.

Spanish

1. Me agradaria tomar una fotografia de usted.
2. Sirvase no mirar hacia el aparato.
3. Muchas gracias.

Swedish

1. Far jag fotografera Eder?
2. Titta inte pa kameran.
3. Tack sa mycket.

SUBJECT AND EXPOSURE

Film, unlike the human eye, has a fixed sensitivity. When exposed as it usually is for middle tones and highlights, it will not register detail in the shadows, though they may be visible to the eye. Dark-skinned subjects present an exposure problem, particularly as they are usually encountered in areas where the sun is strong and where clothes and buildings are light in color. The result is a contrast range beyond the sensitivity of the film. The situation is further complicated by the fact that people in warm countries often wear broad-brimmed hats which place their faces in shadow.

There are several solutions which can be used in combination to compensate for extreme contrasts: 1) If feasible, the subject should be asked to tip the hat brim upward; 2) have the model face in the direction of the light source; 3) avoid light-toned backgrounds so that exposure can be made for darker areas; 4) use fill-in flash.

People not only are interesting subjects in themselves but may be used to give life, atmosphere, and color to medium and long-range scenic and architectural views. A Buddhist temple in Kyoto takes on added interest if a priest is shown entering or leaving it; the copy of Michelangelo's statue of David in Florence looms even larger and more classic with a souvenir vendor at its base.

A characteristically dressed native of the country is, of course, preferable as the human element in a picture, but if such a person is not there, a traveling companion can walk into the middle foreground.

STORYTELLING PICTURES

When even a manufacturer of photographic equipment and film, such as the Eastman Kodak company, advises foreign-bound camera enthusiasts to study the history of countries they plan to visit, it is evident that the criteria for good travel pictures extend beyond good composition, lighting, and technical proficiency.

Although the cameraman may be content with a print or slide that is graphically pleasing, those who view it may want to know more about the subject. The more a photographer knows about the places and people to be encountered on his itinerary, the better are his chances of returning with pictures that are significant in historic, human, as well as graphic terms.

The photographer will pick up much background information in his travels. A notebook in which to jot down material for captions or commentary is standard equipment.

One of the Bahamas' principal tourist attractions, for example, are the trained flamingoes at Nassau; their trainer's commands and explanations are no less colorful than the performance. A few excerpts used as captions for prints or incorporated in the photographer's slide or film narration will add an interesting dimension.

The Route Napoléon that leads from the Riviera to Paris would provide ample photographic fare without any reference to its historical significance. But the picture of a hut snuggled against a mountainside assumes greater importance when the viewer is reminded that Napoléon Bonaparte spent a night here on his triumphant return from Elba.

Welcome home—the Statue of Liberty is a time-honored shot for returning Americans. This photo more than makes up in feeling for the loss of detail which the more common close-up photo has. (Photo: Standard Oil Co., N.J.)

Scene from a film on the Civil War consisting of engravings and also photographs by Mathew Brady. The camera markings are shown on a transparent-sheet overlay that is removed before camera action.

FOTOMATION

Francis P. Lee
Motion-Picture Consultant, New York City

[The comparatively new technique of fotomation can be applied to amateur as well as professional films. Here the technique is explained and its numerous practical applications are discussed.]

• *Also see: Cinematography, Professional; Special Photographic Effects in Cinematography.*

Fotomation is a type of motion picture that combines photography, animation, and automation. Usually shot with a motion-picture camera mounted on an animation stand, fotomated films can be produced in color or black-and-white, with or without sound, and in 35 mm, 16 mm or 8 mm. Advanced production techniques involve the use of an electronically synchronized, motorized animation stand with the camera shooting and the various parts of the animation stand moving synchronously to produce the desired effect. A much slower way of shooting fotomation film is frame by frame, stop motion.

Subject matter for the fotomated film consists of essentially "still" material which is brought to life on the motion-picture screen. This "still" subject matter can consist of color or black-and-white photographs, transparencies, reproductions, newspaper headlines or articles, paintings, drawings, diagrams, charts, blueprints, posters, lettering, or any other graphic material.

The fotomation process combines some of the techniques known as squeeze motion, filmograph, and slide motion. The technique of "still" material shot with an animation camera, although not new, has been greatly refined, synthesized, and reorganized under the heading of fotomation. The development and refinement of fotomation has been carried out by the author and Alvin Stahl, producer and director of Animated Productions, New York. During the two years of its development, over 100 films have been produced, including a full-length motion-picture feature.

AUDIENCE EFFECT

A motion picture produced by the fotomation process, with photographs as subject matter, has almost the flow and action of a live-action film. In certain films, consisting of live action and fotomation of photographs, it is almost impossible to tell the difference, since a zoom shot into a photograph or transparency on an animation stand looks much the same as a dolly shot made with a live-action camera crew on location.

For example, in a color motion picture on the architecture of Frank Lloyd Wright, certain live-action scenes shot on location were unusable because of a defective motion-picture camera. Fortunately, at the same time the camera crews were shooting a still photographer shot some color transparencies of the same scene. The author put these transparencies on an animation stand and reshot them onto motion-picture film with various movements, such as zooms, pans, dissolves and other special effects. In the finished film it is impossible to tell which is live action and which is fotomation.

In another film made in France about the work and life of the artist Vincent Van Gogh, fotomation was used exclusively. Paintings, lithographs, drawings, and photographs were shot on an animation stand in this excellently directed and photographed motion picture. Narration, music, and sound effects were all blended together and used with imagination and taste. The effect on the audience is of a kind of living biography of Van Gogh. One almost gets the feeling of having known the artist, and seen his work change from period to period. The main segments of the artist's work are shown in full, and certain details magnified on the motion-picture screen.

HOW AND WHERE IT IS USED

Fotomation can be used in films on education, science, history, or industrial public relations. It is also applicable to TV commercials, documentary films, art films, theatrical shorts, and full-length feature motion pictures.

In scientific films, fotomation can be used to show abstract scientific concepts through the use of symbols and diagrams. Fotomated motion pictures on history can be made by filming photographs of historic places, statues, documents, maps, castles, etc. All past civilizations have left behind them physical evidences of their industry, culture, and religion. Photographs of these can be made, if they are not already in existence, and fotomation can re-create history for the motion-picture screen.

In television, many documentary TV programs have used photographs shot on an animation stand, intercutting them with live TV, videotape, and live-action motion pictures. Many prize-winning TV commercials have been made with fotomation under the headings of squeeze motion, slide motion, and filmographs—all time and money-saving techniques.

Seventy five percent of one full-length feature motion picture was made in fotomation. The film, *The Black Fox*—an allegorical documentary on the life and times of Adolf Hitler—made effective use of photographs, reproductions, engravings, drawings, newspaper headlines, and specially prepared art work by Byron Goto. It was written, produced, and directed by Louis Clyde Stoumen, in association with Alvin Stahl, and photographed by the author. The film won an "Oscar."

Mr. Stoumen is a pioneer in fotomation, having made several other theatrical films using this technique. One is *The Naked Eye,* about photographers Edward Weston, Weegee, Margaret Bourke-White, Alfred Eisenstaedt, and many others. Another earlier film is *The True Story of the Civil War,* the first theatrical film to use photo-

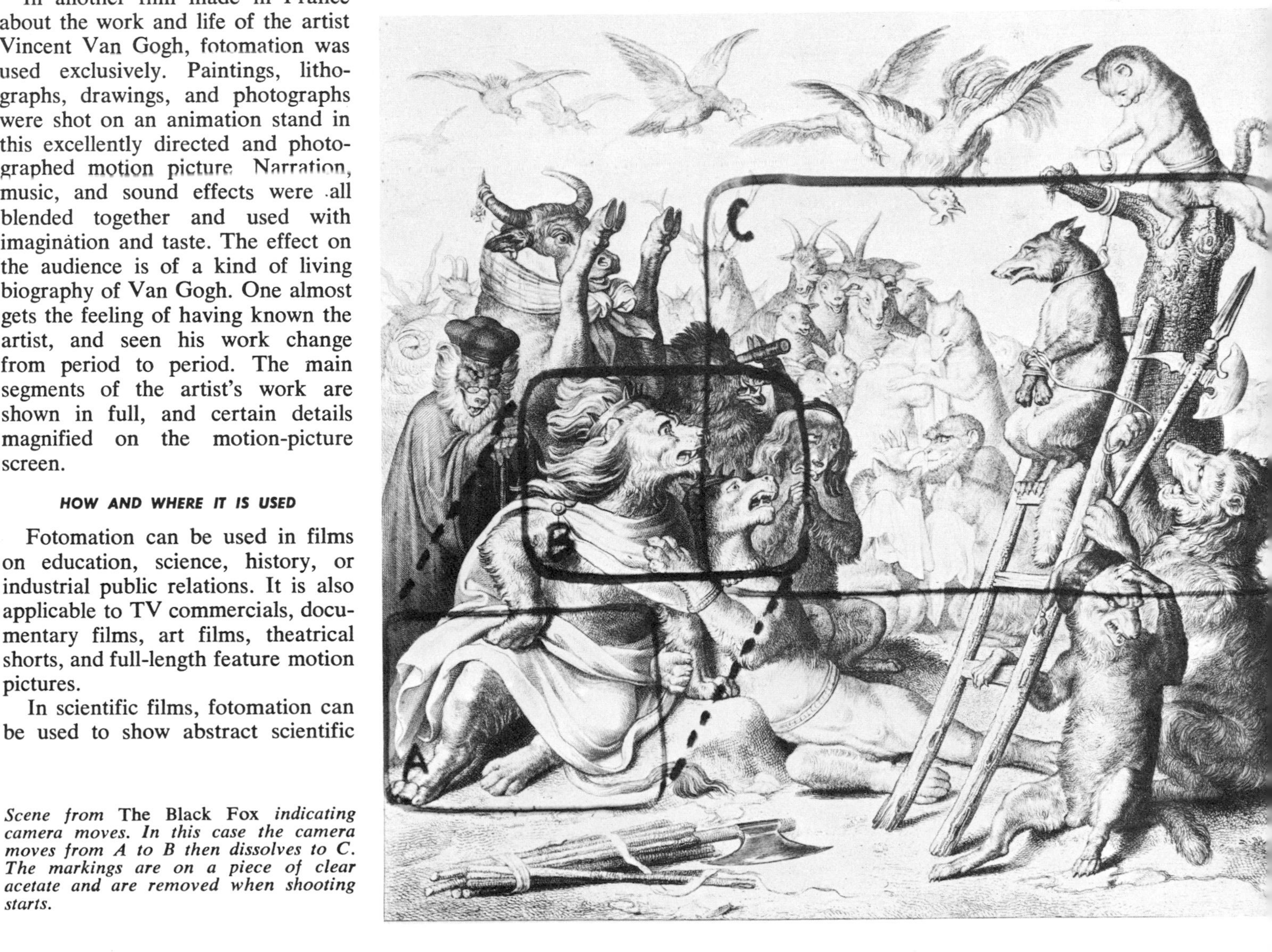

Scene from The Black Fox *indicating camera moves. In this case the camera moves from A to B then dissolves to C. The markings are on a piece of clear acetate and are removed when shooting starts.*

graphs in a dramatic structure. Photographs by Mathew Brady were the subject material. The film won an Academy Award.

HOW IT IS DONE

As in most movies, the first consideration is the script, after which, in a fotomation film, the sound track is made. The final sound track consists of narration, music, and sound effects. Once completed, the sound track is put through a small amplifier to which a special frame and footage counter is attached. This attachment indicates in numbers how many frames, or feet of sound-track film, it takes to say a certain sentence or to play a certain passage of music. These numbers are all marked in the script, as are the numbers of the musical beat. Following this analysis, simple shooting cue sheets or exposure sheets are made for the cameraman and the film is now ready to be shot.

The equipment used in fotomation consists of a motion-picture camera mounted on an animation stand. The camera is mounted vertically for shooting the picture which is placed underneath it. The picture is mounted on a table-top compound, which can move east and west (left and right) and north and south (to the operator and away from him). The compound can also rotate clockwise and counterclockwise.

With fotomation, the movements of the camera and of the table-top compound are all electronically synchronized while the camera is running continuously. The actual shooting is done in a matter of seconds and the final effect on the screen is smooth and natural. Scenes can also be shot without all the electronically synchronized controls, but it takes much longer, since frame by frame, stop-motion techniques must then be used.

In one seven-hour day of shooting fotomation of zooms, pans, and dissolves, a reasonable production goal is six minutes of final screen time

Specially prepared art work by Byron Goto for feature film The Black Fox. *Camera shooting instructions are on the clear sheet of acetate.*

Top: *A fully electronically motorized Oxberry animation stand made by Animation Equipment Co., of New Rochelle, New York. "Joy stick" is in foreground.* Bottom: *Close-up of animation art work showing overlay with detail of area to zoom into.*

per day. It all depends on the complexities of the camera moves, the number and types of effects, and the number of pictures used.

EQUIPMENT

The pioneer in this field and one of the major manufacturers of fotomation equipment is John Oxberry of Animation Equipment Company, New Rochelle, New York. One of Oxberry's latest innovation for shooting fotomation is the "joy stick"—an electronic control similar in appearance to the steering mechanism of the airplanes of the 1920's. With this "joy-stick" control, the camera operator can move the camera into and across the area being photographed with more speed and accuracy than ever before. Oxberry is constantly improving this equipment and has a device in which automation is used. By means of preset dials and switches, the camera can shoot scenes in a semi-automated fashion.

Other manufacturers of animation equipment include Richardson-Bowlds, Burbank, California; S.O.S. Ciné Photo Optics of New York City; and Richmark Camera Service, New York.

CONCEPT AND RESULT

A new concept is required in fotomation. Different styles appear, reflecting the personality of the script writer, director, producer, and cameraman, and all these talents are correlated into a new type of motion picture. For example, the same script and the same graphic materials given to two different directors will result in two different motion pictures. The directors' personalities and styles in the finished films will differ as much as their handwriting or their appearance.

There is a great future in fotomation—in the creative concept, imagination, direction, and in the speed and low budgets at which these films can be made.

FRAMING THE SCENE

Framing within the picture area is a compositional device that can give direction and emphasis to the subject. The properly framed scene will add a dimension of apparent depth to the composition and will also tend to relieve the monotony of the familiar rectangular picture shape. The frame, of course, must be related to the subject and should be an integral part of the entire composition. It need not extend around the whole picture but may appear in only part of it, depending upon its purpose and relationship to the subject.

For example, the photo (Figure 1) of the man studying is more meaningful because of the frame of books and periodicals which holds the eye within the picture and gives it the appropriate mood. The picture gains apparent depth because the side border of books acts as a funnel.

One of the rudiments of framing within a picture area is that dark or tightly composed borders tend to draw the interest in and confine it, while light or "loose" borders broaden the scene. In contrast to the picture of the scholar with its tightly composed border of books, the seaside scene (Figure 2) has a windswept quality with its airy frame of trees and branches directing attention toward the surf and swimmers.

There are countless possibilities for framing a scene. In everyday life views are framed for us, usually without our conscious knowledge, by the windows we look out of, the hallways and doorways we walk

Left: *Figure 1. The stacked books and periodicals close in the picture and hold attention on the man. The open books help to set the mood.*

Top right: *Figure 3. The foliage framing the top of this street scene not only gives a pictorial quality to the photograph but also results in a feeling of distance.*

Bottom right: *Figure 4. By moving in on the street scene, eliminating the trees, the picture takes on a different mood. The starkness of the single street is now emphasized.*

Figure 2. In this photo of a windswept beach, the trees frame and focus interest on the swimmers and surf.

through, by trees and foliage, buildings, parts of machinery, and structures.

The effectiveness of framing depends upon the photographer's creativity and intent. A street scene in a North Wales town (Figure 3) is softened by a border of foliage at the top of the picture which results in a downward emphasis. But by moving in on the scene, eliminating the trees and using the end of the row of houses as a side border, the picture takes on an entirely different mood (Figure 4). The framing in Figure 3 makes the scene pictorial, while the framing in Figure 4 emphasizes the bleakness of the street, giving it a more dramatic quality.

The technique of framing may also be used for selection or elimination. The architectural photographer in photographing a building might get rid of an unsightly telephone pole or nearby building by blocking it out with a foreground tree.

Framing must be done with purpose and with a great deal of thought. It rarely happens automatically. A meaningful relationship between subject matter and frame is essential. Often one is present without the other, and it takes ingenuity, patience, and an artistic understanding to bring the two together. In the picture of a young couple in Central Park (Figure 5) the framing was already present. Here the photographer had to see the bridge as a frame and wait until that brief moment when the two people stepped from its shadow into light.

Also see: *Composition; Esthetics of Photography; Pictorial Photography.*

Figure 5. The bridge forms a natural frame. It not only gives depth to the picture but dramatizes the couple.

Ernst Haas / *Sight of Flight*

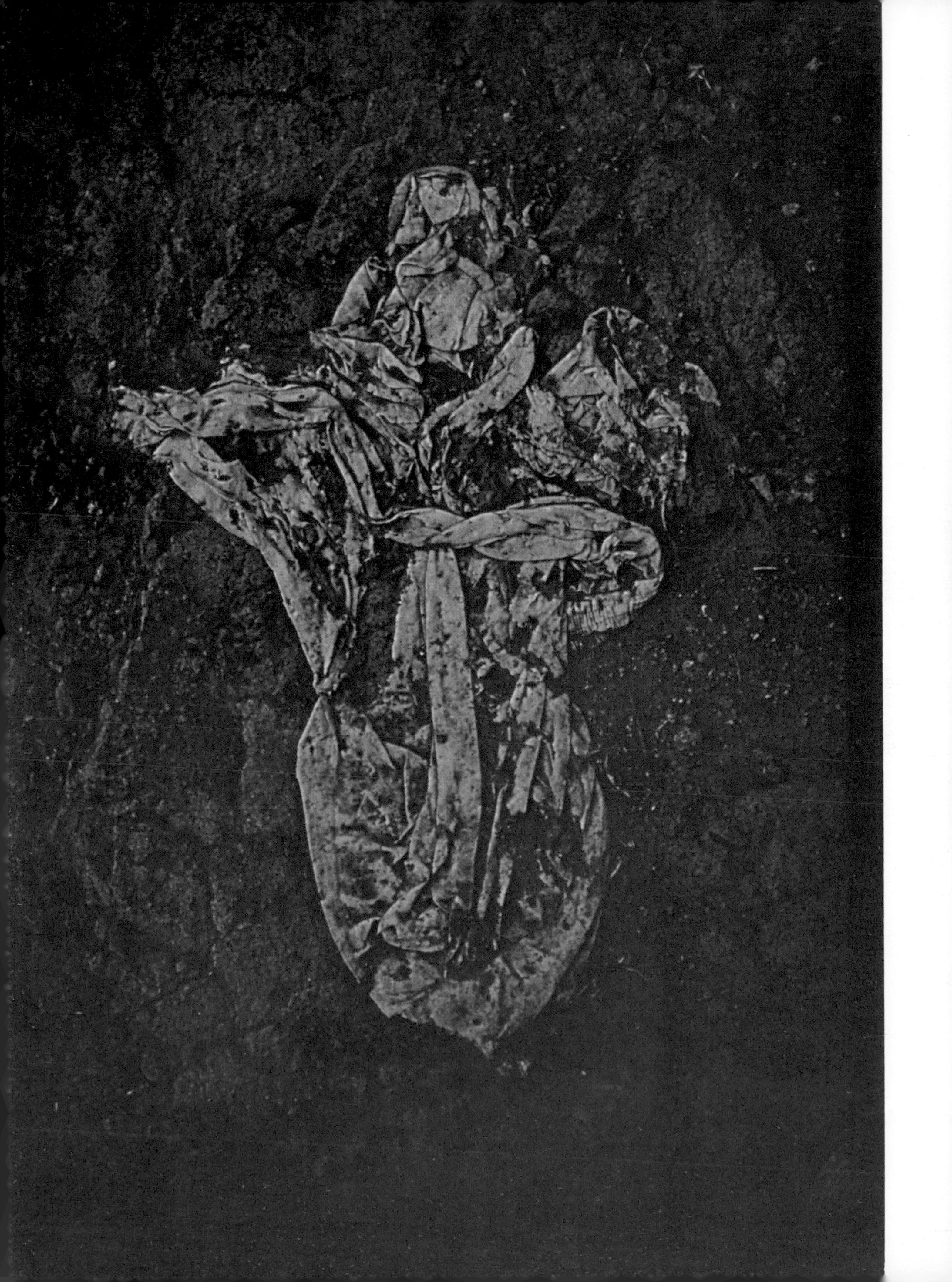

ERNST HAAS / *Study in Textures*

ERNST HAAS / *Bullfight*

Ernst Haas / *New York*

MOUNTAIN CHURCHYARD **ROLF TIETGENS**

A mysterious excitement comes through the dark, close tones and the nervous lines of this picture. If it were a painting it might be called "abstract," so independent are the mood and form from any apparent subject matter.

A dark yellow filter was used to hold the sky tone below middle value, bringing the clouds into whiter relief and making a phosphorescent backplay for the fiery twists of the naked branches. An extremely low camera angle throws the picture into an expressive distortion which makes trees and wooden cross lean obliquely inward. The wirey tangle, once a frame for memorial flowers, gives a contrasting feeling of stability to the form of the cross.

Along with the low-keyed violence of the picture goes the extreme subtlety of tones in the snowy mountain peak as they work through the pattern of branches, which in turn act as a muted subordinate theme in this richly dramatic composition.

Robert Frank.

ROBERT FRANK

Biography

"After seeing these pictures you end up finally not knowing anymore whether a jukebox is sadder than a coffin," writes Jack Kerouac about Robert Frank's work. His words express the ironic vision of life's duality—its hope / despair—which informs the photography of Robert Frank. That vision, expressed with somber beauty and compassion, creates the dominant quality of Frank's pictures. It has made them beloved as well as imitated by dozens of young photographers who also regard the camera less as a breadwinner than as one way to say what a man feels about the human condition, about life in his time.

There was little in Robert Frank's background to suggest the emergence of an artist. But the bourgeois atmosphere of his homeland and family life may have served as that "wall against which to rebel creatively" described by Ingmar Bergman. Born in Zurich on November 9, 1924, Frank began doing industrial photography in Switzerland at the age of 22 "to avoid school and [his] father's business." He also worked briefly on the set of a film in which Maria Schell was the child star, his first experience in movie making.

In 1947, he came to the United States and was soon a successful fashion photographer for *Harper's Bazaar*. Alexey Brodovitch, the *Bazaar* art director who has influenced a number of photographic careers, encouraged him to broaden out from the fashion field. Frank adopted the 35 mm camera which provided him with the key if not the secret to his style. He has said of using the Leica, "It's really brainless. Most people stop at the technical stage. To do good work you need a further intelligence."

In 1948 Robert Frank set out on a trip to Peru where with his Leica he photographed the Andean Indians. On the whole these pictures are flatter, more "journalistic," than his later work. He often shot them in bright sunlight. Later he avoided such light for a reason which the Italian film director Michelangelo

Antonioni has also mentioned to explain his preference for overcast outdoor shooting—the grayness suits the vision, brings out a range of shadings which create the mood.

But some of the characteristics of Frank's mature style can already be seen in the Peruvian pictures; for example, in one photograph a high white Indian's hat stands out brilliantly against a background of grays and blacks. He was later to make a similar picture in Wales—the white tea cup held by a tired miner home from work is luminous amidst the dark gray misery of his room. Whether in South America or northern Britain, Robert Frank has carried his way of seeing with him.

In 1950 and again in 1953 he went back to Europe to do some of his most notable early work—the London series, the story of a Welsh miner, the Spanish photographs. His style emerges now: a hearse on some dreary London street, or, in a different mood but still his own, the essence of Britannia captured in an elegant and faintly ironic image of the top-hatted banker.

Soon after his return to this country, Robert Frank reached the peak of his development as a still photographer. A Guggenheim Fellowship granted for 1955 and renewed for 1956 enabled him to travel all over the United States in an old car with his wife, the English-born sculptress Mary Frank, and their two children. These years produced the pictures he called *The Americans* (published by Delpire in France and Grove Press in the United States, 1959).

In an introduction to the book, Jack Kerouac hails Frank as "a great tragic poet," and has this to say of Frank's vision of America: "The faces don't editorialize or criticize or say anything but 'This is the way we are in real life and if you dont like it I dont know anything about it 'cause I'm living my own life my way and may God bless us all, mebbe'...."

Walker Evans saw Robert Frank's pictures differently. "He shows high irony towards a nation that generally speaking has it not; adult detachment towards the more-or-less

Robert Frank.

juvenile section of the population that came into his view. This bracing, almost stinging manner is seldom seen in a sustained collection of photographs.... Robert Frank, though far, far removed from the arid pretensions of the average sociologist, can say much to the social critic who has not waylaid his imagination among his footnotes and references."

By 1959, Robert Frank was internationally recognized as a photographer of the highest rank. In the United States, his first exhibition at New York's Tibor de Nagy Gallery in 1948 was followed by participation in four group shows at the Museum of Modern Art, a one-man show at the Chicago Art Institute in 1961, and a major exhibition (with Harry Callahan) again at the Museum of Modern Art in 1962.

Much of this acclaim came when he had already turned in a new direction. "The still photograph is a passageway to the movie," he said. In early 1959 he made his first film, *Pull My Daisy,* with painter Alfred Leslie. This 28-minute film was based on a part of an unproduced play by Jack Kerouac and shot in Leslie's loft studio. Shown commercially throughout the United States *Pull My Daisy* earned Frank the label of "graphic spokesman for the Beat Generation." It featured poets Allen Ginsberg, Gregory Corso, and Peter Orlovsky, as well as painter Larry Rivers, cavorting in an apparently spontaneous way to an inspired running commentary by Kerouac (published with stills by Grove Press, 1959).

Robert Frank described the film as "a documentary about a tragic and bedraggled circle"; critics hailed it as a minor masterpiece. Both considered it more successful than his second short film, *The Sin of Jesus,* made in 1960 from a story by Russian writer Isaac Babel. *The Sin of Jesus* is a grim tale of a farm woman who seeks release from the trap of circumstance in religious experience, only to find God's laws as ruthless as those of man. Frank called it "an attempt to combine reality and fantasy."

In 1963, he completed a new 40-minute film based on an original story by Margaret Maggid, entitled *OK END HERE.* Between each of the films he continued to do magazine work and advertising photography for *The New York Times.*

Robert Frank's development as a photographer-artist has shown a steady progression which may rightly be called logical. His turn to film reflects both his need for personal growth and his feeling that commercial-magazine photography has come to an impasse which "makes it difficult to speak about the advancement of photography." Yet his film making retains the essential qualities of his still work: "Black-and-white is the vision of hope and despair. That is what I want in my photographs."

—Elizabeth Sutherland

Robert Frank.

FREE LANCE PHOTOGRAPHY

ARTHUR BRACKMAN
Managing Editor, Free Lance Photographers Guild, New York

[The photographer who wants to make money with his camera can find encouragement and specific sales methods in this revealing article. It discusses frankly the free lancer's chances in the marketplace, and describes opportunities in the local newspaper, magazine, and trade-journal markets.]

All photographs from Free Lance Photographer's Guild unless otherwise credited.

• *Also see: Agencies, Photographic; Careers in Photography; Copyright; Cost Accounting in Professional Photography; Mailing Photographs and Film.*

FREE LANCE PHOTOGRAPHY IS THE term used to describe that segment of the field in which unattached photographers perform services for various principals for a fee. The term is so broad that it includes virtually all but salaried staff photographers.

The free lance photographer has, in some twenty years, risen to an enviable position. In 1940, for example, most photographers of proven talent and ability had staff jobs and were apt to be patronizing toward the unaffiliated who earned what they could at photographic odd jobs. Today, the reverse is true. Staffers on newspapers, magazines, or house organs hope—often wistfully—for the chance of working on their own. One finds that some of photography's biggest names today are free lancers.

Many other free lancers are sensitive men and women with strong creative drives who have forsaken other pursuits in the hope of finding in photography an income and personal fulfillment. Here free lance photography offers the serious cameraman an opportunity to portray the world as he sees it in ways useful and meaningful to others.

Good marine photographs require good techniques as well as good subject matter. This backlighted scene has all the elements of a salable picture. (Photo: Thomas Breer)

SPECULATION FIRST

One way to break into free lance work is to submit pictures that have been made on speculation. It is a good idea to begin in local territory, using local subjects. The first place to submit your work is the local newspaper. If the editor turns you down, try a newspaper in a neighboring city. Then try magazines or other publications which originate in your area.

The subjects suitable for sale to local newspapers are infinite. Most obvious are shots of vehicle accidents, property damage, and local celebrities. But most editors are also seeking feature pictures—cute shots of babies, children, pets, and human-interest photographs with a local tie-in.

If the editor finds your early submissions unusable, he will probably tell you what kind of picture he does want, and this information will be helpful in future effort. A local editor offers practical, day-to-day criticism. A working relationship with a responsible editor gives the beginner more useful insight into satisfying a market than can be found between the covers of all the books written about selling pictures.

As an additional means of gaining confidence and a feeling for commercial work, I strongly suggest that the photographic aspirant solicit and execute small commercial jobs in his own vicinity. This is not only advice to the beginner: Any free lancer who hopes to stay in the business will do well to develop and exploit nonpublication sources

Photographs of pretty young girls are always good sellers. But even more interest is added when the models are doing something athletic, such as in this underwater scene. (Photo: Jack Zehrt)

of income to supplement his publication accounts. Countless such sources can be built up by the man who has push, ingenuity, and persistence.

He can approach local merchants and obtain assignments to make pictures of their best window displays or store interiors. He can get work from real-estate men, making pictures of properties they have for sale. Many photographers do door-to-door canvassing for home portraiture, especially of children and pets.

These tasks may seem to be hack work, but every editor is confronted yearly with artistic photographers who don't know how to take clear, straightforward pictures of elementary subjects. More such "hack" work might improve the output of many a camera-club lion.

The principal difference between the professional and the amateur is not that the former has more skill than the latter, but that the professional has his skill readily available, and can apply it to any photographic job the client or the market requires. Limited interest rather than limited ability is usually the sign of an amateur.

Of course professionals often specialize in particular branches or styles of photography, but this is not because they can't make pictures of other types. Generally they specialize because they find that in devoting their working day to the kind of pictures they do best they are making the most remunerative use of their time.

SPECULATION MECHANICS

Beginning free lancers often receive superfluous advice about the mechanical requirements for salable pictures; there is really very little to learn. Prints should be at least 8×10 inches in size and be printed on glossy paper. Only sharp, clear pictures with as wide a range of tonal values as possible should be submitted. Avoid very contrasty prints as well as those in which contrast is almost absent. Your name and address should be written or stamped on the back of each print or transparency.

Photographs need not be copyrighted. Each picture should have a typed caption giving all pertinent facts—date, location, names of persons or products shown, what is going on, and any other important details. Be sure to send packages by insured or registered mail, and include return postage if it is required by the publication.

MARKETS

National markets. After you have met with some local success and are certain you have mastered the primary task of producing sharp prints that are technically and editorially suitable for reproduction, you can then start to develop more distant markets. Obviously you are not going into the free lancing business on a national scale with only one picture to sell. We take it for granted that by this time you have assembled a sizable collection of miscellaneous subjects.

Effective selling of pictures is more a matter of thoughtful submission than of persistent stamp licking. To sell requires first of all an understanding of your particular talents and capacities and, secondly, some knowledge of the active market for pictures. The success of the agency with which I am affiliated has often been attributed to its ability to ferret out markets and seil pictures to clients often neglected or passed over by others.

Selling your own. If you decide to be your own salesman, your problem is primarily one of selection of markets. If you happen to live in New York, Chicago, Boston, or any other publishing center, you can take your portfolio under your arm and start making the rounds of possible clients. You will find that picture editors, as a rule, are hospitable, receptive, and willing to

An elevated view from a tall building or airplane will often serve to introduce a broad general scene. A Belgian church and the Meuse River with an excursion boat at Dinant are shown here. (Photo: Tom Hollyman)

examine your work with an open mind.

If your home is not a publishing center, you will have to use the less direct method of making submissions by mail. If you do, try to learn something about the prospective publisher's needs before wasting your postage and his time. Do not send baby pictures to a scientific magazine or technical pictures to a women's magazine. Try to send an assortment if you possibly can. Above all, do not be discouraged by rejections.

Magazines. The picture magazines, especially *Life* and *Look,* occupy in the beginner's mind an importance far out of proportion to their real possibilities as markets. Actually, the picture magazines account for an infinitesimal part of the total money spent for pictures. Most of their pictures are produced by staff photographers, so that only a negligible percentage of contributed material has more than an outside chance. Technical and editorial standards are exacting and specialized, and the free lancer who attempts to make pictures for these markets without previous assurances is usually doomed to disappointment.

Newspaper. By picking up any issue of any newspaper, you can get a good general idea of newspaper-picture requirements. The chief element in news pictures is timeliness, although feature pictures devoid of any spot-news elements are sometimes used if they are remarkably good.

One branch of the newspaper field which offers a steady, if limited, market for feature pictures is the rotogravure or Sunday-magazine section. The Sunday-magazine section uses the type of picture essay commonly associated with the picture magazines—a series of pictures bound together by a single theme, or pictures with story-telling value. Among the best examples of this market are: *St. Louis Post Dispatch; New York Daily News; Houston Chronicle; St. Louis Globe Democrat; Detroit News.*

Newspaper syndicates or services like Acme News Pictures, Press Association, Associated Press, etc.,

Milk cans waiting to be picked up by the creamery truck can be the central theme for a series of pictures on the activities of the farmer. Here emphasis is found in simplicity of subject. (Photo: Pete Turner)

supply pictures simultaneously to hundreds of newspapers. These syndicates buy considerable material from free lancers. Their editorial requirements change constantly and are, like the newspapers themselves, chiefly made up of spot news. By going through newspapers and observing which pictures carry the familiar syndicate credit line, you will gain a good idea of what they buy.

Specialized markets. By far the most profitable field for exploitation by the free-lance photographer is that of the specialized magazines and trade papers. Hundreds of publications, each with its particular interest, are becoming more aware of the editorial potentialities of photographs, and buying them in ever-increasing numbers.

Largest among this group are the nationally circulated special-interest magazines, such as *Popular Science, Popular Mechanics, Scientific American, Outdoor Life, American Farm, Popular Aviation,* as well as magazines appealing to motorists, yachtsmen, fishermen, amateur photographers, etc. The editors of each of these are always looking for new material, and hundreds of free lancers have developed substantial, steady incomes as regular contributors. The smaller magazines in this special-interest group may deal with anything from stamp collecting to model spacecraft and be a ready market for pictures in those fields.

A photographer with a knack for understanding and photographing mechanical devices should tackle the scientific periodicals. A cameraman with a flair for the outdoor life should make a definite effort to establish himself with the sportsmen's publications, and so on. Editors are reluctant to experiment with photographers, but when they find one who has mastered their slant, they use him steadily.

Industrial photographs are salable to many trade publications, house magazines, manufacturing plants, and other outlets. (Photo: Ivan Massar)

A more accessible market for the beginner is provided by the trade papers, many of which are hungry for material but cannot afford to pay high rates. Of this group, there are shoe journals that buy photos of shoe-store windows, salesmanship magazines that want pictures and articles relating to sales methods, and pet magazines eager for animal pictures. These and similar publications pay from under $5 to about $25 for each picture used. A modest beginning, to be sure, but much more satisfying than unsuccessful random flings at almost hopeless markets.

ADVERTISING

Beginners are often dazzled with tales that a certain gasoline company paid a certain photographer $1000 for one picture used in an advertisement. Beguiled by such stories, hundreds of wistful beginners have

Don't overlook the ever-present markets for babies, children, and families. The demand for good pictures in this field never diminishes. (Photo: Edward Judice)

shipped their pictures off to advertising agencies. In a majority of cases, their pictures have been rejected immediately. Advertising illustration must be planned weeks ahead of time, and most of this work is assigned to photographers of acknowledged ability and reputation. In a very limited number of instances stock photographs are used for advertising, but these are usually selected from photographer or agency files.

SALE OF COLOR PICTURES

The market for color is big and still growing rapidly, with fees ranging from $100 to $2000 per picture. But standards are very high, and only flawless pictures stand a chance. Editors do not require prints, as they usually reproduce from the transparency. (There is, however, a trend toward the use of color-negative film which necessitates the submission of color prints.) The transparency is returned to the photographer after use unless other arrangements were made at the time of purchase. Color transparencies smaller than 2¼ × 3¼ are salable to a smaller number of clients than the 4 × 5 or larger sizes which are acceptable in any of the markets.

If you remember that it costs much more to reproduce a color picture in a publication than to use black-and-white, you will realize why editors and publishers are exacting in their attitude toward submitted transparencies. Add to this the fact that pictures which may look fine in transparency sometimes lose detail and color value in the process of enlarging them to size.

THE AGENCY

After you have done a number of mailings in an effort to sell your own pictures, you will probably come around to the idea of using a photographic agency as your sales representative. Actually, selling your own pictures by mail does not usually prove feasible because of the small percentage of sales and the waste of time and postage which precedes most sales.

Most experienced free lancers have found that taking pictures is a specialized pursuit for which they are fitted, while selling pictures is a specialized pursuit for which agents are trained. It is nevertheless true that, in a few cases, photographers have combined both functions. Most picture agencies charge 50 percent of the sales price as a commission on black-and-white stock, while 40 percent is standard for color. This may seem high, but experience has shown it to be the least an agent can charge and stay in business.

PICTURES THAT SELL

Photographers often ask: "What kind of picture sells best?"—as if there were some magic formula which might guide their efforts. Unfortunately, sales of types of pictures fluctuate so that no hard-and-fast rules can be given. Over a period of years, the following types seem to be in demand fairly consistently: babies, mothers with children, pretty girls, dogs, monuments, and school-age children. The Free Lance Photographers Guild recently

The travel photograph must be well composed and give a selected glimpse of some important feature of the country. This view of London shows a familiar landmark while the hazy background adds to the atmosphere of the scene. (Photo: Joseph Nettis)

made a survey which showed that during an eight month period certain types of pictures had shown proportionate sales advances, notably: industrial shots, "leg art," scientific and space-age subjects. In the same period there was a decrease in travel-picture sales, close-ups of facial expressions, and cat pictures. This survey is useful only as a rough guide to the trend of picture demand. Any photographer who tries to follow its implications too closely might well find that the trend has shifted before he can catch up with it.

Our experience at the Free Lance Photographers Guild indicates that every type of picture sells and that the safest course for a photographer is to devote himself to the field he likes best. The important thing is to take pictures a little better than the next man—to use more imagination, more originality in approach, more technical skill. A set of photographically excellent pictures built around a poor idea will often fail to sell, while less-than-average quality pictures built around a top-notch, original idea will sell.

Only by trial and error can the novice learn to anticipate sales with any degree of accuracy. After long experience, he may develop a feel for the market by which he can sometimes forecast an editor's reaction. Usually, if he works through a picture agency, his agent supplies this ability.

Organizations like the American Society of Magazine Photographers, better known as ASMP, provide counsel on the free lancer's problems, advise him on economic, legal, and technical matters. (Queries should be addressed to the Society at 1472 Broadway, New York City.)

OPPORTUNITIES TODAY

What are the real opportunities in free lancing today? They are potentially very great, but so much depends upon the individual photographer, his talents, his temperament, his aspirations, his economic requirements, that no generalizations can possibly be made. In some areas of the business, intensified competition makes free lancing less attractive today than it was ten years ago. This is especially true in magazine photography.

Yet innumerable sources of income are still available to the free lancer. Difficult or not, the picture magazines are still a market for free lance work, much of it placed through agencies. Actually, ingenuity

PHOTOGRAPH PRICES

This is a preliminary survey of prices currently quoted for the use of stock photographs by six leading photo agencies. Unless otherwise noted, it is for single color reproduction rights, transparency to be returned immediately after publication. Black-and-white photographs average $33^{1}/_{3}$ percent to 50 percent of color rates. Lowest and highest quotations are listed.

Use	Type	Price
Advertising, National		
Exclusive—all rights	color	$650—$2500*
Exclusive—all rights	b & w	250—1000**
Multiple magazines	color	500—2000•
Multiple magazines	b & w	350—1000
Single full page	color	500—1500
Single full page	b & w	250—1000
Background use	color	350—1000◇
Advertising, Trade Paper	color	100—350
Advertising, Trade Paper	b & w	50—150
Annual Reports		
Cover	color	100—500
Cover	b & w	100—250
Inside	color	100—300
Inside	b & w	25—100
Artist's Reference	color, b&w	25—100
Billboards, 24 Sheet	color	75—1500
Brochures		
Cover	color	100—350
Inside	color	50—125
Color Used as B & W ■		
Display Cards		
National	color	125—1000
Regional	color	125—500
Local	color	100—350
Direct Mail	color	100—300
Editorial, Magazine Covers	color	100—1500
Inside	color	100—500
Inside	b & w	25—500
Encyclopedias		
Inside	color	75—150
Books		
Cover jacket	color	250—500
Cover jacket	b & w	100—500
Inside	color	75—200
Inside	b & w	15—50
Frontispiece	color	125—250
Foreign rights☆		
Package Design	color	100—750
Greeting Cards	color	75—200
Record Covers	color	100—500
House Organs		
Cover	color	100—600
Inside	color	50—150
Presentation Fee	color	25—100
Slidefilm		
One time use	color	35—100
Calendars	color	100—1000
TV Commercial, Network	color, b&w	50—200
TV Commercial, Local	color, b&w	25—100

*Includes transparency
**Includes negative
•*Life, SEP, LHJ,* etc.
◇Multiple magazines
■One half color rate
☆Additional fee

in finding work is what sets the successful free lancer off from the frustrated aspirant. The free lancer lives on "angles," and they are not always camera angles.

Here, as examples, are a few: shooting color pictures of motels and other business establishments which can be printed as post cards; doing photographic work for local industries; acting as regional correspondent for magazines and newspaper syndicates; offering a specialty such as underwater photography, animals, low-altitude aerials, farm, or baby photography, and so on.

Many free lancers regard each phase of their experience as a steppingstone toward the better paying advertising work available in large centers such as Chicago, San Francisco, Philadelphia, Detroit, and New York. One of the wide-open free lance markets is industry, for more and more firms are every day becoming aware of the advantages of using the talented, imaginative, and enterprising free lancer.

FINDING LEADS

Often the most rewarding reading for the free lancer is in the smallest type in the publication—the credit line that accompanies the picture. This will tell him whether the picture comes from an agency, syndicate, or private photographer, and should give him a good idea of who is selling what to whom.

Market lists, if they are reasonably up-to-date, are often handy. There are good ones in Arvel W. Ahlers' *Where and How to Sell Your Pictures,* and in Edna Bennett's *How to Sell Your Pictures at a Profit*. The Gebbie Press, 151 West 48th Street, N.Y., N.Y., issues a useful directory of house organs using photographs.

Persistent and methodical work with market lists and potential buyers will, more often than not, reward the free lancer with at least a comfortable and dependable income. For an inspiring account of how one small-town free lancer parlayed the remodeling of a building into dozens of picture sales, read Walter Harter's *How to Shoot and Sell Money-Making Pictures*.

Outdoor and indoor sporting pictures find many markets. Here is a good action shot that symbolizes the opening day for bass or trout fishing. (Photo: Jack Zehrt)

□

FRILLING

Frilling is a defect in negatives caused by the emulsion pulling loose from the support at the edges of the sheet. The film usually takes on a puckered or pleated look at this point, and dries in a series of overlaps.

Often a source of trouble in the old carbro process, frilling was generally due to insufficient drying time on the temporary support before washing out the soluble gelatin, or to the absence of a safe edge or margin around the image. Frilling also occurred frequently when alkaline developers were used at high temperatures on glass plates. However, the adhesion of modern emulsions to the support material is far better, and frilling is seldom seen today, not even on films which have been developed at high temperatures.

On the rare occasion when frilling does occur, it can sometimes be eliminated by carefully blotting the negative dry after washing and then applying a small amount of denatured alcohol along the frilled edge with a camel's-hair brush. This causes the wet emulsion to become dehydrated momentarily, and to shrink quite noticeably. In shrinking, it tightens up along the edge and eliminates the puckered effect. The negative must be dried at once.

Since frilling affects only a narrow area around the edges of the image, it may often be ignored, provided the film is not handled carelessly. The frilled edge can often be masked out in printing.

FUNGI PHOTOGRAPHY

GRANT M. HAIST

[The many forms and colors of fungi provide endless subject matter for the photographer in both scientific and pictorial fields. Mastering the techniques described here will enable you to overcome most of the difficulties encountered in the dimly lit areas where fungi grow.]

All photographs by the author.

• *Also see: Copying and Close-up Photography; Extension Tubes and Bellows; Nature Photography.*

FUNGUS IS THE NAME GIVEN TO any of a large group of nonchlorophyll plants. Fungi subsist on dead or living plants or animals. When a fungus attacks a living plant or animal, the parasitic plant is often considered a disease, such as rust or ergot in grain, or athlete's foot in human beings. To the nature photographer, fungus means one of the fruiting bodies called mushrooms or toadstools that occur in lawns and gardens, fields and forests.

Because mushrooms do not possess the chlorophyll that green plants use to manufacture their food, these fungi generally grow by the decomposition of dead plant tissues. Actually the photographer rarely sees the fungus itself, which is hidden inside the fallen tree or buried under the duff of the forest floor. The fungus consists of long, thread-like filaments called mycelium that secrete enzymes to make soluble food from the plant tissues. What the photographer usually sees is the fruiting body sent up by the mycelium to spread the fungus through production of primitive reproductive bodies called spores.

LOCATING FUNGI

Photography of fungus requires a knowledge of mushroom growth characteristics, because the location of suitable specimens is the first requirement for good pictures. One or more fungi may inhabit a suitable site until the food supply is exhausted, and the photographer may be able to find specimens in exactly the same place for many years. However, seasonal factors often determine whether the mycelium will produce a fruiting body every year.

If the year is dry or too cold, mushrooms may be difficult to find. Large quantities of water are needed for mushrooms to form, so generally spring or fall is the best time to locate suitable specimens for photography. Occasionally near the end of a hot, dry summer mushrooms and other fungi will cover the woodlands after a soaking rain.

Once located, a suitable specimen should be photographed at once. Delaying just one day often means a prize find will be reduced to an inky mass. Many fungi are more enduring, but it is always advisable to take pictures as soon as possible, before insect infestation or deterioration occurs.

PHOTO TECHNIQUES

Picturing a mushroom or other fungi in a natural state often requires putting the camera closer to the subject than its normal focusing range permits. Close-ups of detail may require up to five to ten times magnification on the film. Pictures of spores necessitate microphotography to make spore detail visible.

Cameras with groundglass focusing are especially useful at short working distances since the exact depth of field and composition can be studied before the exposure is made. Lenses are available for 35 mm single-lens reflex cameras which give life-size film images at their highest magnification. When using the standard lenses for 35 mm cam-

Some mushrooms are very small. The correct scale can be suggested by including a thumb in the photograph.

The photography of mushrooms and other fungi requires a number of tripods. The author is using an intermediate-height tripod to support a Nikon F camera with bellows attachment and a short mount 135mm lens.

eras, other means must be employed to get close-ups of fungi.

Positive supplementary lenses are available in different powers for attachment to lenses that normally do not permit close-up photography. Such slip-on lenses may adversely affect the resolution of the camera lens, so it is advisable to use the lower powers, such as 1×, 2×, 3×, or combinations of two of these. Avoid extremely high powers, such as 10×. Even with the low-power supplementary lens, it is necessary to use a small lens aperture to insure good image sharpness. Positive supplementary lenses do not require additional exposure, unlike most other means used to secure a larger film image.

Although positive supplementary

lenses can extend the focusing range to less than ten inches from the subject, picture taking at this distance is easier with extension tubes or bellows attachments available for 35 mm and 2¼ × 2¼ cameras with interchangeable lenses.

These accessories are placed between the camera body and the camera lens, avoiding any possible degradation of the lens optical quality. Extension tubes consist of a series of interlocking rings that permit a limited number of camera locations for the specific image magnifications given by each ring or combination of rings. Use of bellows allow the image to be focused after the camera location has been chosen. With 35 mm cameras, the use of a 135mm lens in a short mount on a bellows attachment allows the lens to be focused from infinity to at least 1:1 (life size) on the film.

There is real value in using the 135mm lens in a short mount rather than the 50mm lens with a bellows attachment. At 1:1, the 135mm lens will be 270 mm (almost 11 inches) from the subject, but the 50mm lens will be only 100 mm (4 inches) away. For the same image size, the depth of field will be the same for both lenses. The extra distance between the 135mm lens and the subject is often needed for arranging the lighting. At higher magnifications, the 50mm lens is so close to the subject that it is sometimes difficult to light properly.

EXPOSURE DETERMINATION

Extension tubes or bellows attachments increase the distance of the lens from the camera so that aperture markings on the lens are no longer valid, and additional exposure is necessary to compensate for the extra extension of the lens.

Most bellows attachments and extension tubes indicate this exposure increase as a multiplying factor of the exposure determined in the usual manner. However, if you have a view camera, you may have to compute this factor yourself. This can be done by first measuring the lens-to-film distance with the subject in focus, squaring this measured distance, then dividing this number by the square of the focal length of the lens. Thus, for a six-inch lens used at a 12-inch lens-to-film extension, the factor can be calculated:

$$\frac{(\text{lens-to-film distance})^2}{(\text{focal length of lens})^2} =$$

$$\frac{(12)^2}{(6)^2} = \frac{144}{36} = 4$$

The exposure must be increased by four times, or two stops more exposure than the normal exposure are needed.

Determining the exposure for mushrooms or other fungi that grow in well-lighted areas is no problem.

Right: *The pores of this red-pored wood fungus are photographed with a 55 mm extension tube on a Hasselblad 500C Camera with 80mm Planar lens.*

Below: *Close-up camera equipment is necessary to picture minute details such as the pore structure of the red-pored wood fungus.*

Tripods with extensions of six feet or more are often necessary to take pictures of fungi specimens that grow on tree trunks high off the ground.

But it seems that the finest specimens flourish in the dimmest part of the forest. A low level of illumination is rarely satisfactory for the small apertures needed for lens extensions at close-up distances. Flashbulbs or electronic flash supply the dependable supplementary lighting often needed in fungi photography.

Time exposures are often unsatisfactory with color film, because of color casts from the unequal reciprocity failure of the dye layers. But time exposures on black-and-white film are preferred, because flash exposures of white mushrooms such as *Amatina verna* almost always result in high contrast, making printing difficult. Time exposures result in lower contrast negatives and will give a better rendition of the background.

SPECIAL TECHNIQUES

Some of my best fungi pictures have been taken combining long time exposures with completely diffused lighting. Negatives have good detail in both the fungus and background, without the harsh, unnatural contrasts often encountered with flash lighting. The best time to make such exposures is at sunset or very shortly after. The entire sky is the light source; the wind almost always dies down at sunset, minimizing subject movement.

Exposure duration is dependent on many factors, but exposures of 30 to 120 seconds at *f*/32 on black-and-white film of 400 ASA rating should provide a starting point for test exposures using this technique.

When using after-sunset lighting, shaded areas will receive very little light and will lack detail on the negative. It is necessary to "paint" these shadows with light during the exposures, using a reflector such as a sheet of white paper or paper with a silvered surface. Keep the

paper in motion during the exposure period, but do not move it so vigorously that the mushroom trembles from the disturbed air. This diffused-light technique has given surprisingly good results with slow speed, high-contrast color-reversal film, but the higher speed, "improved" color films may require test shots with filters.

TRIPODS

Probably the fungi photographer's most valuable equipment, next to his camera, are his tripods; not one, but many. Because fungi may be on the ground or high on a tree trunk, a variety of tripods is a necessity. For close-up work near the ground, a sturdy table-top tripod is most useful. For high-angled views of ground subjects, a short-legged adjustable tripod, preferably with an elevating center post, is needed. An even larger tripod must be employed for high-growing specimens. I always carry the two smaller types with me in the field and often have to backtrack for the largest one. Although burdensome, an extra tripod often is useful to hold a flash gun or flash head.

To insure over-all sharpness when photographing groups of fungi, it is best to use a view camera where exact focusing can be done on the groundglass, using tilting and swinging front and back.

GAMMA

John N. Harman, Jr.

[Here is a definition and discussion of a term misunderstood by many photographers. The author describes the derivation and measurement of gamma from the sensitometric strip and the characteristic curve. He tells of the relation of gamma to time, emulsion characteristics, temperature, agitation, and color, and of the effect of gamma on film.]

• *Also see: Characteristic Curve; Development, Background; Exposure with the Zone System.*

Gamma has been defined as the numerical indication or measure of the degree of contrast to which a photographic emulsion is developed. As such, it can rightly be considered as the development factor of a film under certain specified conditions.

But through interpretation and usage, perhaps incorrectly and yet not without some justification, gamma has acquired a slightly broader meaning in the minds of many photographers. It has grown to be a term by which the final contrast of a film negative can be freely discussed, and it has become a synonym for the gradation of a developed emulsion—a convenient mathematical measuring stick by which the contrast relationships of negatives and prints can be visualized.

Lack of complete understanding of the term "gamma," and of the principles of sensitometric measurement it represents, has led to considerable confusion among photographers in regard to its meaning and applications. An explanation of the derivation of gamma values and their function in sensitometric procedure may help prevent misunderstanding of the applications of gamma to be described here.

MEASUREMENT OF GAMMA

It must be realized that the measurement of gamma is a laboratory procedure requiring the use of accurately standardized equipment and methods. The reliability of the results depends as much on the

The creative photographer controls the development of a negative in order to obtain a specific result. In this photograph of an abandoned church in Tiburon, California, the abstract and design qualities were stressed by the strong side-lighting which was even further emphasized by careful and calculated processing. Leica with 35mm lens and Plus-X film. (Photo: Michael E. Bry)

accuracy of the instruments as on the competence and training of the operators.

Sensitometric Strip. The first requirement is an exposing device which will give the film sample a series of uniformly increasing exposures of known value. This can be accomplished by exposing the sample behind a calibrated step wedge having a suitable progression of densities.

While a calibrated step wedge qualifies as a "sensitometer," in that it allows varying amounts of light to reach the film, such an exposing arrangement is used mainly for processing control where extreme precision is not required. A wedge-type sensitometer is quite useful for amateurs and even for processing laboratories. But in manufacturers' laboratories, where not only gamma but the actual speed of the film must be measured with a high degree of precision, a much more elaborate instrument is used. This instrument incorporates a standard light source and a mechanical means of producing any number of identical exposures.

This type of sensitometer allows a minimum of variation in exposure. A film given a standardized exposure in this way is termed a sensitometric strip and, after development under closely controlled conditions, reveals a series of densities that are related to the progression of exposures.

Characteristic Curve. By plotting on a graph the measured values of the densities corresponding to the series of known exposures produced with the sensitometer, and by connecting the points thus obtained, a long S-shaped curve is formed (Figure 1).

This graphic interpretation of an emulsion's behavior is known as the characteristic or sensitometric curve, and it fulfills several important functions in testing sensitized materials. In this particular instance, the important feature is the slope of the straight-line section of the curve, that section lying above the lower curve or toe (which corresponds to the least dense sections of the sample) and below the upper curve or shoulder (which corresponds to the most dense sections of the film).

In Figure 1, the vertical component of the graph represents density units expressed arithmetically, while the horizontal component indicates the relative exposure received by the film sample, expressed in logarithmic progression.

Figure 1. *Typical sensitometric curve for a photographic emulsion.*

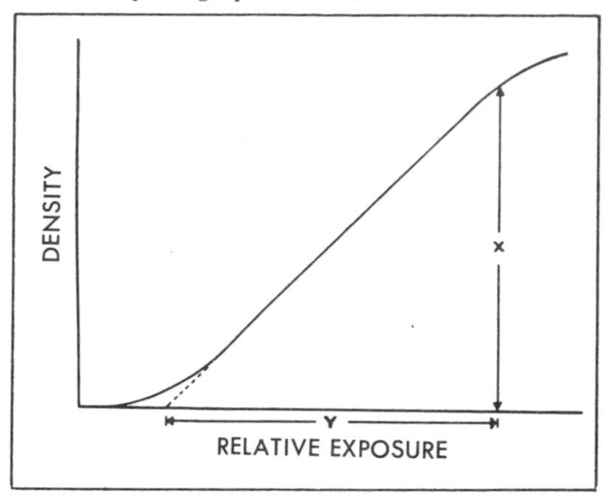

FINDING GAMMA

In the region represented by the straight-line section of the curve, a direct and proportional relationship exists between successive densities and the exposure values causing them. The ratio of density differences to exposure differences within this region is indicated by the ratio of the distance X to the distance Y when the straight line is extended to the horizontal axis of the graph.

The value for this ratio, by simple trigonometry, is indicated by the tangent of the angle enclosed by the horizontal axis and the extension of the straight-line section of the sensitometric curve. This ratio of resulting density differences to originating exposure differences is a measure of the tone separation, or gradation, and is thus a direct indication of the degree of contrast of the developed emulsion.

The numerical value for this ratio is, for convenience, referred to by the Greek letter γ, more commonly known as "gamma." When the values for X and Y are equivalent, the ratio is equal to 1.0, and the gamma value is unity, the condition prevailing in Figure 1. When the slope of the curve is greater and the values for X greater than those for Y, the resulting gamma will be higher than 1.0. Conversely, when the curve is less steep, the values for X are smaller than those for Y, and the gamma is less than 1.0.

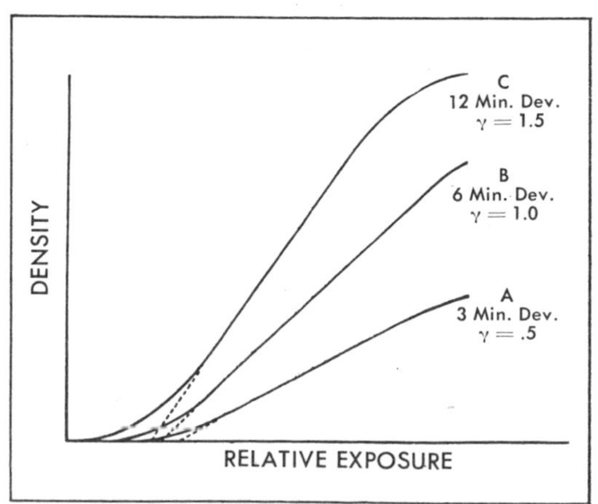

Figure 2. *Characteristic curves for three film samples show an increase in gamma as developing time is increased from three to six to twelve minutes.*

A PRACTICAL EXAMPLE

The interpretation of a sensitometric curve perhaps will be somewhat clarified, and the principles of graphic analysis more understandable, when a comparison is made to actual negatives or prints. An example is afforded in a comparative study of three samples of film which have been exposed identically but developed for varying lengths of time. In such a test, three film samples are each given a standardized sensitometric exposure and an identical pictorial exposure. The samples are then developed together in the same developer, but with a variation in their developing times of three, six, and twelve minutes. The characteristic curves plotted from the three sensitometric strips are shown in Figure 2.

The shortest developing time has produced a negative of soft gradation with little density difference, shown by the gradual slope of the related characteristic curve having a gamma of only 0.5. Sample B, the second of the series in order of developing time, reveals a more natural density relationship and a correspondingly higher slope in its associated characteristic curve, which has a gamma of 1.0. The third sample shows an excessive rate of density progression, a condition which is also represented graphically by the very much steeper slope of C and gamma of 1.5.

Thus a definite pictorial condition can be visualized, representing various characteristic curves obtained in sensitometric tests, though it must be realized that this is an ideal comparison with little direct application in actual practice.

AVERAGE GAMMA

Up to now the average and presumably normal gamma was assumed to be unity. Actually this is seldom true in photographic work, for the degree of contrast to which negatives are developed varies over a considerable range according to the photographic requirements, the sensitized materials used, and a number of related factors. However, a few broad classifications may be safely given for the usual contrast requirements of several types of photographic work. The following gamma values are representative of the contrast to which various emulsions are normally developed:

Film Type	*Average Gamma*
Motion-picture negative	0.6
35 mm	0.7
Portrait	0.8
Press	0.9
Roll and pack	0.8
Commercial and illustration	0.9
Process	3.0
Graphic arts	6.0

DEVELOPING TIME AND GAMMA

There is a direct relationship between development time and the degree of contrast produced in a negative, the gamma increasing as the developing time is lengthened. This happens because in the early stages of development there are tremendous numbers of silver-halide particles in the regions of high exposure which are in a developable condition. Proportionately few developable particles exist in the less-exposed portions of the emulsion. As the developing solution reaches and converts these developable grains of silver halide into black silver, densities are formed far more rapidly in the heavily exposed areas.

As this reaction progresses, the available developable particles which have not been converted are depleted; soon there are very few exposed but undeveloped silver-halide particles left. Thus after the rapid gain in contrast in the early stages of development, a point is reached where continuing action of the developer results in a diminishing increase in gamma, until any increase in density is roughly equal for all densities.

This maximum contrast is referred to as "gamma infinity," and its numerical value is indicative of the steepest grade obtainable with a particular film and developer combination. In some instances of prolonged development the gamma value reaches a maximum and then diminishes slightly, due to the proportionately greater fog densities deposited in the shadow portions of the image.

TIME-GAMMA CURVE

If the gamma values are determined for a progression of development times, the results can be plotted in graphic form, as in Figure 3A, with the curve indicating the time-gamma relationship of the film and developer under examination. Such charts are particularly useful because they show the manner in which gamma advances during development.

It is possible to tell by inspection of such a time-gamma curve what developing time to employ when a certain degree of contrast is desired in negatives. It also is possible to ascertain the degree of accuracy required in timing development. If, for example, the contrast increases very rapidly in the first stages of development and then levels off at a usable value, any developing time within a range of several minutes will give essentially the same contrast, as long as that period of development falls within the nearly horizontal section of the time-gamma curve. Such a condition is represented in Figure 3B.

However, when the time-gamma curve has no "leveling-off" region within its usable range of gradation, the selection of a particular developing time for a desired contrast is very critical. When film-developer combinations show time-gamma relationships like that depicted in Figure 3C, a light change or inaccuracy in developing time will result in appreciable differences in the final contrast of the negative.

INHERENT EMULSION CONTRAST

The contrast in a developed negative is influenced by a number of conditions. One of the most important factors is the developing time.

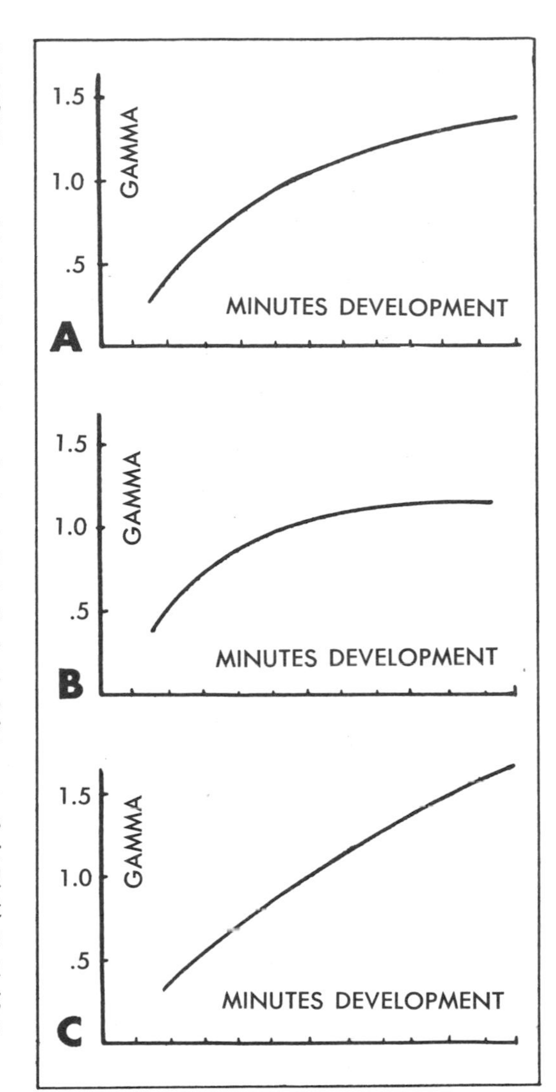

Figure 3. *Time-gamma curves:* A, *typical;* B, *type which levels off, permitting wider selection of developing time for desired gamma;* C, *type which requires critical control of developing time to obtain desired gamma.*

Another is the inherent contrast of the photographic emulsion. By combining a film of certain inherent contrast with an appropriate developer and developing time, the contrast of the developed negative can be adjusted to fit the subject requirements.

A third, and in some ways equally important, variable is the temperature of the developing solution. Just as many chemical reactions proceed more rapidly at higher temperatures, so there is considerable variation in the rate of development at different temperatures. It has become standard practice to specify a developing temperature of 68 F.

Chilling or warming the developing solution to 68 F prior to use is usually done by placing the tray or tank of developer in a bath of cold or hot water. When almost perfect control of developing temperature is necessary, a permanent water bath is frequently installed. Direct chilling methods, such as the addition of ice

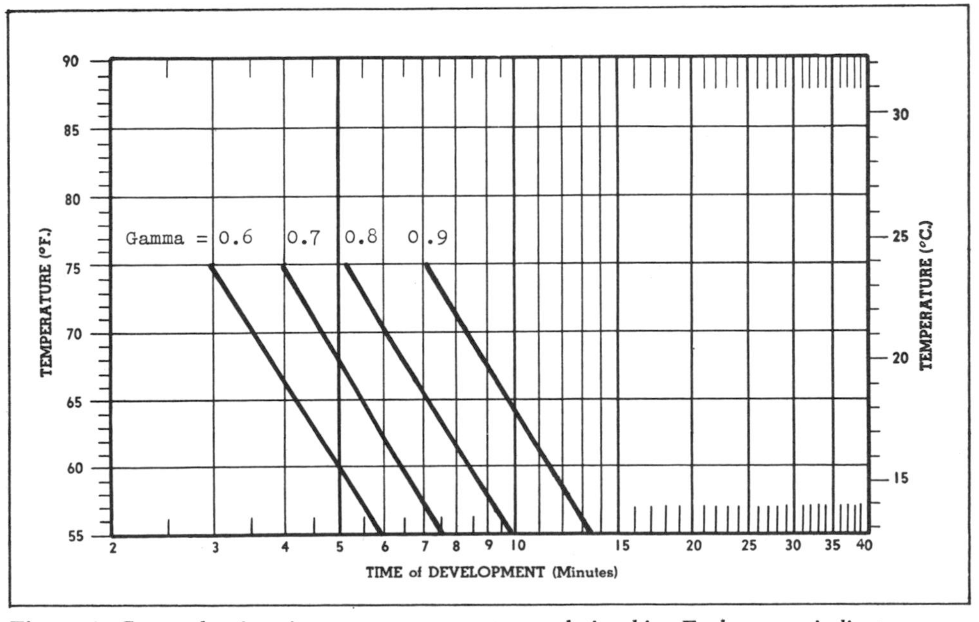

Figure 4. *Curve showing time-gamma-temperature relationship. Each curve indicates developing times needed (for the one developer and film combination for which the chart was made) to obtain the indicated gamma at any temperature within the range covered by the curves. Time and temperature values for gammas between these given can be estimated by drawing additional parallel lines.*

This scene's brightness range lacks deep blacks, which is typical of most water and snow photos. Sometimes, in addition to exposure compensation, there must be changes in development: if the scene is flatly lit, a snappier negative can be obtained by extending development, but the photographer will have to sacrifice other characteristics. (Photo: British Columbia Government)

or dry ice, should not be employed because of the resulting dilution of the developer or formation of bicarbonates.

Since film development must sometimes be carried out under circumstances which will not permit temperature control of solutions, manufacturers of sensitized materials have, in many instances, published data on the amount of decrease or increase in time when development is carried out at higher- or lower-than-normal temperatures.

It should be remembered that all developing agents do not alter their action to exactly the same extent when subjected to changes in temperature. A developer, for example, containing both metol and hydroquinone and balanced for use at 68 F will behave much more like a hydroquinone developer at higher temperatures, while at lower temperactures its action will be more characteristic of the metol constituent. Such imperfections will naturally be small in extent, and under normal conditions moderate variations in developing temperature can be safely compensated for by appropriate modifications of developing time.

TIME-TEMPERATURE CURVES

Time-temperature data is often placed in graphic form and appears as a "time-temperature-gamma" curve. The usual method of indicating this information is shown in Figure 4, where a series of time-temperature-gamma curves incorporates this data for a given film-developer combination.

Each curve indicates the time-temperature relation for a particular gamma. In use, the temperature of the developer is measured, and then the line selected for the desired gamma. The intersection of the temperature level and the line projected down to the base gives the developing time. Such charts must be prepared for every combination of film and developer. The chart shown in Figure 4 is purely hypothetical and does not apply to any practical film.

An intermediate gamma is sometimes desired. Say, in Figure 4 you would like to develop to gamma 0.65. Since the gamma curves are parallel, all you have to do is measure halfway between the 0.6 and 0.7 lines and draw a new line, parallel to the existing ones, for gamma 0.65. It does not pay to try to split the space into any section smaller than one half.

In practice the user will not get these exact gammas because his development conditions are different from those used in the laboratory; the method offers a workable approximation.

AGITATION

Photographers usually realize the important effect of time and temperature upon the degree of contrast produced in development. Frequently, however, the influence of agitation upon gamma is overlooked. This mechanical aspect of development plays an important role in the production of the photographic image, and improper agitation can result in local defects and generally poor photographic quality.

Agitation of the film in the developer brings fresh solution to the emulsion surface and removes chemical by-products formed by the interaction of developer and exposed silver halide. When alkaline developing agents react with exposed grains of silver halide, silver is deposited to form the densities which make up the image. The halide component is set free and combines with alkaline components of the developer, forming an alkaline halide such as sodium bromide.

In "stagnant" development, where there is no agitation of negatives, the sodium bromide concentration increases wherever silver deposits are formed and greatly retards the rate of development because of its strong restraining action. As a result, films developed without agitation usually reveal an undesirably soft, flat gradation.

This effect can largely be overcome by increasing the time of development, but even then the appearance of the final photograph may be badly marred by streaks occurring near the borders of strong highlights and heavy shadows, especially when films are suspended vertically in the developing solution tank.

These streaks appear where heavy silver deposits adjacent to unexposed sections have caused a local concentration of sodium bromide which, drifting slowly down the face of the emulsion because its density is greater than the surrounding solution, retards the formation of the image.

DEGREE OF CONTRAST DESIRED

A final factor affecting the gamma to which an emulsion is developed is the degree of contrast desired. This matter is an individual one, to be adjusted to the requirements of the particular subject and to the purpose for which the photograph is made.

The brightness range of the subject does not directly affect the gamma to which a film is developed, but it may, for example, be desirable in some instances to adjust the degree of development so that the subject will be represented by a suitable and printable range of densities in the negative. In this way a subject of extreme brightness range may be compressed in scale by

Here, though the lighting was near average and exposure was made accordingly, the photographer extended development to obtain more contrast in the negative. This strengthens the composition and design aspects of the photo. Leica IIIG with 50mm Elmar f/2.8. Plus-X film exposed at f/5.6 for 1/60 of a second. (Photo: Michael L. Edelson)

development to a low gamma and, conversely, a subject of low brightness range may be expanded by use of appropriate film-developer combinations that permit development to high gammas.

GAMMA AND FILM CHARACTERISTICS

The extent to which a photographic emulsion is developed noticeably modifies certain basic properties of the emulsion. The degree of development can, for example, measurably influence such characteristics as graininess, accuracy of tone reproduction, film speed, and exposure latitude. When these properties are important considerations, the gamma to which development is carried should be adjusted accordingly.

The relationship between gamma and graininess is a direct one, for simple tests show that with any emulsion type, graininess increases as the emulsion is developed to progressively higher gammas. The reason for this is the tendency for deposited silver grains to form in clumps or clusters as development continues, resulting in non-homogeneity which is recognized in enlarged prints as graininess. While fine-grain developers employ different means of restricting this clumping action, the basic relationship still exists and care should be taken to avoid development to excessive gamma values.

Figure 5. *Latitude varies with the gamma of the negative. Note that the exposure range (straight-line portion) of higher-gamma negative A is much shorter than the exposure range (straight-line portion) of lower-gamma negative B.*

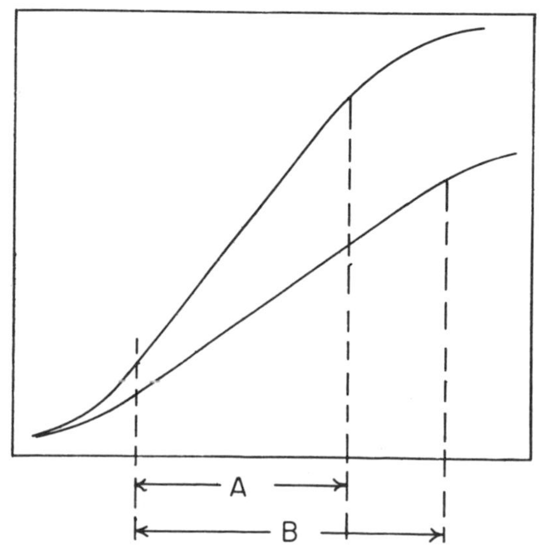

The necessity of full development for the realization of the full speed of an emulsion is well known by most photographers, even overemphasized by those who "force" development by an excessive length of time in the futile hope of obtaining an extra measure of speed. It is equally important, if the inherent sensitivity of a photographic emulsion is to be fully employed, that underdevelopment be avoided. The maximum useful speed is obtained when development is carried to the gamma recommended for a particular film-developer combination.

Exposure latitude is perhaps seldom considered a function of development, and yet it is influenced to a considerable extent by the degree of development.

The reason is simple. Though increased development does not change the length of the straight-line part of the characteristic, it does increase the slope of the line; therefore its projected length on the baseline (Figure 5) is shorter. Since values along the base represent the range of exposures, it is obvious that the high-gamma negative has a much shorter latitude than the low-gamma one. Note, too, that the curve swings around the low end as a pivot, so the effect of overdevelopment is to lower the range in the highlight end of the curve. Examination of these curves will show why overdeveloped flash pictures often have washed-out highlights.

GAMMA AND WAVELENGTH

Most emulsions exhibit a variation in contrast over different regions of the spectrum. This variable is usually referred to as the gamma-wavelength relationship.

When a photographic emulsion is exposed in a camera, the various parts of the latent image are formed by light which varies in color content. It might be expected that when the quality of the light used for exposure is matched to the color sensitivity of the emulsion, density differences would be produced in the negative that are accurate interpretations, in monochrome, of the tonal brilliance of subject color gradations.

Actually this ideal condition varies to a greater or lesser extent, depending on the character of the subject and on the gamma-wavelength response of the emulsion used. In some severe cases it is possible to detect tone distortion in the final print.

It is common for a silver halide emulsion to exhibit a noticeable variation in gamma for subjects of greatly different color content. If, for example, the gamma response of an emulsion is examined in several limited sections of the spectrum, considerable difference in contrast may be found, though the same developing time is employed in each instance. Sensitometric strips exposed to limited sections of the spectrum by colored filters and then developed identically may show, for a panchromatic film, a series of characteristic curves much like those in Figure 6.

Several highly red-sensitive panchromatic films exhibit this type of gamma-wavelength response, giving a soft recording when exposed through a red filter. Obviously such "soft-red" films are not suitable to some subjects requiring filtering, but they are particularly useful when photographing (with filter) subjects having an extreme brightness range that must be recorded on the negative within a usable range of printing densities.

The gamma-wavelength relationship of photographic emulsions is also an important consideration with films used in natural color photography, as in the preparation of three-color separation negatives. Color separation negatives should exhibit uniformity in gradation from shadow to highlight to preserve proper color balance in the final print.

Usually a film with suitable speed and color sensitivity will show some gamma variation in each of the three color separation negatives when they are given identical development. This variation in gamma generally becomes serious at longer developing times. Correction can be made and the negatives developed to approximately identical gamma values by appropriate modification of the developing time for each negative.

Note the extremes in tonal range: the absolute black of the dark auditorium and the white of the conductor's shirt. Through proper exposure and development, the photographer was able to record both extremes satisfactorily. Tri-X film and Contax II. (Photo: Witlin / The Lamp)

It is common to find a range of developing times for color separation negatives with the red-filter negative, for example, developed seven minutes; the green-filter negative, five minutes; the blue-filter negative, ten minutes.

PRACTICAL GAMMA CONTROL

It is not necessary to know the exact numerical value of the gamma of your negatives in ordinary photographic work (though it is very important in motion-picture duplication and sound recording). If you find that using a recommendation for gamma 0.7 provides the kind of negatives you want, then as long as you use the value 0.7 you will get this kind of negative. If the actual gamma of your negative is 0.65, it will make no difference to you.

But for those who like to work precisely, the measurement of the actual gamma attained in the darkroom is not difficult. You need a good small densitometer; the Kodak Color Densitometer is excellent. And you need a simple gray scale on film, having about 20 steps from clear to a maximum density of about 3.0. Such scales can be bought at any dealer who handles supplies for color photography.

This gamma rating method is based on the fact that in contact printing, the ratio between the original densities and the printed-through densities is the same, numerically, as the gamma. Thus all that is necessary is to make a contact print of the gray scale on the film you are using and develop it with a batch of pictures. When this printed-through scale is developed, fixed, washed and dried, the densities corresponding to those of the original scale are plotted on a simple graph and the gamma is easily determined from this graph.

The first thing to do is to calibrate the original gray scale. A 20-step scale would have steps in which each had approximately 0.15 higher density than the preceding

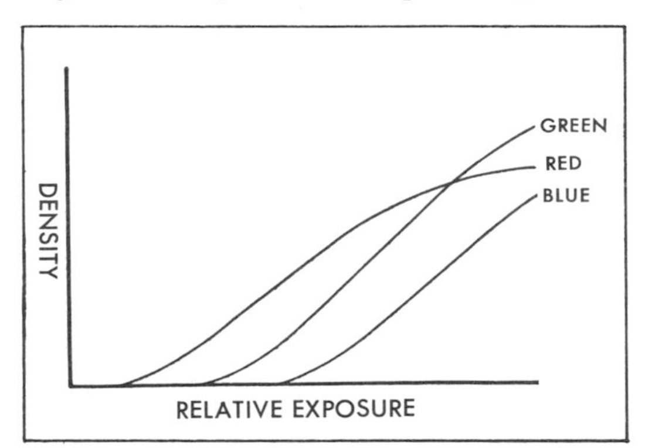

Figure 6. *Sensitometric curves for a panchromatic film which exhibits a "soft-red" gradation. Each curve indicates the density-exposure response of the film to a limited section of the spectrum. Lateral displacement of the curves is due to the differences in the exposure factors of the red, green, and blue filters.*

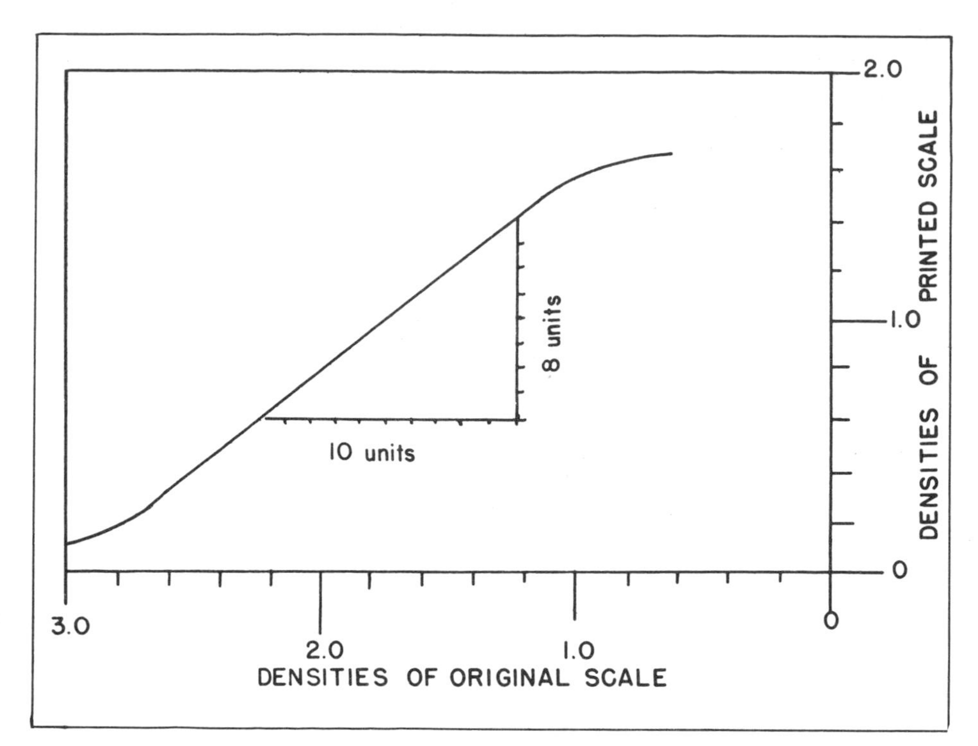

Figure 7. *When the densities of the original scale are plotted against the densities of the printed negative of it, a curve is obtained which exactly duplicates the usual characteristic curve—provided the plot is made left-handed, as shown. Gamma is measured by simply erecting a right triangle at any point, counting the units in the base and altitude, and using arithmetic, as explained in the text, to find gamma.*

one. But this is not exact, so measure the density of each step, and make a table which will look something like this:

STEP	DENSITY
1	0.15
2	0.28
3	0.44
4	0.62
5	0.72
6	0.88
7	1.02
8	1.18
9	1.34
*10	1.52
11	1.66
12	1.81
13	1.93
14	2.08
15	2.24
16	2.42
17	2.56
18	2.68
19	2.80
20	2.98

Note that we have placed an * opposite Step 10. On the scale itself, mark Step 10 by making a small notch in the edge of the scale or by scratching a tiny "x" in the corner where it will not interfere with reading the density. This is necessary because, in making the print-through on film, we will not get all the steps; some may be lost at the light end, or a few may be blocked-up at the dark end.

Since you are interested only in gamma and not in film speed, the exact exposure is unimportant. It is necessary to print the scale by contact since a false gamma reading will result from projection printing. The gray scale is placed in a printing frame in contact with an unexposed piece of film, in total darkness, and exposed to a relatively dim light source (a 7½-watt bulb about three to six feet away will be adequate). A few test negatives can be made until you get most of the middle steps of the scale. A few of the light ones will be lost, or a few dark ones will block up completely, but this does not matter.

The exposure does not matter, but you can estimate the correction after seeing the first test. If the original scale has, approximately, 0.15 density steps, doubling the exposure will print two additional steps, halving it will remove two steps.

Once you know the exposure that produces a reasonable number of clearly defined steps, keep a record of it for further use. To find the gamma to which you are developing, expose a negative strip and develop it with a batch of negatives.

CHECKING DENSITY

When the strip is dry, the densities of the steps visible are read on the densitometer, remembering that Step 1 of the original scale will be the darkest step on the print-through. The first step that can be readily separated may be number 4, all below this being blocked up. Check this by counting back from the frame marked number 10. From this point, read each step and make a table:

STEP	DENSITY
4	1.60
5	1.58
6	1.50
7	1.40
8	1.28
9	1.15
10	1.02
11	.90
12	.78
13	.70
14	.60
15	.50
16	.38
17	.28
18	.20
19	.18
20	.16

Plot this on graph paper, using the measured densities as the vertical scale, and the densities of the original scale, written backward (that is, with zero at the right) on the baseline. The marks will not necessarily fall as smoothly as in Figure 7, but will depend on how carefully you read the densitometer.

The resulting curve has exactly the shape of the characteristic curve of the film. Since you do not know the exposures given at each step, you can't draw any conclusions about film speed from the curve, but you can easily measure the gamma. Pick a point in the straight line and measure ten spaces horizontally from it. Now measure upward until the line hits the straight line again; counting the number of spaces in this case, we find it is eight. (Figure 7.)

The gamma is found by:

$$\text{Gamma} = \frac{\text{Density difference, print}}{\text{Density difference, original}}$$

$$= \frac{8}{10} = 0.8$$

Actually it is not necessary to draw the graph if only the gamma value is needed. Since you are interested in the ratio of the density differences, simply take the differences of about six steps in the middle of the scale. For example, steps 8 to 14 are respectively 1.28, 1.15, 1.02, .90, .78, .70, .60. Subtracting each from the preceding, we find the differences are .13, .13, .12, .12, .18, .10 and, if we take an average of all these, it comes out close to .12 per step.

Doing the same with the original over the same steps, you get 1.18, 1.34, 1.52, 1.66, 1.81, 1.93, 2.08 and the differences are .16, .18, .14, .15, .12, .15. The average of these is close to .15. Using the same formula:

$$\frac{.12}{.15} = 0.8$$

It is the same figure found by the graph method.

This second method is basically the one used for process control in most movie film developing laboratories and is capable of as much accuracy as any other, depending only on how good the densitometer is and how carefully the readings are taken.

Whichever of the two methods is used, the average photographer will find that its real advantage is that it does not necessitate the use of logarithms and trigonometry; all that is needed is arithmetic. Once the original gray scale has been calibrated, the table of densities, density differences, and average density is known and, for process control particularly, it is not even necessary to read the densities of the whole test strip.

Throughout the preceding discussion of the important aspects of gamma, emphasis has been upon its use in evaluating negative film emulsions. Similar but less extensive applications exist in the evaluation of positive film emulsions, such as those used in motion-picture work. While many of the general principles outlined apply in a broad way to photographic papers as well, the lack of a long straight-line section in their characteristic curves makes the use of specific gamma values in paper sensitometry somewhat impractical. For similar reasons, the use of gamma values for reversible emulsions is of little direct value.

Looking down on a garden scene is a good way to capture the repetition-design as we find here in the water-lily pads. It is also a good way of eliminating disturbing background details. (Photo: Margaret Ohlander)

GARDEN PHOTOGRAPHY

JOHN R. WHITING
Photographer; Formerly editor and publisher of "Flower Grower," Editor of "A Treasury of American Gardening"; Author of "Photography is a Language"; Publisher, "Popular Science Monthly."

[The various approaches to garden photography are discussed in this informative article. Valuable advice is given on how to discover and photograph the hidden beauty of the garden.]

All Photographs Courtesy *"Flower Grower"* magazine.

• *Also see: Filters; Flash Photography; Flower Photography.*

MANY GARDEN PHOTOGRAPHS CAN be called "miniature landscapes," for nature (plus some of the landscape architect's art) has provided the photographer with a potentially well-organized unit. It is this combination of the natural plant forms with the design to be found in garden layout that makes this branch of photography so intriguing. But garden photography is a little more complex than the mere search for composition, and as with many other subjects, the photographer will get better results if he knows what to look for, and why and how to control the various pictorial, botanical, and architectural elements involved.

These basic requirements and their many details are there regardless of our approach to garden photography—whether it be that of the "snapshooter," the botanist, the landscape architect, the magazine illustrator, the commercial photographer working for a real-estate man, or the photographer who searches for subjects for his "creative vision."

PROBLEMS ARE SPECIFIC

One of the delights of garden photography is the infinite variety of the subject matter to be found in the garden. Here is a beautiful specimen of a plant, the texture and color of its leaves setting it apart from the rest of the garden. Here is a tiny corner, with very small plants and their small blossoms. Here is a white statue, perhaps with a background of evergreens or of azaleas in flower.

Here is color. Here is sunlight and shadow. Here is repetition in the design of a brick walk, with texture, with the contrast of grass. Here is the delicacy of a group of tulips, with sunlight backlighting them. Here is the massiveness of trees, and here the problem of telephone wires cutting across the background. Here is a total garden, a miniature landscape, that "feels" beautiful, but how do we get it all in?

At different seasons of the year, in different climates, the well-trained eye of a photographer-viewfinder combination can find pictures by looking upward. Simplicity is a key word in this type of angle shot. (Photo: Margaret Perry)

Everywhere we turn there are both opportunities and problems. We can begin to work out some of each if we set the camera up on the tripod and examine the scene through the viewfinder or groundglass. In garden photography there is time to select the proper elements, time to try various angles. Often time can provide another advantage—as the sun moves it changes the shadow pattern and often the entire "mood" of the garden.

Although we are dealing with stills—let us use a little motion-picture thinking as we look about us. Here is a corner that has the makings of a picture. We look into the viewfinder, and move the camera slowly, searchingly. Long shot, medium shot, close-up—from this angle, from that. If only we could frame the scene with part of a tree limb—well, why not? Just by borrowing a stepladder and getting three feet higher, we can give this whole scene extra depth.

As we go slowly through the garden, the moving scene in the groundglass gives us ideas—perhaps to contrast the white garden ornament in one part of a scene with a group of white lilies in another, or to repeat a curve in a composition.

In a few cases, motion itself may be used in the still picture. Perhaps some leaves flutter in the foreground; we can use the slight blur as part of the picture. In another way, the motion-picture idea may be used in a series of pictures, as we move down a walk or closer and closer to a statue.

This technique, of course, must be used with extreme care when you are actually taking motion pictures in the garden. Panning, except very slowly, is disturbing, but good contrasts of scene and the accentuation of the small motions that occur in the garden make pleasant touches.

Perhaps the best way to bring life to a slightly static garden scene is also the best way to find drama and variety in a group of stills—by finding the real variety in the many ways of looking at a subject. For example, photograph a tree—and mark the spot where your camera is. Then, go back in winter, and photograph the same tree's branches against the sky. Or, as the famous team of Gottscho-Schleisner did, photograph the same garden in the four seasons, including winter when it is covered with snow.

This typically Japanese contrast of textures was found in the Huntington Botanical Garden in California. (Photo: Margaret Ohlander)

The garden can also become a specialized studio for experiments, for portraits of individual plants. Here you can try silhouettes, reflections in a pool, or a great magnification of the center of a flower. You can get down low and look up at a mushroom or move in tight on the shaggy bark of a tree.

CAMERAS AND EQUIPMENT

Any size or type of camera can be used to take satisfactory garden pictures. Fast shutters or so-called fast lenses are not necessary. However, groundglass focusing is valuable because of the emphasis on leisurely composing and framing the picture. A choice of lenses in various focal lengths can make a professional's work easier, for although one seemingly has time and space to move the camera forward and back with infinite variations, there are instances when a quite immovable tree, or a wall, or a fragile bed of flowers is in the way. A tripod, of course, is invaluable, and a lens shade should always be used. A cable release is desirable, as in any camera work that may require short time exposures.

EMULSIONS

Extremely satisfactory black-and-white photographs are made in the garden. Any type of film, of course, will "do," but the emulsion of preference is medium-speed panchromatic for fine detail in enlargements and a full range of tones. A light-yellow, a medium-yellow, and perhaps a light-green filter will provide a sufficiently wide range of tone control.

The use of color is, of course, ideally suited to garden photography whether one takes transparencies for projection or ends up with color

Point of view is all-important in garden photography. For a large formal garden, as this one at Williamsburg, the high angle and rather distant view makes an excellent composition. (Photo: Richard Garrison)

prints. The only difficulties are caused by the sometimes uneven light intensities, such as sunlight coming through the leaves of trees. Today's range of color emulsions is so broad that whatever film you are used to can be a safe choice for garden pictures.

LIGHTING

Most garden pictures are taken outdoors using only the available light that is present in the scene. Shooting garden pictures at the extremes of the day, in early morning or late afternoon, often provides excellent quality and valuable variety, as does shooting on gray, overcast days, in fog or mist, and even on rainy days.

Considerable control of light is possible. Control of light begins with proper selection of the time of day to make the picture: for example, when the sun is shining evenly on a whole rose border, or when the shadows are falling exactly where you want them. For local control of light, such as softening shadows and "opening up" unwanted dark areas, fill-in reflectors painted white or covered with aluminum foil are invaluable. If you cover your reflector with aluminum foil, crumple the foil first; then straighten it out and glue it down. An absolutely smooth aluminum surface is apt to reflect light too harshly and make a "hot spot." Flash, too, can be used to balance the light on a bright day or add sparkle to an overcast one.

Photographing a garden that is illuminated with floodlights is easier than most people realize. Simplicity should be the basic characteristic of a photograph of an illuminated garden. Do not be afraid to include fairly large areas of darkness in the final picture.

GARDEN RESEARCH

A knowledge of plants, of the way a garden grows, and of how the seasons change a garden is most helpful in choosing the proper moment to make pictures. There are a hundred pitfalls you can learn to avoid, and another hundred small delights that a thorough knowledge of how a garden "works" can place before your camera. Visit public gardens, where the various flowers, shrubs, and trees are often labeled. Make notes about the season of bloom of various plants. Find private gardens near your home whose owners will point out the hidden things—ferns in a corner in early spring just before they uncurl, for example—that have meaning for horticulturally-minded people and provide visual opportunities for a photographer.

Read the garden magazines, from the highly specialized horticultural publications to the over-all gardening magazines. There are also the larger general and "shelter" magazines, although at times you will find pictorial examples in them that seem impossible to duplicate. One trick they use is to move plants in bloom from a greenhouse to a garden to "fill in" a bare spot. Another, even more dubious, is to stick the stems of cut florist flowers in the ground, to last just long enough for an impressive color photograph to be made. Nursery and seed catalogs are also a valuable source of information, ideas, and identifications.

Finally, observe and think. Learning to really see is a part of all good photographic work, but it has a special meaning in the garden. How many hours will it take for a patch of sunlight to move to the exact spot you want? Is this scene an extreme close-up after all? How can one best change this background —by putting it completely out of focus, by waiting until it is in shadows so it will photograph dark, or by putting a gray cloth behind a plant? Ingenuity of ideas, of observations, will lead to ingenuity of pictures. In time, your observations and thoughts will be about the details of plants, about the changing pattern of the garden, about the contrasts in color, texture, and design. You will put some special observation together with an idea from a book or magazine—and get a picture.

Most of all do not forget the value of simplicity. Even if you find a large and perfect garden—find the perfection of its details, its corner, its small quiet places, its contrasts, and photograph these. If you are in an apparently dull garden, just look around. Somewhere there is something to be seen, to be recorded for your lasting satisfaction on film.

This close-up portrait of a gloxinia is dramatic because all background competition has been eliminated, enabling the rich detail of blossom and leaves to be shown simply and effectively. (Photo: Laurie Wiener)

GEOMETRICAL APPROACH TO COMPOSITION

Ansel Adams
Photographer, Author of "Polaroid Manual"

[A novel and experimental approach to creative composition is discussed in this interesting article. It explains how a picture can be analyzed from the geometrical point of view of lines of force, sectors, and extensions. This article will help the photographer to understand the mathematical relationships in a well-composed and well-cropped photograph.]

All illustrations by Ansel Adams.

• *Also see: Composition; Esthetics of Photography; Juxtapositions in Photography.*

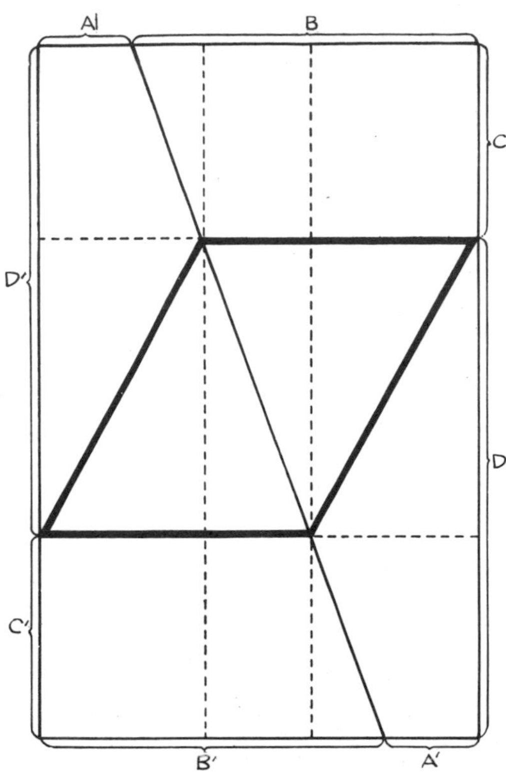

Above: *Figure 1. Symmetrical composition. Notice the relationships between A and A', B and B', C and C', D and D'. Other relationships are indicated by the dotted lines.*

Below: *Figure 2. Asymmetrical composition. In this, the segments marked as A, B, C, D, E, and F are all different, but proportionately related. That is, A is to B as C is to D and E to F. The dotted lines indicate a symmetrical framework suggested by M and N.*

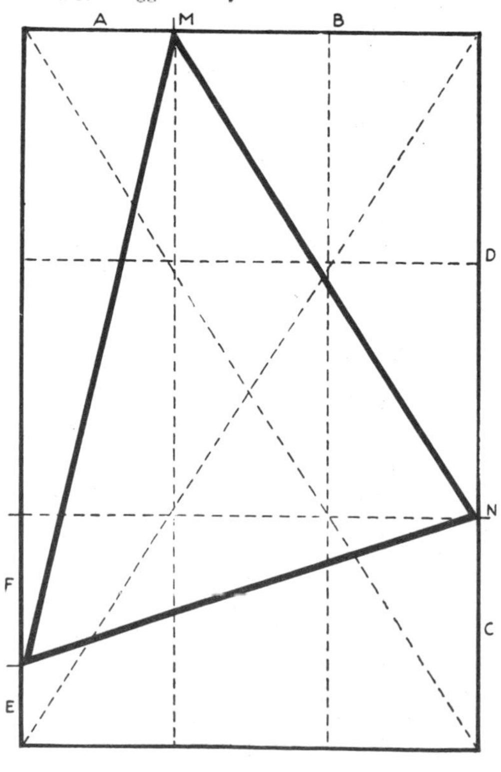

Every medium of art expresses itself in its own terms, just as each language has its own syntax. In art, this expression is controlled by composition, the basic rhetoric of pictorial statement. Formal composition and intuitive composition, in their final form, are not dissimilar. One is the product of intellect tempered by emotion; the other is the product of emotion tempered by intellect and experience. In active art, "perfection" is theoretical and rarely attained.

Composition is not an isolated thing in itself. A work of art, functioning in terms of color, values, line, and form, necessarily possesses a high order of composition. It cannot be said to have composition because of its line, or form, or distribution of values, but only because it has successfully combined all the elements of expression and construction.

Composition has been defined as some particular aspect of creative expression—especially in the graphic arts, painting, and photography. Certain "base patterns" have been established, derived largely from the techniques of accepted "old masters," or from mathematic-philosophic systems such as "dynamic symmetry." The latter is based on geometrical analysis of formal classical art.

CREATIVE COMPOSITION

For the creative artist, any such imposition of formulas or method is usually meaningless, as every expression determines its own manner of composition. Composition is a result, not a cause. It is the form of expression, not the expression itself. Photography has suffered vastly from the false domination of "rules of composition." The "rules" being in the main superficial derivations are questionable in themselves; a prime error is committed when they are supported as the basis of creative expression.

The "formal" approach of classical art was far more an attitude of creation and function than a devotion to set formulas. We must remember that art in the making is a very different thing from art viewed in retrospect. The artist, reverting five hundred years to the methods of an old master, or five years to his own earlier techniques, is merely depending on what has been done; in both cases he is only restating, not creating. Yet he may select such inspirational suggestions from previous work as he can integrate to his best advantage. The greater the artist's objective knowledge of all art, the richer his own expression may become. Yet his results will lose force and imaginative importance in direct proportion to his imitation of past methods and forms.

Photography is an imaginative, analytic art, an art of selection, elimination, and emphasis of subject. The optical image of the lens is in itself quite inflexible; the chemical images of the negative and positive are equally rigorous in line and detail, but admit a certain control of values.

What, then, establishes the difference between photography as a purely mechanical process and photography as an intense form of creative expression? The answer is: the degree of preselection and visualization of the final print in all its aspects—form, placement, and tonal values—before the exposure is made. While the optical image is a strict, inevitable thing in itself, it is nevertheless subject to certain selective controls—the point of view, the focal length of the lens, and the direction and quality of the light. These elements determine the composition; the chemical processes express it.

It is apparent that the formal, three-dimensional aspects of the subject projected on the two-dimensional surfaces of the negative relate to a certain space. Within this space the proportions, directions of line, and resultant areas will be revealed. We can attempt to "force" these elements into preconceived space, but we will be less successful in so doing than if we were to determine the space in relation to these elements. Certain combinations of compositional elements predetermine the "dynamism" of the whole, and this dynamism must relate to the emotional significance of the subject. If these relationships are felt, and the arrangement of the photograph carried out accordingly, we can be reasonably certain of satisfactory results. That which is completely felt and which results in a clear statement almost always withstands close formal examination.

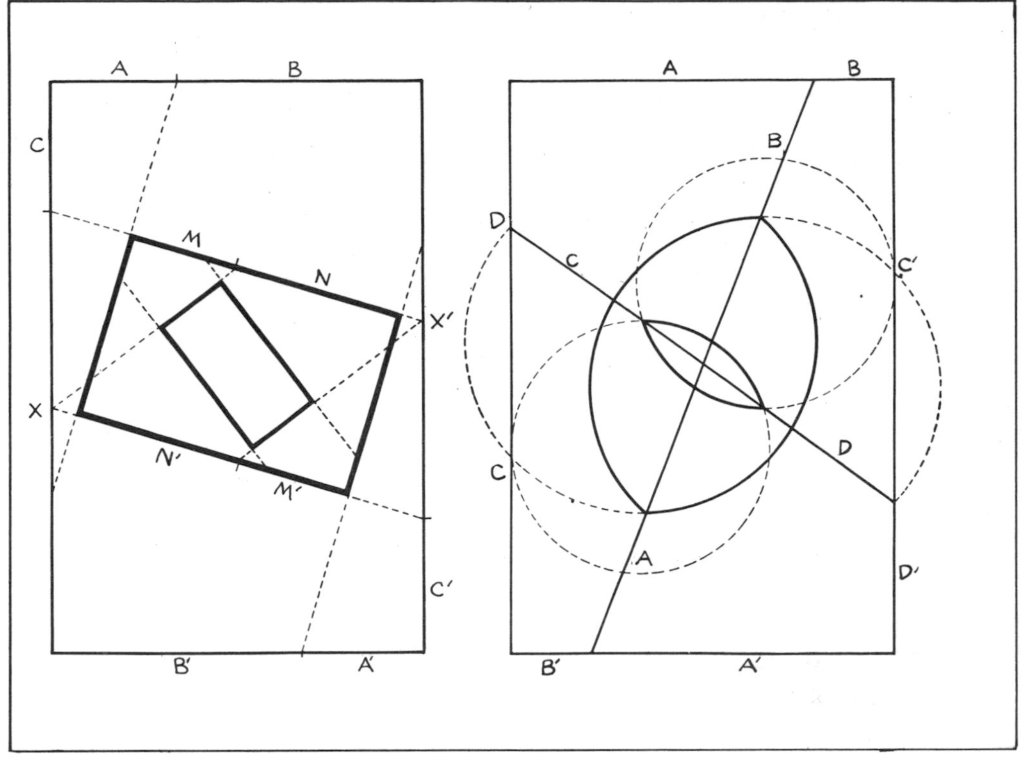

Figure 3. Extended lines within picture area. The diagrams show compositions where no part of the prime image touches the edges of the picture. In the figure at the left, notice the relationship of A to A′, B to B′, C to C′, etc. Notice also the relationship of N to N′, M to M′, and the tie-in of the inside and outside areas at X and X′. The figure on the right shows how the axis of an elliptical form may be treated. Again the relationships of A to A′, B to B′, etc. should be seen.

LINES OF FORCE

Perhaps the simplest method of understanding compositional relationships is to investigate the sectors (or the sector points) of lines of force or direction evolving from the subject. These lines may terminate at the confines of the space, or resolve beyond them. Parts of the image itself may contact the space confines (edges of the picture); or, "extensions" of the image may do so. There are no rules—only logical appearances. The more important basic relationships may be stated as follows:

1. The completely symmetrical (Figure 1)
2. The asymmetrical (Figure 2)
3. The extended lines within the picture space (Figure 3)
4. The lines resolved outside the picture space (Figure 4).

Briefly, the first and second represent the simplest relationships, the third the most usual, and the fourth the most interesting and subtle. All, of course, appear together in actual practice. The divisions are arbitrary, made for purposes of discussion.

These relationships are at best approximate. None will resolve with rigid accuracy. All must take advantage of the give-and-take of line and form in relation to values that is essential in all art. A very pertinent musical analogy may be made in this regard; a phrase of strict notation and meter is performed with elasticity depending on its tonal dimensions and "shape" and on its emotional weight and emphases. Formal relations in photography, as in all art, should be similarly elastic and flexible. Restricted arrangements are to be avoided.

The following analysis of formal compositional relationships does not imply that photographs should be consciously composed by rigid application of rules derived from such analysis to the problems. However, if an awareness of these relationships and their compositional function is established in the mind, an augmented clarity of perception will result. Emotional values take obvious precedence over the mere formulas

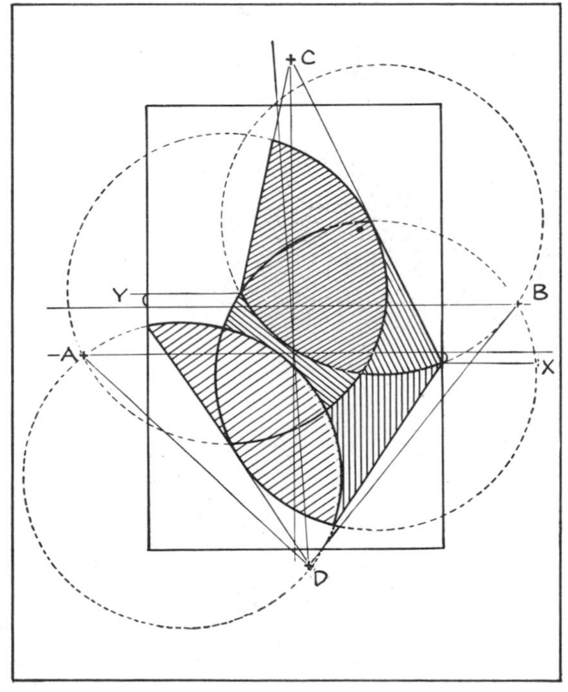

Figure 4. Lines resolving outside picture area. The distance A to bottom is the same as B to top, and both A and B resolve the same distance from the edge. C is the symmetrical resolution on the center line and D, off center, balances A and B.

of construction and execution.

Above all, it is necessary to visualize the emotional and organic aspects of the photograph before the exposure is made, to feel the directions of line and force, the counteraction of force and mass, the perspective directions not only across the composition, but into it. When this expansion of perception and understanding is achieved—even in small part—the taboos and canons of conventional photographic "composition" become meaningless.

TYPICAL ANALYSES

It must be stressed that the following analyses were done after the photograph was made. The relationships were undoubtedly sensed unconsciously while the picture was being composed, but the prime object was to achieve an emotionally balanced arrangement. If the results are balanced, the pictures will almost always tolerate analysis such as this. It is suggested that photographers go over their best pictures and seek out such relationships. A better eye for structure will be the outcome of retrospective analysis. However, it is not advisable to work out compositional analysis in detail on the groundglass while the picture is being made. Feel while composing; intellectualize afterward.

Old Timers, Hornitos, California:

This is a simple composition based chiefly on verticals and horizontals (Figure 5). Vertical lines drawn through each of the men extended to the top and bottom edges result in the equal divisions A and A′. Two other verticals, through the centers of the "woodwork," result in the equal divisions C and C′. Horizontal lines running across the top of the hats and the "woodwork" create the equal divisions B and B′, or if the divisions are considered overlapping, BB and BB′. A line running across the bottom of the chairs forms the division (to bottom of picture) of M. This division is equal to M′.

Right: Figure 6. *Ansel Adams / Half Dome, Yosemite Valley.*

The diagonal O-O′ runs from the upper left corner through the wooden box on the wall, and follows the leg of the man at the right. It crosses the edge of the print at the M line. The diagonals X and Y are interesting as they are almost equal, especially XB and YB.

Half Dome, Yosemite Valley:

This composition is based on horizontal and vertical sectors and a definite curved form (Figure 6). The verticals A and A′ (through the tip of the dome and the tip of the dark cliff to the left) result in equal divisions to the edges of the picture. So do the horizontals B, B′ and C, C′, and the verticals D, D′ and E, E′.

Note that the approximate curves contact the picture edge as follows: O at AO; OO at the upper left corner. This merely signifies that the curving rhythm of the forms bears some relationship to the other elements of the composition and to the picture area. The large curve, resolving at the left edge of the print, was the dominant factor in the decision to trim the composition on that side. This resolution was "felt" at the time of exposure.

Other comparative relationships often occur, accurately or approximately, such as the relationship of A to the base print to B to the height of the print.

Figure 5. *Ansel Adams / Old Timers, Hornitos, California.*

□

GEORGE EASTMAN HOUSE

The George Eastman House, a museum of photography and cinematography in Rochester, N. Y., was founded in 1947. The museum maintains a permanent collection of photographs, motion pictures, apparatus, documents, and books; it organizes exhibitions shown in the Eastman House and circulated throughout the country; it conducts research in the history of photography and cinematography and supports a publications program.

The purposes of the George Eastman House were set forth in the charter granted to the Trustees by the Regents of the State of New York:

> To establish, operate, and maintain a museum of photography and allied pursuits in or about the City of Rochester, New York, as a memorial to the late George Eastman;
>
> To promote, develop, conduct, and maintain public exhibitions of photography and its uses;
>
> To teach photography by demonstration and exhibition and to foster public knowledge of and interest in the various methods and techniques involved therein;
>
> To promote, encourage, and develop photography and its allied arts and sciences;
>
> To receive, collect, and preserve relics, records, apparatus, equipment, material, and other items of historic or current interest;
>
> To carry out and discharge any of the purposes hereinabove set forth either directly or by contribution to other organizations, corporations, foundations, or institutions organized for any of the above purposes.

The permanent exhibitions at the museum consist of "The Art of Photography," a survey of photographs from Daguerre to the present day; "Pictures for All," a display of popular portraiture from the silhouette to the snapshot; and "The Science of Photography," in the Mees Gallery, which presents the fundamentals of the photographic process explained with cameras and demonstration apparatus operable by the visitor.

In the 550-seat Dryden Theatre programs of motion pictures, from the historical archives of over 3000 titles, are presented every Saturday and Sunday afternoon. Members of the Dryden Film Society view special evening programs.

The George Eastman House Associates receive a newsletter, an annual book publication, and invitations to openings of special exhibitions and lectures.

A circulating-exhibition service offers to museums, colleges, and libraries special exhibitions drawn from the Eastman House collections on a modest rental basis.

The George Eastman House is open every day of the week from 10 a.m. to 5 p.m. Admission is free.

GLAMOUR PHOTOGRAPHY

Peter Gowland
Photographer

[The attractive female model is widely photographed by all classes of photographers. To get the best results the author gives many suggestions directly from his vast experience in this field. Equipment, exposure, lighting, accessories, make-up, backgrounds, and posing are fully described.]

• *Also see: Make-up for Photography; Model Posing for the Amateur; Models and Directing for the Professional; Nude Photography.*

Today we are continually engulfed by glamour. We see it in the movies, on calendars, in advertisements, in the fine and graphic arts, on television, in the theater, and in photographs. Despite the presence everywhere of the beautiful female face and form, an illusion of glamour is one of the most difficult images a photographer can attempt to capture on film. Much more goes into making a successful glamour photograph than just a camera, light, and a pretty girl. And this is one of the reasons why some of the more accomplished glamour photographers are also some of the highest paid men in their field.

Glamour photography encompasses many types of photographs, the over-all field including fashion, pin-up, face or figure photography, and advertising. Since each of these areas has its own special demands and criteria, the proper choice of model is of the utmost importance. Once selected the model must then be intelligently posed and directed. All of this, plus proper equipment, good technique, and perhaps a measure of good luck, adds up to the difficult but rewarding result of a finished glamour photograph.

FASHION

In the fashion field there are two distinct types of beauty. One is the girl used for casual dress and teen-type clothes. She is the healthy all-American girl, neatly groomed and with a sparkling personality. She conveys the feeling of youth. Her figure is trim but not gaunt.

The high-fashion model on the other hand is not always beautiful in the typical American-girl sense. She is more sophisticated in her manner, expert at applying make-up, styling hair, wearing clothes, and posing. High-fashion models can work indefinitely as far as age goes, since most of their pictures are full-length and often not wire-sharp.

If occasionally a rare beauty appears on the scene and close-ups are desired, retouching can take care of any unfavorable lines. As a rule, most advertisers like to avoid retouching. This is why young girls from age 15 to 20 are used for soap commercials, or in other types of picture where the face is under close scrutiny.

PIN-UPS

The pin-up model must have a good figure as well as a pretty face. Dancers are always a good choice for this type of work. Their lithe and supple bodies, their innate poise and grace in movement greatly simplify the photographer's task.

The choice of a model for figure-study shots depends on the type of picture desired. The calendar market and men's magazine prefer the voluptuous beauty who looks directly into the camera. The girl must have facial beauty as well as a lush, fully developed figure. The artistic nude can have a rounded figure, or the slim fashion type. Both of these figure-types make interesting studies if the model is graceful and has an interest in working for the best results.

ATTENTION TO DETAIL

In any of the categories mentioned, grooming is important. The photographer should have a fashion coordinator assisting him, preferably a woman, to take care of these details. It is almost impossible to

Various techniques can be used to emphasize the model's best features. Here the photographer utilized petroleum jelly over the lens to soften the entire face except the eyes. View camera with floodlights. (Photo courtesy of Gevaert)

Glamour photography tends to be repetitive after a while, making a fresh approach always welcome. Here a peeling wall, mop, strong sidelighting, and a beautiful model create a striking glamour shot. Leica M2 with 35mm Summicron f/2 lens and one light. Tri-X film rated at 800 ASA and exposed at f/2 for 1/30 of a second. (Photo: Michael L. Edelson)

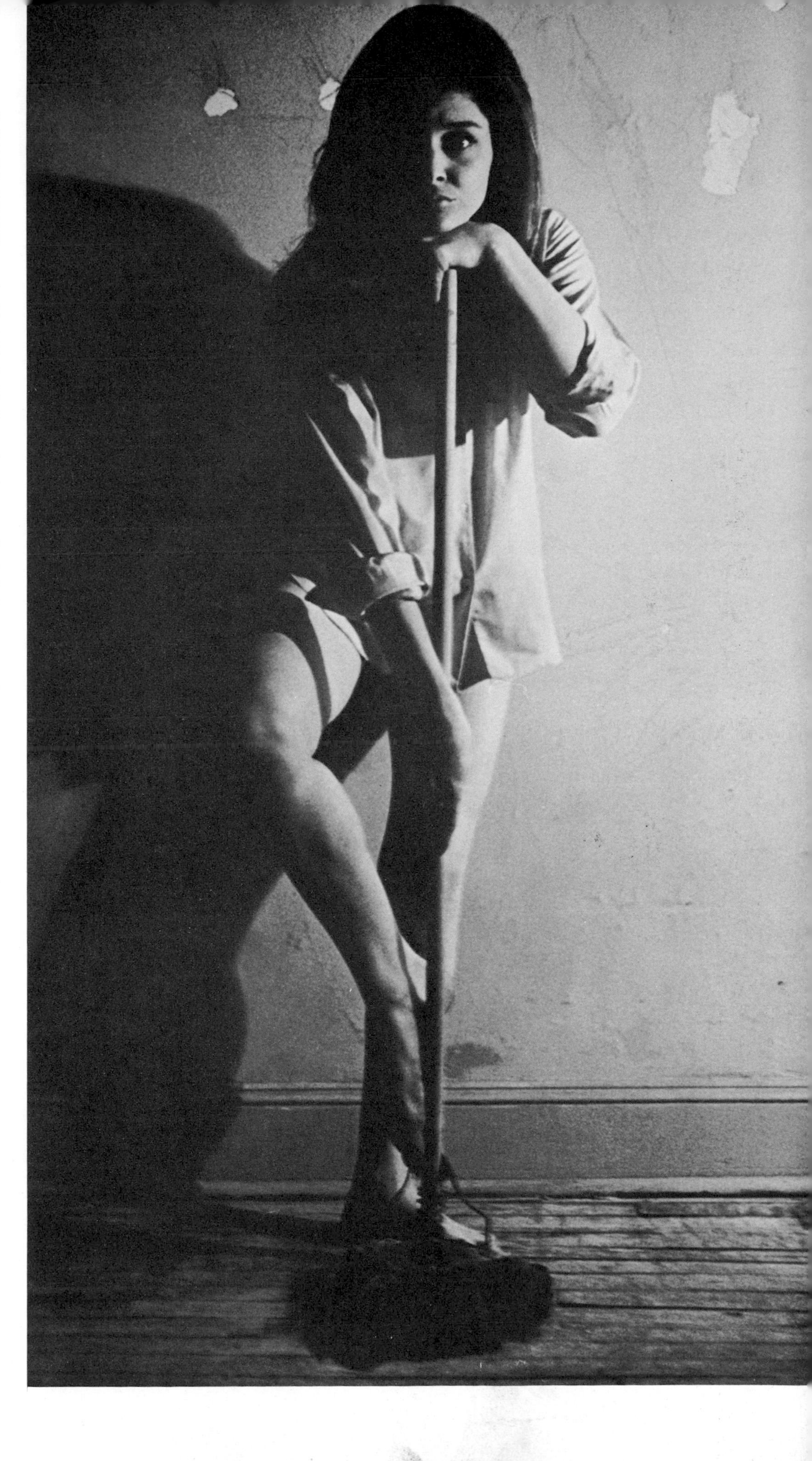

think creatively about posing, backgrounds, and lighting while worrying about clothing, hair, make-up, etc. A good fashion coordinator should be able to improve the look of the clothing being modeled and to select the style of hair and accessories to be used.

In calendar, cover, and advertising work the same holds true. Even with the help of a coordinator there are times when some small detail is overlooked and the pictures are ruined. The person who has final approval should have the ability to see with the eyes of the camera, for the camera picks up things that the naked eye will not catch. For example, the lipstick line often runs just the tiniest fraction of an inch—hardly noticeable at a glance—or the hair may be out of place just enough to look messy when frozen by the camera's lens.

In the glamour studies which encompass the entire figure the close scrutiny of face make-up is not so important. But small details of the clothing, hair, hands, and feet should be closely watched.

A key factor to remember in making glamour pictures designed to sell for a period of years is to avoid dating them. By "years," I do not mean indefinitely; let us say a picture should sell over and over again over a period of five years. With straight fashion pictures where styles change overnight this cannot be done. Evening dresses, street clothes and hair-do's which are extreme will always put a time tag on the picture. But a beautiful girl photographed on the beach in a bathing suit or indoors with a towel or a short negligee will remain in style indefinitely.

POSING THE MODEL

Success in posing will depend on one's ability to notice the body arrangement and make suggestions to improve this arrangement. Proper

Success in posing will depend on the photographer's ability to notice the body arrangement and to make suggestions to improve it. Proper posing begins with a careful analysis of the model's best features. Twin-lens reflex with flash fill-in. Panatomic-X exposed at f/5.6 for 1/250 of a second. (Photo: Peter Gowland)

posing begins with a careful analysis of the model's best features. If the model is nearly-perfect, the only worry is to avoid distortion. However, if the model has wide hips, thin legs, or a thick middle, posing can make these features less obvious.

If the model is in a standing position, the hips will appear to be smaller when they are turned slightly to the side, with the top half of the figure facing the camera and leaning forward. Having the camera at a somewhat higher angle than usual corrects the situation even more. If the model is seated, the same rules apply; never photograph the hips straight on.

Thin legs are best photographed

in compact positions. The popular pose of a girl kneeling is still a top seller for commercial and cover material. If the situation requires that she stand, thin legs will appear to take on more weight if they are photographed from a rear view—this emphasizes the calves and the heavy part of the thigh.

Good direction in posing does more than merely correct unfavorable features; it also encourages the model to take an interest in her work. Most professional models expect a certain amount of instruction, at least until they understand what is desired of them. For a start, pose the girl in a seated position and gradually change one section of the body at a time to add variations. When the sitting begins to lag, a mirror will come in handy. Models can often pose themselves by looking into a full-length mirror placed behind the camera.

CAMERA ANGLES

Another method of varying the pictures is to change camera angles. There are certain basic rules that should be followed when considering the angle of the camera:

1. To avoid body distortion on full-length pictures, keep the head and feet about the same distance from the camera.
2. To add length to the legs, use a low camera angle.
3. Low camera angles are better for standing shots.
4. High camera angles are better for sitting and reclining poses; they feature the face and bosom.
5. Side and three quarter body angles tend to thin the figure.
6. Front and rear "flat-on" angles tend to make the figure heavier.

PROPS

For the beginner who is not used to directing or posing his models, the use of props is of great value. A chair, a stool, or a pillow will encourage the model to move naturally into different poses.

When working outdoors there are many natural props available, such as rocks, trees, driftwood, or interesting fences and architectural forms. In using these, one must be careful not to concentrate more on the prop than on the girl. One of the easiest ways to avoid having the prop dominate the picture is to fill the negative area with as much of the model as possible. If part of the rock, fence, or tree is eliminated, so much the better; it has been used without dominating the scene.

Every photographer has his own preference, but I like to work with single props against a white background, rather than to use them in a room setting. Naturally, there are exceptions to this rule—when the room is bare enough or of a design which permits the prop to be fairly isolated. But in general a chair, a vase, or a screen will be more effective when placed against a plain studio background with only the model to complement it.

WORKING WITH THE MODEL

Any photographer who works with people must have an outgoing personality himself. This does not imply that he should be a noisy jokester, but he cannot be shy and retiring and still expect the best of his model.

When the final analysis of a portrait is made, the expression is what counts. Professional models can "turn on" expressions, but their best pictures are those which were instantaneously inspired by the pho-

When working outdoors there are many props such as rocks, trees, driftwood, or interesting fences and architectural forms. Be careful not to concentrate too much on the prop and too little on the girl. Leica IIIG with 50mm Elmar f/2.8. Plus-X film exposed for 1/60 of a second at f/4. (Photo: Michael L. Edelson)

tographer. In order to catch or create this mood of expression, the photographer must prevent boredom and maintain enthusiasm.

Without going into a psychological essay, there are several ways of achieving this goal. If the model is encouraged to talk about herself, and the photographer shows a genuine interest in what she is saying and contributes incidents out of his own personal experiences, this will help to prevent boredom. Occasional food and drink will keep her from becoming tired and uninterested. A full-length mirror on wheels will come in handy; if she can look at herself and try different poses while the photographer is adjusting lights, or making some kind of technical change in the set-up, she will be content and might even come up with some unusual angle.

COMPOSITION

Understanding the elements of composition is as important in glamour photography as the selection of a beautiful model. Where to crop the picture is often a major compositional problem. In a full-length standing or seated pose, the least offensive place to draw the line is just above the knee, around mid-thigh. This provides good composition for a bathing suit, negligee, or other brief costume. Cropping between the foot and the knee is awkward.

The second good area for closer cropping is at the waist. This is ideal for the glamour portrait where the model is wearing a low-cut evening gown or an off-the-shoulder blouse.

Head-and-shoulder, or standard-portrait distance, where the bottom line of the picture cuts above the bust, is a third type of composition. In most of these closer compositions, it is advisable to work in the hands if they are attractive.

A common fault with many pictures is the failure to use the full picture area. Often the model is a tiny figure in the middle of meaningless scenery. Use as much of the negative area for the model as possible, and let the background play a minor role.

The results may be disappointing if the model is posed in "square" or "rectangular" positions. By using diagonal poses, there is more space from opposite corner to corner than there is from top to bottom or side to side. This is one composition frequently overlooked by the beginner.

Compact poses in which the legs and arms are bent will also show more of the girl in the picture. In this type of composition, where the girl is seated and her legs curled around close to her, there is no need to cut off any portion of the body.

BACKGROUNDS

The selection of backgrounds is one of the distinguishing marks of the professional. In glamour photography the background is most important for three reasons: 1) It must be one which compliments the subject, making her stand out; 2) it must not distract from the model; and 3) it should be harmonious with the theme.

Outdoors there are such back-

Results may be disappointing if the model is posed in "square" or "rectangular" positions. One composition frequently overlooked by the beginner is the diagonal pose. Hasselblad with medium-speed pan film exposed at f/5.6 for 1/125 of a second. (Photo: Peter Gowland)

When making glamour pictures designed to sell over a period of years remember to avoid dating them. Since the model in this photo does not have an extreme hairdo style, this picture will be commercial for a long time. Nikon F with 135mm, f/3.5 Nikkor. Plus-X film exposed at f/4 for 1/125 of a second. (Photo: Peter Gowland)

grounds as white sand, water, sky, walls, and fences. These are all plain areas. It is sometimes difficult for the photographer who is working with a particularly beautiful scene to crop out enough of the background so that the model is properly featured. He is torn between a scenic and a glamour photo. Sometimes this problem can be solved by using the girl as foreground and keeping as much of the scene in as possible. But generally speaking, the plain backgrounds are the best for glamour.

Sand, for example, as found in sand dunes or in the damp water line of the ocean, makes a very attractive textured background. But sand marked by footprints, twigs, or old bottles is just as distracting as any other type of cluttered background. Most sand backgrounds require a high angle in order to cut out objects that may be in line with the camera's coverage.

Water, of course, can also serve as a background at the beach. A model in the surf at the water's edge or against the water in a swimming pool or lake will stand out.

When working indoors, my favorite background is the seamless paper roll. These rolls come in many colors and are compact for easy storage. With the paper-roll background, all types of set-ups can be arranged—from bedrooms to kitchens.

The out-of-focus backgrounds obtainable with long focal-length lenses are good for outdoor portraits where there is no clear area. Leaves or trees that are lighted by sun can give some wonderful out-of-focus effects.

EQUIPMENT

The question of what camera to use for glamour is often asked. The choice should depend on the individual photographer and the technique he prefers. For example, there are many 35 mm cameras used in the glamour field, and many photographers who use them prefer them exclusively. Theirs is the more candid, natural approach often seen in editorial coverage, rather than the posed, technically perfect pictures required in advertising work.

There are certain advantages in using 35 mm. The cameras are light-weight and can take 36 exposures before reloading is required (many photographers carry two or three cameras around their necks so that they can shoot up to 100 or more pictures without stopping to reload). Perhaps more important, the 35's have faster lenses which permit working under marginal light conditions. There are other advantages, too, but these are the primary ones.

On the other hand there are experts who have built their entire professional careers on the use of the 4×5 format. They work with a more studied technique where

Advertising agencies are among the biggest users of glamour photographs. Here, rather than just being a picture of a pretty girl, it must also sell a product such as soap. Electronic flash and Leica M3. Panatomic-X film exposed for 1/50 of a second at f/4. (Photo: Peter Gowland)

careful flattering posing and highest quality are stressed. These men work in the commercial field for advertisers who require the large format in order to make corrections through retouching, or to show their products in extreme detail. A compromise size is to be found in the 2¼ × 2¼-format of the Rolleiflex and Hasselblad. With these cameras, the photographer can achieve a candid feeling, and yet have the advantage of a film larger than 35 mm.

LIGHTING

In glamour, as in other fields, the photographer may choose from a variety of lighting techniques.

When using sunlight as the only light source, the midday sun should be avoided because the shadows cast by this harsh overhead light are deep and unflattering. Also sunlight brings out character, and in most glamour situations this is not desirable.

Direct overhead sunlight can be used to advantage, however, if the model is posed flat on the ground or on a low couch with her head back and eyes closed so that the face is fully lit by the sun. It is possible to supplement the light by use of a strobe, flash, or reflector, thus softening the harsh shadows. Another method of softening the effect of the sun's rays is to position a plastic sheet or light-weight cloth over the model, thereby diffusing the light the model receives.

Pictures taken outside in the early morning or late afternoon are generally the most satisfactory. The model does not have trouble with squinting and the light hits her body at a lower angle without casting heavy shadows in the area of the eyes and under the nose. When working with color in the late afternoon, the pictures will have an orange cast unless a blue filter is used. I quite often like the orange cast, as it gives an unusual effect to the pictures.

Many difficulties of working in sunlight can be overcome by moving the model into the shade. Since shade light is soft, there is no worry about harsh shadows, or about the light changing angles. Shade continues as a diffused over-all source. Shade lighting is particularly good for women because any wrinkles and lines are softened.

Shade lighting is found next to buildings, under trees, or in any number of miscellaneous structures which protect the area from direct sun. The best shade locations are those where there is good ground reflection, such as from white sand or light pavement. This type of lighting will require more exposure than sunlight—from two stops up, depending on location and reflection. I usually work with a tripod in the shade because of the slower speeds. When I find that the shade lighting is too weak, I use a supplemental light, such as a reflector flood or flash.

Floodlights can be used when working indoors to supplement the natural room light, or to provide the entire light source in portraiture. I use floods in connection with window light to fill in the shadowed area to avoid loss of detail. The main thing in using floods is to keep the lighting simple. Too many lights will cause cross shadows, and unless the eye is trained to see them, the results can be very unflattering.

When working with flash, I refer to a small chart attached to my lens shade which gives me an f-stop for a variety of distances. For example, with my flash unit and the film I normally use, I shoot at $f/22$ at 3½ feet, $f/16$ at 8 feet, and so on down to $f/2.8$ at 30 feet. I have worked out these calculations for my particular type of film, camera, and flash unit. In this way there is no need to waste time in calculation. Anyone can work out such a chart for his own use; a few test rolls are well worth the trouble.

Perhaps the easiest type of indoor lighting is bounce light. I use the silver Reflectal umbrella units with electronic flash. This gives an over-all light to the subject and seems to encompass her from all sides. Bounce light can be achieved by bouncing the light source from the ceiling, a wall, or any light area.

The use of window light is an excellent way for a novice glamour photographer to begin his career. With window light a studio is not necessary; the photographer can work in any home having sufficient window space. He can use 35 mm cameras with their fast lenses, and thus avoid a heavy investment in flash or floodlights. If the shadow area still seems to be too dark, any home-made reflector will fill in. This type of lighting, incidentally, is one of my favorite sources for figure studies.

This is the author, Peter Gowland, setting up reflecting umbrellas with electronic flash to provide a soft, bounce lighting effect. The twin-lens reflex is the Gowlandflex of his own design.

GLASS AND SILVERWARE PHOTOGRAPHY

STANLEY WEISENFELD
Supervisor of Photographic Services, Corning Glass Works

[Glass comes in all colors. It can be opaque or translucent, covered with metal designs or unusual textures, cast into many shapes. Different lighting techniques are used to record all these variations. The author, an expert in the use of lights, backgrounds, and arrangements, here explains the techniques used in glass photography.]

• *Also see: Antiques: Photographing Them.*

FEW PEOPLE HAVE EVER REALLY seen glass. Have you ever paused in the drinking of wine or water and actually looked at the container? What do you see? You see through it or you see a reflection in it. You rarely notice the object itself, if it is clear. You may see the refraction of light that creates a distorted image of what is beyond the glass. You may see a prismatic pattern of objects through a molded or cut-glass goblet. You may see things or light patterns reflected from the surface of the glass. But you will rarely notice the container itself.

Try it. Look at the outline of the vessel. Study it as you turn it in your hand. Hold it up to the light. See how the visual image changes. You have just taken the first step in learning how to photograph glass; you are beginning to see what this unusual material is really like. Now, wherever you go, whatever you are doing, if there is glass present, try to pause and perceive.

The next step is learning to photographically interpret what you see. This includes not only the ability to record it on film, but also the faculty to implant a specifically desired impression or evoke a precise emotional response in the viewer.

THE NATURE OF GLASS

Here we enter the realm of the philosophy of photographing glass. Most of our interpretations or photographs must be believable to be successful. It is expected, generally, that a photograph depict reality and truth. Occasionally we may leave realism behind for a startling effect. Then however we are not rendering an object for its own sake, but creating an impression only and using the object for that end. This, too, is valid. But first learn to record the glass object as it is. Then, and only then, may you distort with validity to achieve the desired effect.

Glass is usually thought of as transparent, fragile, delicate, and smooth. This is our normal and basic feeling about the substance. Most of the glass that we are familiar with fits this description, and most of our photographs will depict it so. However, we also manufacture glass that is opaque or translucent; or extremely strong (sometimes stronger than metals); or gross, thick and heavy with a rough or textured surface; or decorated with pigments, decals, metallic designs. Any one or more of these characteristics may appear in a single object and must be correctly interpreted photographically.

INDIVIDUAL CHARACTERISTICS

It must now be obvious that one simple technique will not work in all cases. Each problem is an individual entity and must be approached as one anticipates a new experience. Not only must we be

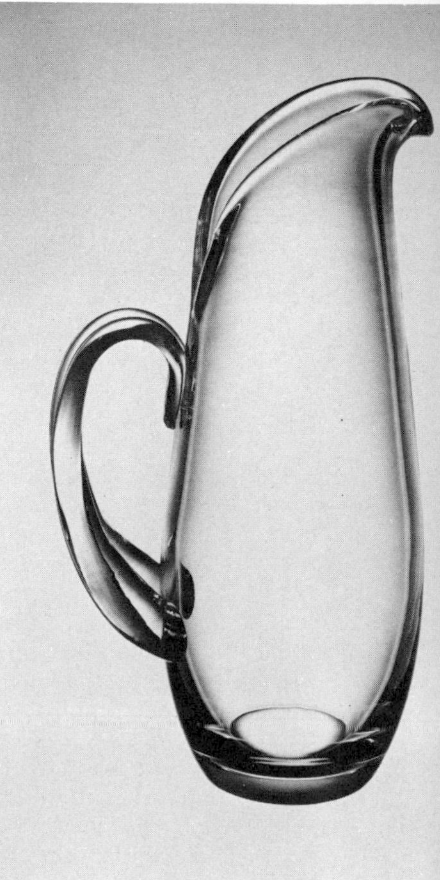

Top left: Figure 1. *A Steuben pitcher on a white paper background. Note the camera position designed to show off all the details of the gracefully formed mouth and handle. Two controlled spotlights were used, as shown in Figure 2. One spotlight illuminates the pitcher from a high 45-degree angle behind the object, while the other one lights the background. Compare this rendition with the others of the same object that follow.*

Top right: Figure 2. *Camera and lighting arrangement for Figure 1.*

Bottom left: Figure 3. *The same Steuben pitcher, but this time floating in white space. Attention is focused on the object and remains there. This is an example of extreme purity and simplicity. Note in Figure 4 that there is but a single diffused source of illumination under the curved sheet of groundglass upon which the pitcher is sitting. The amount of diffusion will control the contrast.*

Bottom right: Figure 4. *Note the curved sheet of groundglass background used in Figure 3.*

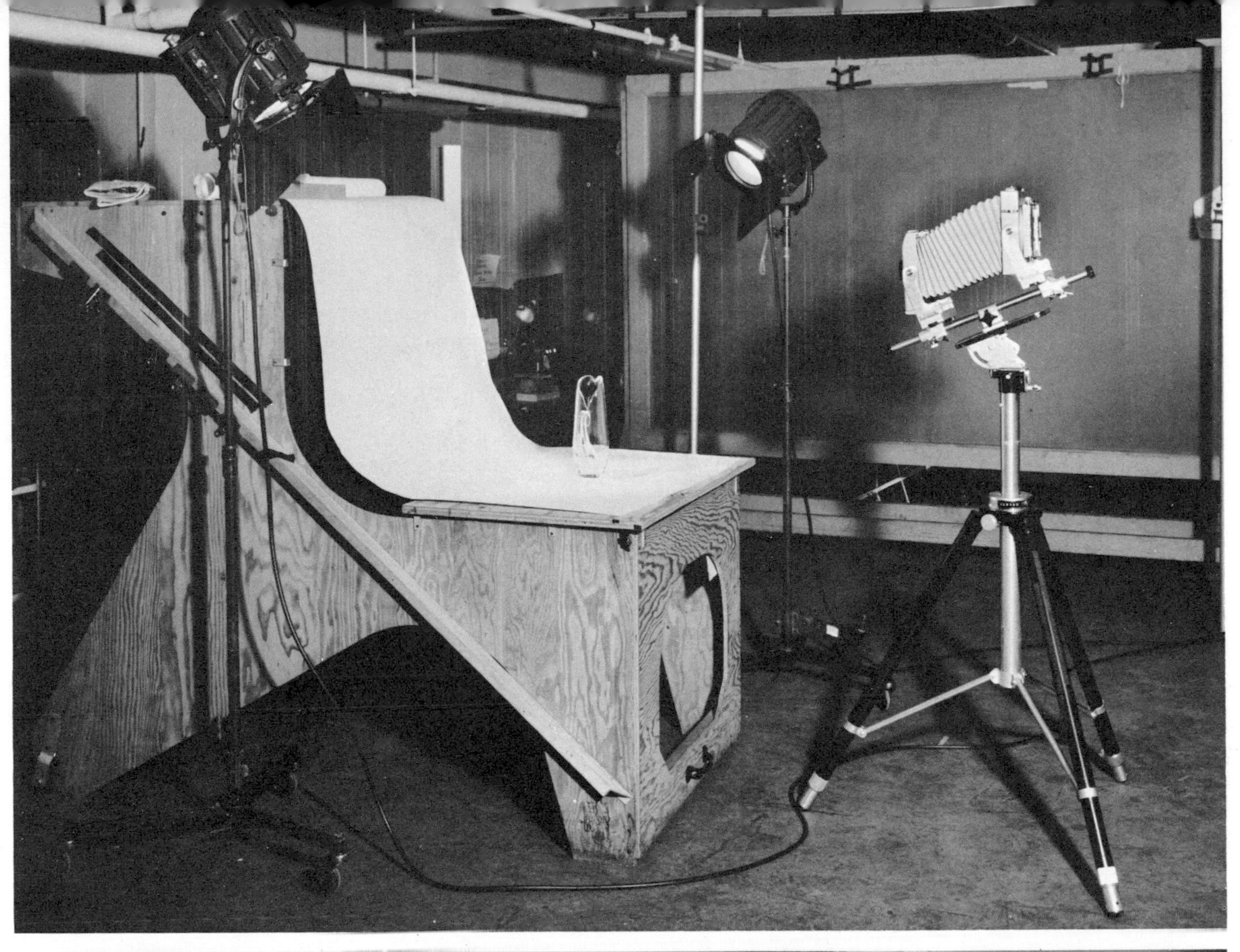

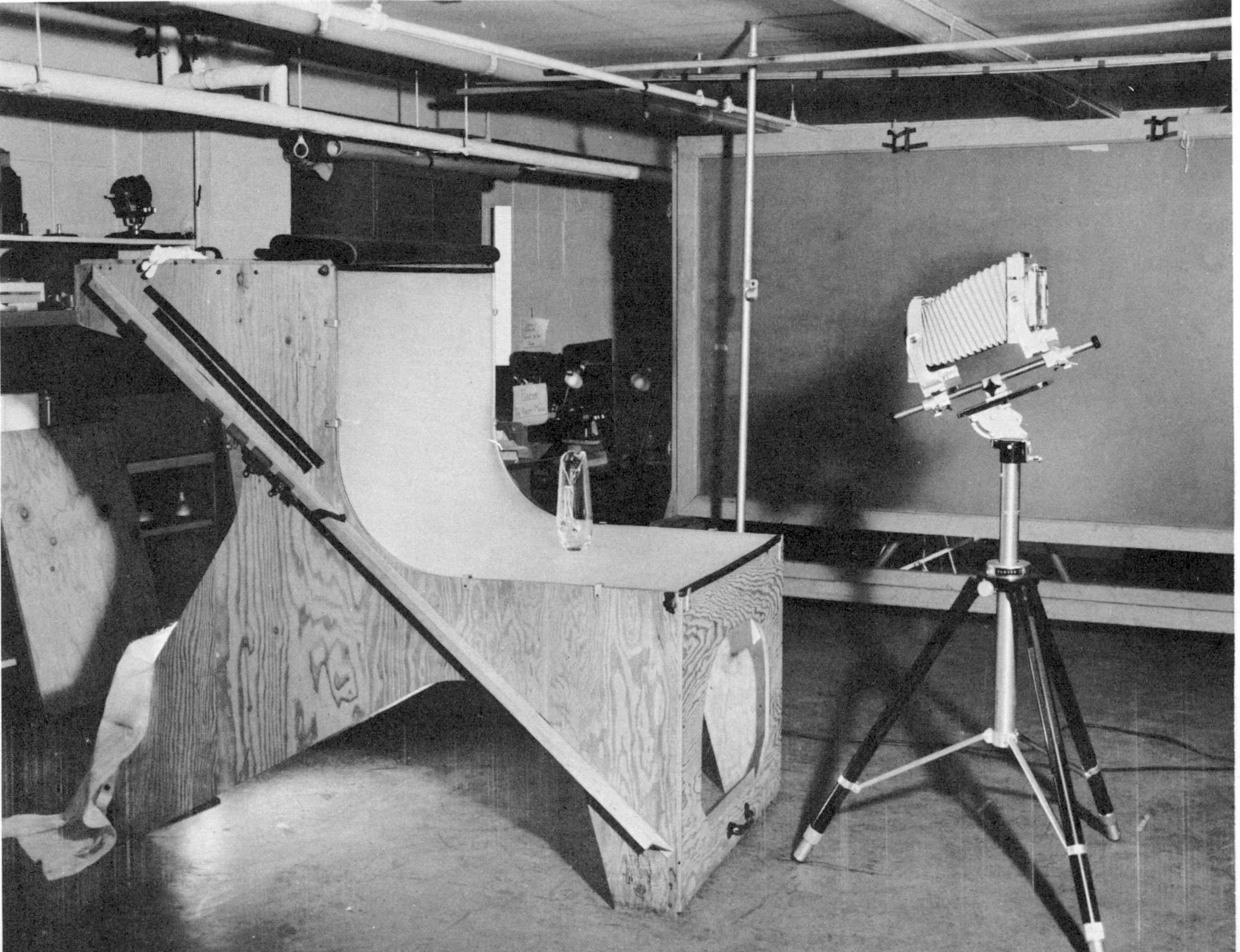

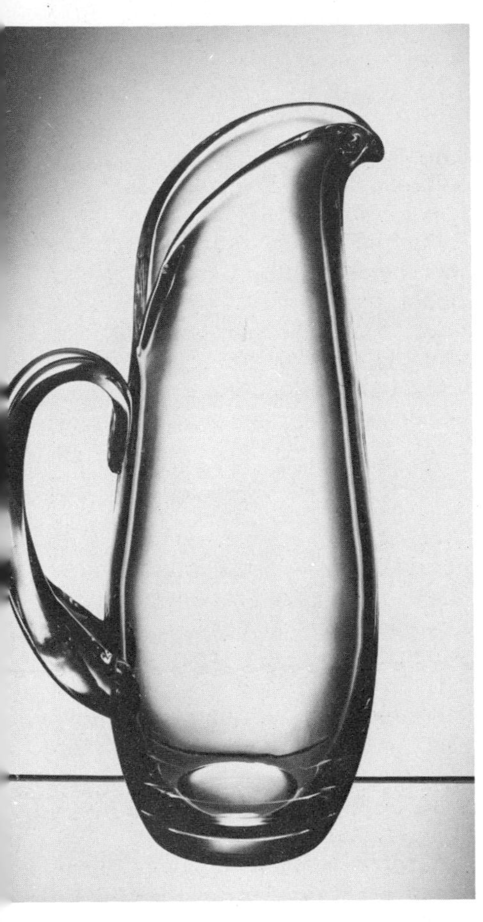

Top right: Figure 5. *The Steuben pitcher is now placed on a plate-glass shelf against a white paper background. Some may object to the line of the shelf and others may want a foundation for the object; this is a matter of taste. This technique can give quite a bit of contrast, and if less contrast is desired a more diffuse source of illumination is necessary. Only one spotlight was used and the barn doors created the shape of the light on the background.*

Top left: Figure 6. *Arrangement for making the photograph shown in Figure 5.*

Bottom right: Figure 7. *On a black paper background illuminated by light bouncing off white cardboard reflectors the Steuben pitcher can be made to glow.*

Bottom left: Figure 8. *Set-up for Figure 7. Barn doors were used to keep any direct light from falling on the subject while allowing only a slim strip of bright light to strike the reflector.*

concerned with what is generally thought of as "glass," but also with what we want to cause people to think and feel about this particular glass object. If the final print depicts the true characteristics of the subject and creates the specific impression that was desired, then we have taken a successful photograph.

All objects and materials are recorded on film by the light reflected from them. Light-colored objects have a high reflectivity and a strong effect upon the photosensitive emulsion. Conversely, dark surfaces reflect only a small percentage of the light falling on them and affect the film emulsion proportionately.

Glass, however, is not photographed by the light bouncing off it, but only by the light passing through it. Fully understanding this is essential to mastering the techniques of glass photography. (An exception, of course, is glass that is opaque.) This discussion is predicated on the transmission of light through and the refraction of light within a glass object.

LIGHTING EQUIPMENT

The lighting equipment you select will depend almost entirely upon the photograph to be taken. Spotlights, floodlights, and large white reflectors are all employed. Each will create a different over-all effect when used as a key source, and each serves a specific function when used as an auxiliary source of light.

Spotlights permit accurate control of the light. By manipulation of the bulb and/or reflector within the housing, a large smooth circle of light or a small intense spot of light may result. The light can be further confined by barn doors or snoots, diffused by spun glass, colored by gelatins, or precisely shaped by the use of a condensing lens and cutouts.

Floodlights emit a much less controlled illumination. However, this light will be softer, gentler; it will create less harsh shadows than the spotlight, and at the edges of the illuminated area the light will fall off much more gradually.

Reflectors are used to give a bright edge or outline to a glass object which usually is placed against a dark background. I prefer matte white cardboard reflectors. Reflectors can also be used as a very broad source of extremely soft, practically shadowless illumination.

Glass should almost never have raw light striking it from the 180-degree arc on the camera side. This will usually result in harsh, unsightly hot spots (pure white, specular reflections).

For the simple black outline type of rendering, light should come through the rear of the object toward the camera. A groundglass or light-colored background should be used to gain this transmitted light effect. (See Figures 1-6.)

To achieve the white outline, a black nonreflective background material is necessary. The object is then sidelighted or backlighted with reflected or direct light. (See Figures 7-8.)

Engraving on glass will reproduce differently depending upon the lighting method. Transmitted light will render the engraving dark, while light striking the object from the side or back will be refracted by the rough surface of the engraving itself and reproduce light against a dark background. (See Figure 9.)

Each set-up or piece of glass has its own inherent characteristics which must be exploited. Some are to be minimized, others emphasized. The movement of a light a few inches in any direction can change the entire effect of that light.

The selection of the correct type of light (spot, flood, reflector) will determine the success or failure, in varying degrees, of the effect desired. The intensity of each source of illumination in a set-up also can be of critical importance. A correct balance is essential.

SILVERWARE

Silver and glass are similar, actually—similar in the difficulties which they present to the photographer, similar in the solutions to these problems which they require. Both are highly reflective, both have subtle curves and shapes, both are likely to be entirely lacking in color.

When photographing flat subjects like plates or cutlery, the lighting is fairly simple. Usually a general reflected light plus a direct low modeling light will be sufficient. The camera should be above and pointing down at the flat subjects. In some cases the camera can be directly overhead for making a photograph similar to the silverware picture shown. (Figure 10.)

Vertical silver objects can be placed in lighting arrangements that are similar to those in glass photography. A dull matte silver surface without any reflections can produce a rather dull and lifeless photograph. Reflections and highlights are needed to make silver look natural. In some cases a Polaroid filter combined with Pola Lights can be used effectively to control the proper lighting.

BACKGROUNDS

Lighting and background are in many ways dependent upon one another. Almost any background tone or material may be used. How it is used is the key. The desired effect or result is really the determining factor. At times the selection of a background is decided by the object being photographed. However, the choice is usually governed by the lighting technique.

Light or white backgrounds will usually project a light, airy delicate feeling, while dark or black backgrounds evoke a dramatic, mysterious or somber response.

Figure 9. *This Dragonfly Plate from the collection of the Corning Museum of Glass was placed on black velvet. Two spotlights at the level of the table and 45 degrees behind the plate brought out the fine detail in the etching.*

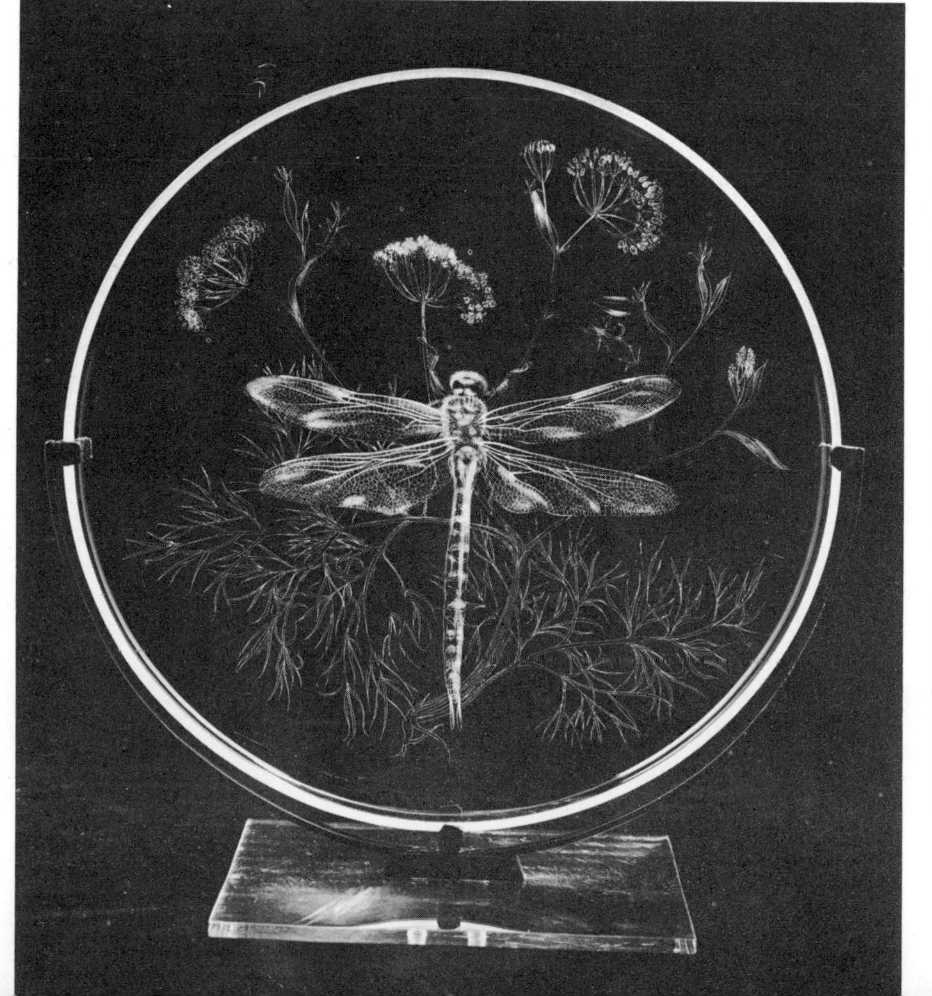

Figure 10. *A direct overhead view of flat silverware arrangement. Strong sidelight combined with softer diffused light.* (Photo: Victor Keppler)

Remember that a solid tone with no variation is less interesting as a background, but also will intrude less upon the subject. White should usually fade off to darker tones around the subject. Black can be varied by the addition of light.

Good background materials include paper, groundglass sheets or bends, or glass shelves.

CAMERA EQUIPMENT

To achieve the maximum result, the fastidious worker must use a view camera or a single-lens reflex. It is imperative that you see on the groundglass exactly what the film will record. You must be able to determine in advance precisely what your lights are doing for you, the camera angle, the exact depth of field, and the correct overall impression.

A view camera has the added advantage (essential for truly professional work) of swinging and tilting movements at the front and back of the camera. By the use of these, distortion can be corrected or introduced and emphasized for effect, and the plane of sharp focus can be placed in any desired position.

As a rule, a lens of longer-than-normal focal length is used. With 4×5 film, 8½-inch and 10-inch focal length lenses are preferred. When using 8×10 film, 14-inch and 16-inch focal length lenses are selected.

Since the object is stationary and long exposures are practical, very fine grain, relatively slow emulsions such as Kodak Panatomic-X, Kodak Plus-X Pan, or Ansco Versapan are employed so maximum detail will be retained.

Always think of the end result desired. Everything you do, every step you take, should lead to this one goal. Nothing in the treatment of glass, silverware, or any material for that matter, should detract from the response you wish to evoke in the mind of the viewer of the finished photograph.

BURT GLINN

Biography

Burt Glinn describes himself as a photographer who tries to "approach things like an editor." This ability to analyze a story in editorial terms and then to look at it with a fresh eye has made him one of America's undisputed masters of magazine photography.

Born in Pittsburgh, Glinn started on the road to photojournalism in 1948 and 1949 when as a student at Harvard he "majored in putting out the *Crimson*," the university's daily newspaper. As photographer-editor of the paper, Glinn attracted the attention of *Life* magazine's talent scouts and upon graduation was offered a job as a photographer's assistant. It was here that Glinn came into contact with such men as editors Wilson Hicks and Ray Mackland and photographers Cornell Capa, Ralph Morse, and Gjon Mili, who were to profoundly influence his ideas about the professional discipline of photography.

After a year and a half working as an assistant to top photographers on *Life* (and, incidentally, building up a considerable knowledge of photographic technique), Glinn decided to strike out on his own as a free lance photographer. With the help of *Life*'s picture editor Ray Mackland, Glinn continued to work for them as a photographer on a part-time basis.

Those early years of free lancing in New York were very important to Glinn's development. In an interview in *Popular Photography* magazine he explained: "When somebody asks me, 'How do you become a photographer?' I tell them, 'I don't know, but the first thing you do is go to New York!' I think it's much, much more difficult to become a really professional photographer operating away from New York. The exposure is important. Not so much exposure to technical ideas—what kind of film do you use, what kind of developer, and so forth, although that is part of it when you're young—but only a

Burt Glinn / Premier Khrushchev at the Lincoln Memorial, Washington, D.C., 1959.

Burt Glinn / Prayer at the Republican National Convention, San Francisco, 1956.

small part. And it's not those terribly serious discussions sitting on the floor wearing turtle-neck sweaters and asking, 'Is photography art?' What I mean is the continual examination of things you have done, with the help of other people."

In 1952, Glinn joined Magnum, where he became the friend of Henri Cartier-Bresson, the man whom, along with Gjon Mili, he describes as "having the most influence on my ideas of photographic quality."

For the next four years Glinn made his headquarters in Seattle, Washington, where he covered such stories as the Pribilof Island Polio Epidemic, the Alaskan uranium strike, the Hell's Canyon controversy, and Senator Neuberger's successful election campaign.

In 1956, Glinn returned to New York and switched to news coverage, to the global magazine assignments that have brought him his present success in the field. Twice in 1956 he went to Israel, photographing the UN Truce Team under fire on his first trip and the Sinai war on the second. Between these journeys he covered both the Democratic and Republican conventions. In 1957 he returned to Israel for the Jordan crisis. In 1958 he covered the U.S. Marine landing in Lebanon, an uprising in Baghdad, the revolt in Cuba, and Brigitte Bardot.

In the years that followed some outstanding Glinn accomplishments have been the widely published photograph of Khrushchev before the Lincoln Memorial (an excellent example of how Glinn's fresh approach to a much photographed subject can produce a memorable picture), a photostory on Sammy Davis, Jr., and special coverage for *Holiday* magazine on Japan, Mexico, and Soviet Russia. Although he has on occasion used all types of cameras, he is primarily a 35 mm photographer (his basic camera is a Nikon F). Most of his current work is in color.

If any clue can be given to why Burt Glinn is a first rate photojournalist, it is the fact that he is not

Burt Glinn / Explosion of the Vanguard Rocket, Cape Canaveral, 1957.

just a photographer but also a man who is keenly interested in world events. Clay Felker, formerly Features Editor of *Esquire,* said of Glinn, "Burt is one photographer who does his homework faithfully; he reads the *Times* every day, follows the *London Economist,* and keeps up with current events." Glinn also has strong ideas about what photography does best. These views are explained in an article for *Camera,* the Swiss photographic magazine:

"As a matter of fact great photographs are never conceived, they are perceived. That is why I do not believe that great photographs are ever made in a studio. They are never built artificially. Some of us carry a studio in our heads. In the terms of this discussion, when you dress the duchess in her best Balenciaga, sit her in a gilt chair under the great crystal chandelier in the giant ballroom of her palazzo—you are working in a studio as surely as if you built the entire set in 480 Lexington Avenue. I know of hundreds of pictures taken in studios or in created studios that are spectacular, or interesting, or of superb design, or have many other qualities. But they are not great. They, of necessity, treat the subject too specifically. Those mountain peaks of poetry are shrouded in ambiguity. Dick Avedon, who for me is the most exciting of the studio photographers, takes portraits that stun and arrest the viewer, but once I have recovered I feel I am looking at superb caricatures. Look at one of his famous old women and you see one moment in one life. Look at Cartier-Bresson's obscure old women and you see a million lifetimes."

Along with this conviction comes an endless striving on Glinn's part to see even the most photographed subjects in a new way which shows them both with insight and with a graphic quality that will command the viewers' attention on the magazine page. About this Glinn has said:

"People say, 'Photography has to find new ways of saying things.' I agree, but I don't think this will be done by soft lenses, double exposures, multiple flash, darkroom manipulation, or smearing vaseline on the lens. It will be done by people seeing better and deeper."

PETER GOWLAND

Biography

For nearly a quarter of a century the name of Peter Gowland has been almost synonymous with glamour photography. His pictures have been widely published (he has had photographs on over 500 magazine covers alone), and the popularity of the Gowland approach to feminine beauty continues.

In a field where photographic clichés are rampant and where dozens of "cheesecake" photographers appear and disappear each year, the probable reason for Gowland's success is his ability to use the camera without the vulgarity or obvious eroticism present in so much "cheesecake" photography.

Gowland is the "healthiest" of American glamour photographers. He is the "red-blooded American boy" of the cheesecake business. He is neither chic nor sophisticated, and even though he is occasionally corny, he is never pornographic. In his best work he is a man who likes

Peter Gowland / The Kiss.

pretty girls and is able to express this, clearly and cleanly, through photography.

Peter Gowland was born in Hollywood, California in 1916. His father was Gibson Gowland, a prominent character actor of the silent screen and the early talkies whose most illustrious role was the lead in Eric von Stroheim's film masterpiece, *Greed*. Gowland spent much of his childhood on motion-picture sets where he learned by observation the techniques of photographic lighting. In Junior High School he was head electrician for the school plays, and in Lawler Professional School he studied with such classmates as Mickey Rooney, Betty Grable, and Judy Garland.

After six years in movies as an extra, stand-in, and double for stars like Joel McCrea and Ronald Reagan, Gowland decided that his real talent and interests lay *behind* the camera, and his career as a glamour photographer was launched. His first subjects were mostly young actors and actresses from the film

Peter Gowland / Indecision.

GRAININESS

MONROE H. SWEET
Formerly of the Physics Department, Ansco

[There is a fundamental distinction between the grain of a silver emulsion and the "graininess" of a photographic image. The late Monroe Sweet was an authority on the physics of photography, and this article is a complete review of the subjects of grain and graininess.]

• *Also see: Density; Development and Developers; Development, Fine Grain; Emulsion Chemistry; Gamma.*

UNDEVELOPED PHOTOGRAPHIC EMULSIONS consist primarily of silver salts suspended in a layer of gelatin. After exposure and upon development, these salts are converted into metallic silver grains, and it is the aggregation of very large numbers of these silver particles which gives rise to the blackness or density in the finished film.

The term "silver grains" is often used indiscriminately to mean the underdeveloped silver-bromide crystals as well as the developed metallic silver particles. In this chapter we shall confine its meaning to the developed silver grains. The individual grains are far too small to be seen with the naked eye or even with low-power magnification; but when viewed under a high-power microscope, they can be studied quite easily.

The size and shape of the unde-evenly distributed and tend to coalesce, forming clumps which merge upon development. As a result, when a negative is appreciably enlarged or viewed by projection at high magnification, the resulting image will appear speckled, showing decided unevenness. In a general way, it is this unevenness which is referred to as graininess.

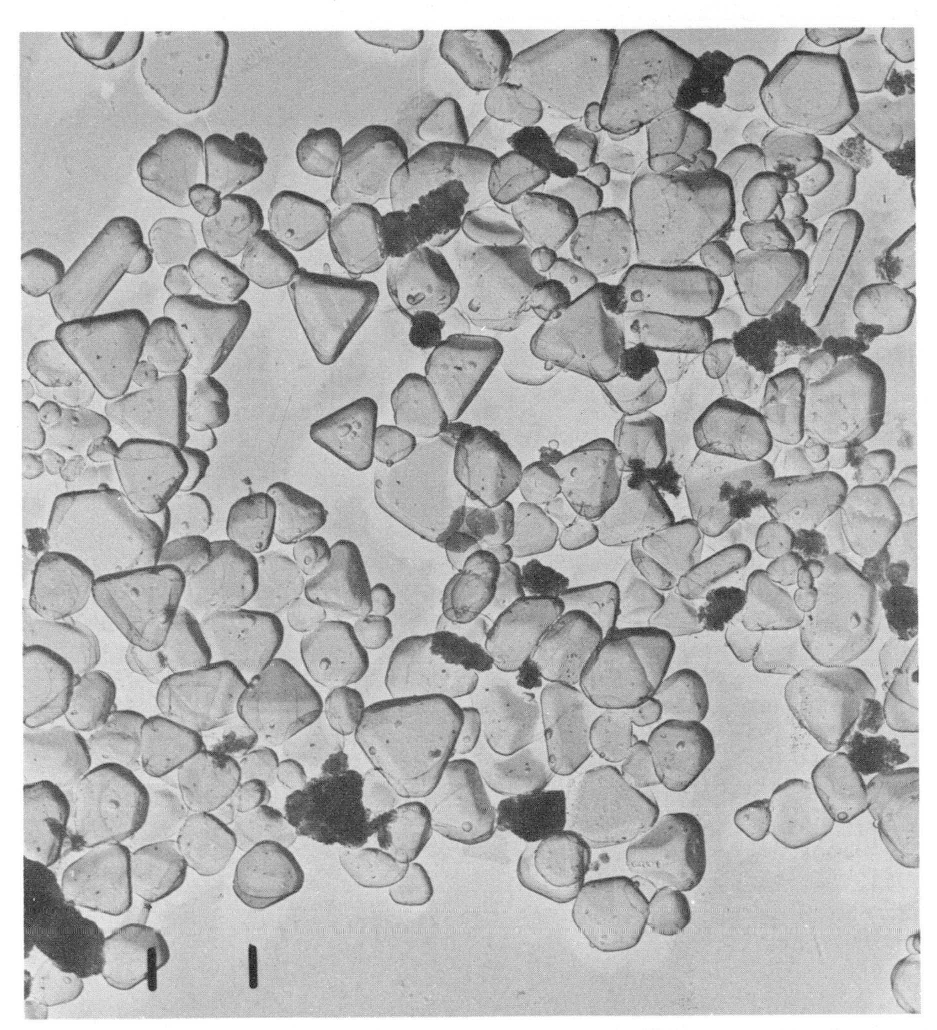

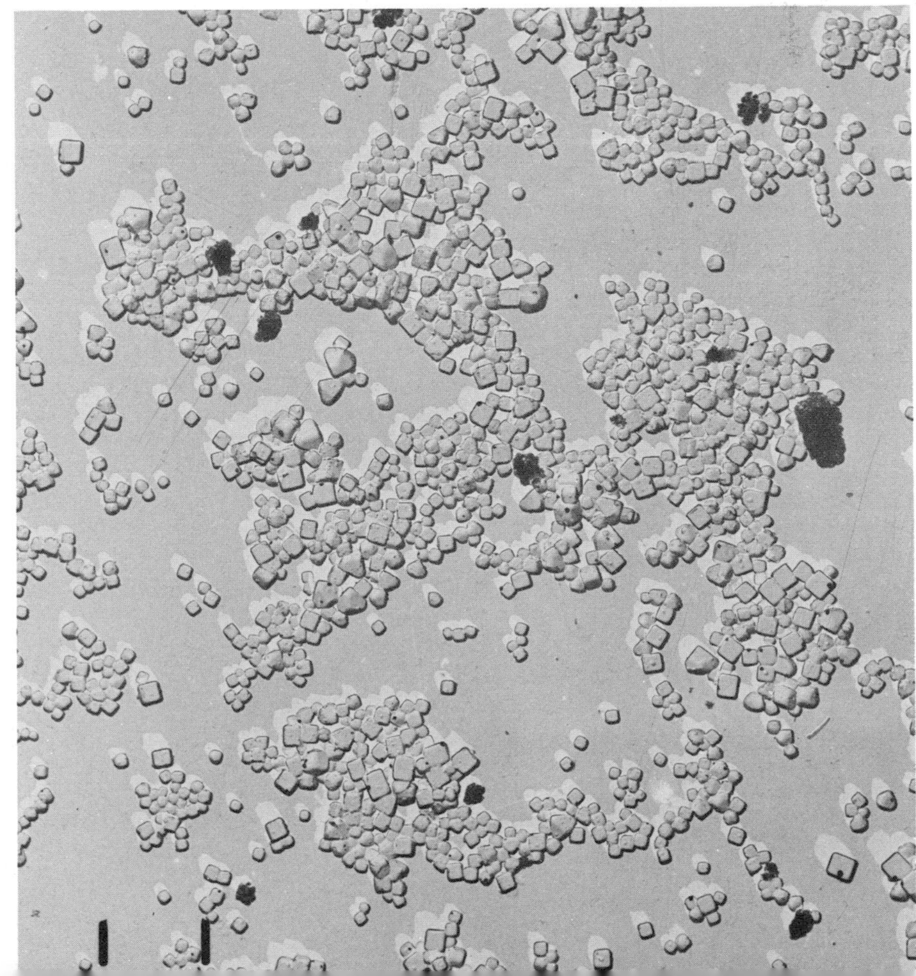

Top: Figure 1. *Photomicrograph of silver-bromide crystals in a high-speed emulsion (Ansco Super Hypan) at high magnification.*

Bottom: Figure 2. *Same magnification as in Figure 1, showing the finer grains in a slower film emulsion (Ansco Microfilm).*

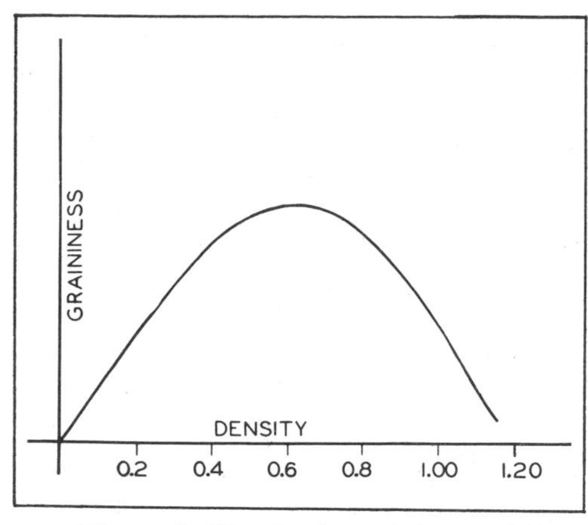

Figure 3. *The density-graininess relationship for diffusion enlargers.*

The size and shape of the undeveloped silver-bromide crystals as well as their distribution and clumping tendencies vary with the emulsion and the type of processing. Figures 1 and 2 show the structures of two widely different types of emulsions enlarged 1400 times. The approximate grain diameters vary from about 0.5 micron to 5.0 microns. (A micron is one millionth of a meter, or about 0.0004 inches.) The general sizes and shapes of the grains and clumps are roughly similar before and after development, although during development the clumps tend to grow by combining with more and more of the neighboring grains.

Until the early thirties, the subject of graininess attracted little attention outside the motion-picture industry. When 35 mm cameras became popular, the graininess of negatives assumed new importance. No 35 mm negative could be satisfactorily enlarged unless its graininess was small enough to prevent an appearance similar to that shown in the illustrations.

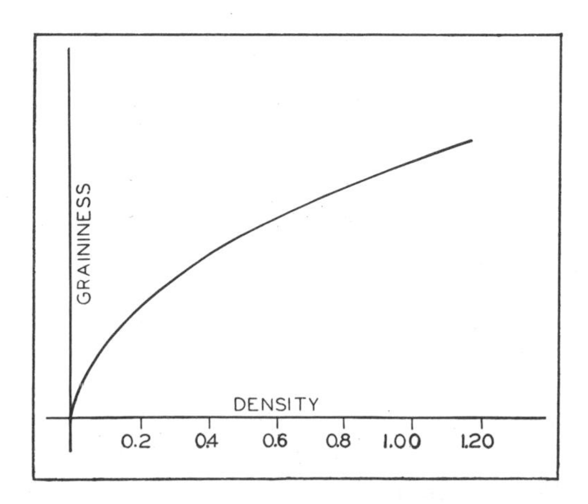

Figure 4. *The density-graininess relationship for condenser enlargers.*

GRAININESS DEFINED

To demonstrate more exactly the meaning of graininess, consider the following experiment:

A negative is placed in a microscope and examined at magnification of 500 times or more. The individual silver grains can easily be distinguished and their sizes estimated, if not actually measured. The magnifying power is now reduced to about 50×. The individual grains cannot be discerned, but the clumps of grains are still very conspicuous. At 15× the impression of unevenness remains, but now it is the combination of the clumps of grains and their distribution that disrupts the smooth appearance of the film. This impression of unevenness which an observer receives when viewing a film under normal magnification is defined as graininess.

Ordinary enlargements range from five to 20 diameters and within this range it is graininess, rather than grain size or clumping alone, that is important. Imagine a sample consisting of many grains of small size, but clumped badly enough to produce a result as grainy as that of a sample whose mean grain size is much larger, but whose grains are more uniformly spaced and distributed. Graininess, being a visual impression, is the integrated effect of grain size, clumping, and distribution.

GRAININESS AND DENSITY

At very low film densities, graininess is also low. The density of a film is the measure of the transmission of light by the silver grains of the total area. At low densities there are only a few grains to disturb the smooth appearance of the film surface. When films of high densities are examined, the grains and clumps may be so numerous that the film seems to be entirely black. This is particularly true if the high density is adjacent to a very low density, since the eye automatically adjusts itself to accommodate the average light intensity, making the higher density appear opaque.

Consequently, the real graininess at high densities is not noticed under such conditions. This situation arises in motion-picture theater projections where the medium and low film densities show the highest graininess. However, the high-density sample appears practically grainless primarily because of the conditions under which it is examined.

Suppose uniform negatives of different densities are enlarged separately to 20× magnification in a conventional diffusion enlarger. At very low negative densities, there are practically no grains to disrupt the field, and the graininess appearing in the print is consequently very low (for zero film density, the graininess is zero). As the negative density increases, the graininess at first increases, too. Eventually a density is reached which gives a print of maximum graininess. Still higher film densities give lower and lower print gaininess until finally, at a density of about 1.6, the print graininess returns to practically zero. Figure 3 illustrates this relationship.

When the same test is performed with a condenser enlarger, the results are decidedly different. As the negative density rises, the print graininess rises not only beyond film densities of 0.6, but to higher and higher densties almost indefinitely (Figure 4). For negative densities of 1.6 or higher, the print graininess will be practically zero when using a diffusion enlarger, but higher than any lower density when using a condenser enlarger. This fact is vitally important in any discussion of graininess, although the details of the interrelationship are rarely fully appreciated.

Materials examined under diffuse light should be referred to as "diffuse graininess," and those under specular (parallel) light as having "specular graininess." Most conventional enlargers are a combination of condensers and diffusion screens, and they give results which more closely approach the diffusion type of graininess-density relation. It

A fine-grain print rendition most often will result from the right combination of film, developer, and subject matter. Adox KB-14 film, rated at 32, was developed in Tetenal Neofin Blue. The photo was taken with a Contarex, 85mm lens, f/4 at 1/60 of a second.

would be a mistake to conclude immediately that a diffusion enlarger is always preferable, for improvement in print graininess is generally obtained only at the expense of other desirable qualities.

The difference in the results obtained with the two enlarging systems is due partly to the light scattered by the grains themselves, but more to the direction of actual illumination by the individual clumps which are focused on the enlarging easel. In the case of an enlarger utilizing specular illumination, the clumps appear to the lens as sharp silhouettes.

With diffuse illumination, they appear as more or less sidelighted solid particles against a bright background. This gives a gradual tapering-off of illumination, as the center of a clump is approached with respect to its background, and this softening of the image greatly reduces the apparent graininess of the negative. At high densities, the softening is accentuated because the background now becomes filled with other silver clumps, producing still less contrast in the images of the clumps.

GRAININESS IN VARIOUS SUBJECTS

Enlargement of negatives is by no means the only case where graininess is a problem. The following examples show some additional cases where graininess is an important consideration.

Subject	*Type of Graininess*
Direct enlargement	Specular or diffuse
Slide projection	Mostly specular
Motion-pictuure projection	Mostly specular
Contact printing (transparencies)	Mostly diffuse
Motion-picture sound recording and playback	Specular
Motion-picture duplicating printing	Complicated
Spectroscopic plate	Specular

The cases are rather well divided, although there are few examples of strictly specular or diffuse graininess.

GRAININESS AND FILM SPEED

Among the fundamental properties "built into" a film during its manufacture are film speed and, within limits, the film's inherent graininess characteristics. Unfortunately the more sensitive an emulsion is made the more grainy it becomes. This relation holds true for an amazing variety of films which cover an enormous range of speed and grain size.

The coarsest-grained films are the X-ray emulsions. These are extremely sensitive and, since they are not used for enlarging, their high graininess does not matter. Next in

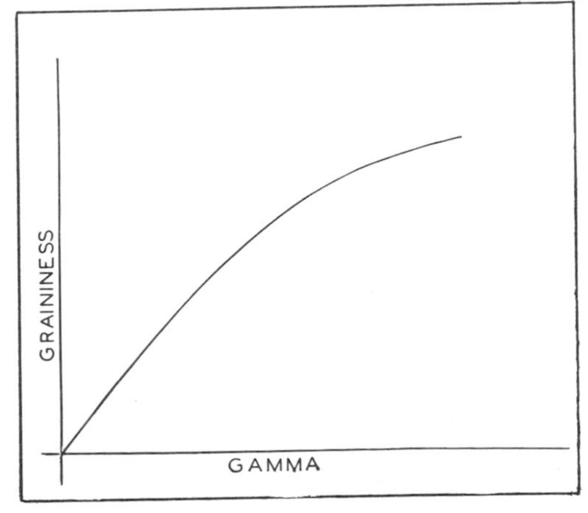

Figure 5. *The effect of gamma on graininess when equal densities are compared.*

Grain is less evident in high-contrast subject matter, such as the shade and highlight portions of this photo. The photo was made with a 200mm lens on a Leica, f/8 at 1/50 of a second; the film, Adox KB 17, was developed in Tetenal Neofin Blue.

order of graininess are the common negative-material types. First is a slow-speed film, recommended where fine grain is most important. Next is the high-speed emulsion which is extremely sensitive—but this sensitivity is gained only at the expense of increased graininess. An intermediate film is made as a compromise between high speed and fine grain.

Materials used for printing are still slower in speed and of finer grain. Finally, the materials used for reproduction are representative of the slowest and very finest-grained emulsions available. They are practically useless for other work, because of their high natural contrast and very slow speed.

"Artificially" increasing the speed of a film tends to increase its graininess in keeping with the speed-graininess trend. Using strong developers which increase the film speed invariably increases the graininess.

GRAININESS AND GAMMA

Another factor to be considered with graininess is contrast. Imagine a scene where the subject contrast is easily controlled by varying the lighting. When such a scene is photographed and the film developed to the same "brilliance" as the original scene, the graininess of differently lighted scenes will vary greatly. When the scene is flat-lighted, the negative must be developed to a high gamma (contrast) to retain its brilliance. When the scene contrast is greatest, the negative is underdeveloped to minimize the excessive contrast.

There is a well-established relationship between graininess and gamma. In general, the higher the gamma, the greater the graininess, even when equal densities are compared. When compared at equal exposures, the differences are still greater. The relationship is shown graphically in Figure 5.

In the test just described, equal brilliance means that each part of the scene produced the same density in the corresponding section of the negatives. From the graph it is apparent that when the scene contrast is high and a low gamma required, the graininess of the resulting density is low. When the scene contrast is low and a high gamma necessary, the graininess will be much higher.

At very high gammas, the effect of any change in gamma on graininess is lessened. In some cases a high gamma may be reached where further increases fail to show any increase in graininess. Unfortunately, this point corresponds to an already high graininess, so that the effect is not very useful.

GRAININESS AND RESOLVING POWER

Another film characteristic intimately connected with graininess is resolution. The slower, finer-grained films are capable of distinguishing a larger number of black and white lines per unit length than fast, coarse-grained films. For medium-speed 35 mm negative materials, the resolving power is about 96 to 135 lines per mm. When extremely fine detail is required, both graininess and resolution must be favorable. The microcopying emulsions are very fine-grained, with resolving power as high as 225 lines per mm. They are quite slow in speed.

While low graininess and high resolving power go hand in hand, it is equally true that "artificial" treatment may disrupt this relationship. Once the negative has been processed, no "special" printing process can improve the sharpness of the image which the film has recorded.

GRAININESS AND THE DEVELOPER

When a powerful, quick-acting developer is used to "develop up the shadows," the graininess of all densities increases. Gentle-acting developers which are composed of low-potential developing agents minimize graininess and tend to cut film speed. The metol-hydroquinone developers exemplify the first type, and the paraphenylenediamine developers are representative of the fine-grain class.

As far back as 1939 studies were made on the influence of developers on graininess. One of the most thorough was published by George Higgins, now in the Kodak Research Laboratories. He confirmed the view held by many impartial investigators that there is no outstanding exception to the rule that fineness of grain obtained by use of a fine-grained developer is accompanied by a loss in speed. A normally fast, coarse-grained emulsion is about equal in speed and graininess to a medium-speed film if the fast emulsion is developed for fine grain and the medium-speed film is developed in a normal developer.

When considering grain, it has been pointed out that the lower the gamma to which the film is developed the better. There are practical limits. Below gammas of about 0.50 or 0.45, normal scenes become so "flat" that satisfactory prints cannot be made from them. Very contrasty scenes can advantageously be developed to a low gamma because the resulting negative contrast will still be sufficient to make good enlargements. But especially in 35 mm work, it is impractical to develop each negative individually, according to the original scene-brightness conditions.

In addition, when the negative is developed to the minimum gamma which will give satisfactory prints on high-contrast paper, there is so little latitude in technique that slight errors will spoil the result. Because of the shape of the H&D curve for normally developed negatives, it is best to use the "toe" of the curve (see *Hurter and Driffield).*

One method of minimizing grain is to use a diffusion screen while exposing the print. This is particularly effective with female portraits where a soft quality is desirable. Leica M2 with 50mm Summicron f/2 *lens; Tri-X film rated at 800 ASA and exposed at* f/2 *for 1/125 of a second.* **(Photo: Michael L. Edelson)**

This advantage is extensively diminished when the negative is badly underdeveloped.

TECHNIQUE AND GRAIN

Considerable attention has been devoted to careful control of the strength and temperatures of short-stop baths and wash, as well as to drying conditions. Some contend that if the temperature of the wash water is very different from that of the fixer, graininess would be affected. Often it is claimed that quick drying promotes fineness of grain.

Actually there is much to be said in favor of uniform temperatures for all processing solutions and for rapid drying, but it is doubtful that it has any effect on graininess. Often excessive "graininess" is found in negatives which have been washed and dried under severe conditions. But careful examination of the image under high magnification will show that the effect is not actual grain but a form of incipient reticulation.

GRAININESS IN MOTION PICTURES

Seldom is the graininess of the negative alone important, because it is almost never the end result. In motion-picture practice, however, negatives are often duped—that is, the negative is printed on 35 mm duplicating positive stock. This print is used to print again onto duplicating negative material. Finally positive prints are made from the dupe negative, and these are released for theater use.

Graininess is naturally very important here because of the high magnification needed in projection. Graininess may have an adverse effect on background projection. To cut expenses, it is standard practice to project suitable backgrounds for various sets onto translucent screens with either still or motion-picture projectors. If the films used for these projections are grainy, this graininess will be recorded on the talking film.

Graininess appears on the motion-picture screen as "boiling"—grain clumps of consecutive frames which overlap each other at random. The persistence of vision makes the whole image waver as though one were looking through strongly heated air.

The materials ordinarily used in professional motion-picture negative work are, in some cases, the same as those available for 35 mm cameras. Tests show that when a fine-grain negative is printed by contact on a coarse-grained print material, the result is more grainy than the negative itself. To take full advantage of fine-grained negative materials, fine-grained print materials must be used. The graininess of prints made from coarse-grained negatives is improved by the use of a fine-grain positive material, but the improvement is not so great as with fine-grain negatives.

In the duping process, as printing progresses, each step tends to lose some of the graininess pattern of the original negative. There is less evidence of original negative grain in the final positive made by the dupe method from a high-speed negative, than from a direct-positive print. But there is a corresponding loss in resolution.

Reversal films. In amateur motion-picture work, reversal films are used in the majority of cases. With these films the coarse, high-speed grains which appear in the first development are removed in the bleaching process, and the final image is composed of the slower finer-grained silver clumps. Consequently, reversal films as a class produce images of much finer grain than ordinary negative-positive transparencies.

The photographer using a tripod—and with it, longer exposures—can use slower, finer-grained films. The result will be photos which, to the unaided eye, appear to be almost grainless. (Photo: Barry Kaplan / Scholastic-Ansco Photography Contest)

Low-contrast subject matter and, in this case, the difficulty of filling the 35 mm frame while retaining candid quality result in high apparent grain. Leica IIIB with 50mm Summar f/2 lens; 1/30 of a second at f/2. (Photo: Michael L. Edelson)

Color films. There is a theory, held by many uninformed photographers, that since the image in a color film is of dyestuff, it has no grain. While it is true that dyes do not have grain of their own, the mechanism of a color film is based on the formation of a dye by the interaction of a color developer, a color coupler, and silver grain. Each grain of silver in the original emulsion is replaced by a small blob of dye which approximately reproduces the grain's shape.

The very fine grain of such films as Kodachrome II and similar emulsions is due to their reversal processing and not to any inherent property of the dye image. Films in which the color coupler is present in the original emulsion in "protected" form, such as Ektachrome or Kodacolor, tend to be even grainier because the couplers are present in globules and do not necessarily represent the presence of the original grains.

Negative color films such as Kodacolor or Ektacolor are naturally grainier than reversal films. Even in reversal color, the high-speed emulsions such as High-Speed Ektachrome or Super Anscochrome tend to be grainier than the slower emulsions. The finer grain of Kodachrome II, compared with the earlier and slower Kodachrome, seems to disprove this point, but it is a result of recent improvements in emulsion technology which, in black-and-white, has led to the production of faster, finer-grained high-acutance emulsions.

MINIMIZING GRAININESS

The following is directed chiefly at camera users who seek practical methods for avoiding grainy prints. First, most of the statements made about motion-picture print graininess do not apply to 35 mm negatives, because the enlarged image is not further magnified. In addition, the graininess in chloride and chlorobromide print materials is considerably less than that of most negatives. In practice, one of the influences on apparent graininess of an enlarged print is due to the printing paper's contrast and surface type.

Print graininess is approximately proportional to the enlarging magnification. The necessity of enlarging very small sections of the negative to a high magnification should be avoided. (This can be done by filling the frame when taking the photo.) When an entire 35 mm frame is enlarged, by the time the point in magnification which normally gives objectionable graininess is reached, the distance at which the print must be viewed is so large that the graininess is not noticeable. This is why photomurals from 35 mm negatives are successful.

On the other hand, if a small section is enlarged by an equal magnification, the print is usually examined much more closely, and the graininess becomes painfully obvious. If the negative image is smaller, a greater degree of magnification is required to give the same-size print image.

A film should be selected which is as slow as possible with the lighting conditions encountered. Whenever it is possible to adjust the lighting, it should be made contrasty to permit developing the negative to a low gamma and still gain adequate contrast.

Graininess is most noticeable in large uniform areas of medium print density, and the use of high-contrast lighting of the subject diminishes the frequency of such areas. It already has been shown that graininess increases with increasing density, so exposures should be as low as possible without loss of shadow detail. This requires the intelligent use of a good exposure meter.

NEGATIVE DEVELOPMENT

Negatives should be developed to the lowest gamma the lighting contrast in the subjects will permit. This applies to all types of developers. Photographers using 35 mm film with 36 exposures per roll should try to keep subjects with similar lighting

Crypte du Sacré Cœur
EXPO
FOU
L'AF

A full-frame 35 mm shot and high subject contrast result in low apparent graininess. Zeiss-Ikon camera, 50mm Tessar lens, 1/125 of a second at f/8.

and contrast on the same roll.

Certain of the newer fine-grain films must not be developed in fine-grain developers if optimum results are to be obtained. For instance, when the Adox KB-14 film was introduced, the manufacturer found it necessary to caution against using fine-grain developers with this film. It is, specifically, a slow-speed, fine-grain, thin-emulsion negative, intended for maximum image sharpness and detail.

It was generally found by test that fine-grain developers, both of the solvent type (DK-20) and the paraphenylenediamine type, tended to produce images on this film which were fuzzy and lacking in sharpness, while improving the grain very little, if at all. For this reason, D-76 or D-23 are recommended as the basic developer for best image sharpness and minimum graininess with Adox KB-14. Similar recommendations apply to other thin-emulsion films such as the newer Kodak Panatomic-X, and the improved type Plus-X.

For those who wish to try true fine-grain development on higher-speed films, the Sease 3 formula has never been surpassed. However, its use causes a loss of from one to two stops of speed. A film of 500 rating may have to be exposed at 250, or even as low as 125 for full shadow detail. Under these circumstances, it is likely that equal results can be obtained by using a film rated at ASA 125 to begin with, in a normal developer such as Kodak D-76, and developing to a fairly low gamma, 0.6 for example.

Sease Number 3 Formula

Water, 125 F	125 oz.	975 cc
Sodium sulfite, dry	12 oz.	90 grams
Paraphenylenediamine	1 oz., 146 grains	10 grams
Glycin	352 grains	6 grams
Final volume	1 gal.	1 liter

Paraphenylenediamine is difficult to dissolve in cold water, but if added to warm water in which the sodium sulfite has previously been dissolved, the paraphenylenediamine will dissolve without requiring prolonged stirring.

For high-speed 35 mm films, develop about 30 minutes (stagnant tank development) for a gamma of 0.7; medium-speed films, about 20 minutes; slow-speed films, approximately 16 minutes.

Fresh developers generally are more active and produce coarser-grained results than after they have been aged by development of a few rolls of film. Some increase in developing time is required to compensate for their loss in strength, but the result gives an effective film speed about equal to the original for equal gammas.

To obtain consistently fine-grain negatives, the developer should not be used at temperatures above 70 F. The temperature of the subsequent solutions may vary considerably without affecting the graininess, though reticulation may result. Nor is rapid drying particularly useful in avoiding graininess.

For the least possible graininess, films should be developed to a low gamma and exposed sufficiently to record shadow detail. Intermittent agitation in tank development, with a corresponding increase in developing time, will usually produce slightly less graininess than continuous agitation.

PRINTING

Once the negative is processed, any special treatment which reduces print graininess also will reduce resolution. Having developed the negative to a low gamma, a medium-hard paper will be necessary to maintain snappy prints unless the scenes are of unusually high contrast.

Glossy surfaces will accentuate negative graininess, whereas matte and semimatte papers reduce it. Rough-surfaced papers mask even fairly coarse graininess.

Wherever permissible, the whole frame should be enlarged, as this establishes a reasonable viewing distance and lessens the visual objection to print graininess.

Using a highly diffuse light source in the enlarger is helpful in keeping graininess at a minimum. Pure condenser enlargers are capable of giving very sharp prints of grain patterns as well as negative images. Most of the common 35 mm film enlargers are a combination of the two, but are more diffuse than specular. The differences in graininess due to enlarging systems are enormous at higher densities. An outline for minimizing print graininess includes:

Exposing

1. Choose a fine-grain film, as slow as possible.
2. Fill the whole frame with the scene to be enlarged.
3. Use high-contrast subject lighting whenever possible.
4. Give the minimum permissible exposure.

Developing

5. Develop with a suitable low-potential developer.
6. Develop to a low gamma, not over 0.65 for 35 mm films.
7. Avoid high or low temperatures of developer during processing.

Printing

8. Wherever practical, enlarge the whole frame.
9. Use a matte or rough-surfaced paper.
10. When feasible, use a diffusion screen in printing the picture, not in exposing the negative.
11. Enlarge with a diffusion-type enlarger.

Like many photographic characteristics, graininess is an evasive film quality, quite difficult to measure. The average grain size of a film can easily be determined with a microscope, but the visual impression one receives of a print (transparency or reflection print) made from two negatives with equal grain size may be decidedly different.

For those who want to compare the graininess of several films which they commonly use, 20× or 30× enlargements should be made with a condenser enlarger, using high-contrast glossy paper. At this size, differences in grain will be apparent and may be studied even more minutely through a magnifying glass.

Chicago Tribune

Top Left. **THREE POINT LANDING.** Boxer Wallace Smith caught just as he was headed for a fall during Golden Gloves bout. Speed Graphic with Tri-X film exposed by electronic flash. (Photo: Chester Gabrysiak)

Bottom Left. **HI THERE!** Young visitors to Lincoln Park Zoo meet Helen, 1-year old gorilla, for first time. Taken with Leica M3, 90mm Summicron **f**/2 lens, Tri-X film exposed for 1/50 of a second with flash at **f**/8. (Photo: William Vendetta)

Top Center. **PAUSE THAT REFRESHES.** Anxious fans trying for HR ball give Whitesox outfielder Al Smith an unscheduled shower. Leica IIIG with Visoflex housing and Telyt 400mm **f**/5 lens. Tri-X exposed at **f**/11 for 1/60 of a second. (Photo: James O'Leary)

Top Right. **HOT CARGO.** Firemen fight gasoline flames after tanker-truck overturned igniting its 7700 gallon cargo. Driver leapt to safety. Speed Graphic and Tri-X film exposed at **f**/11 for 1/100 of a second. (Photo: Luigi Mendicino)

Bottom Right. **40 WINKS.** Dreams and a warm police jacket soothe lost child as he waits for parents to find him. Speed Graphic and Tri-X film exposed with flash. (Photo: James O'Leary)

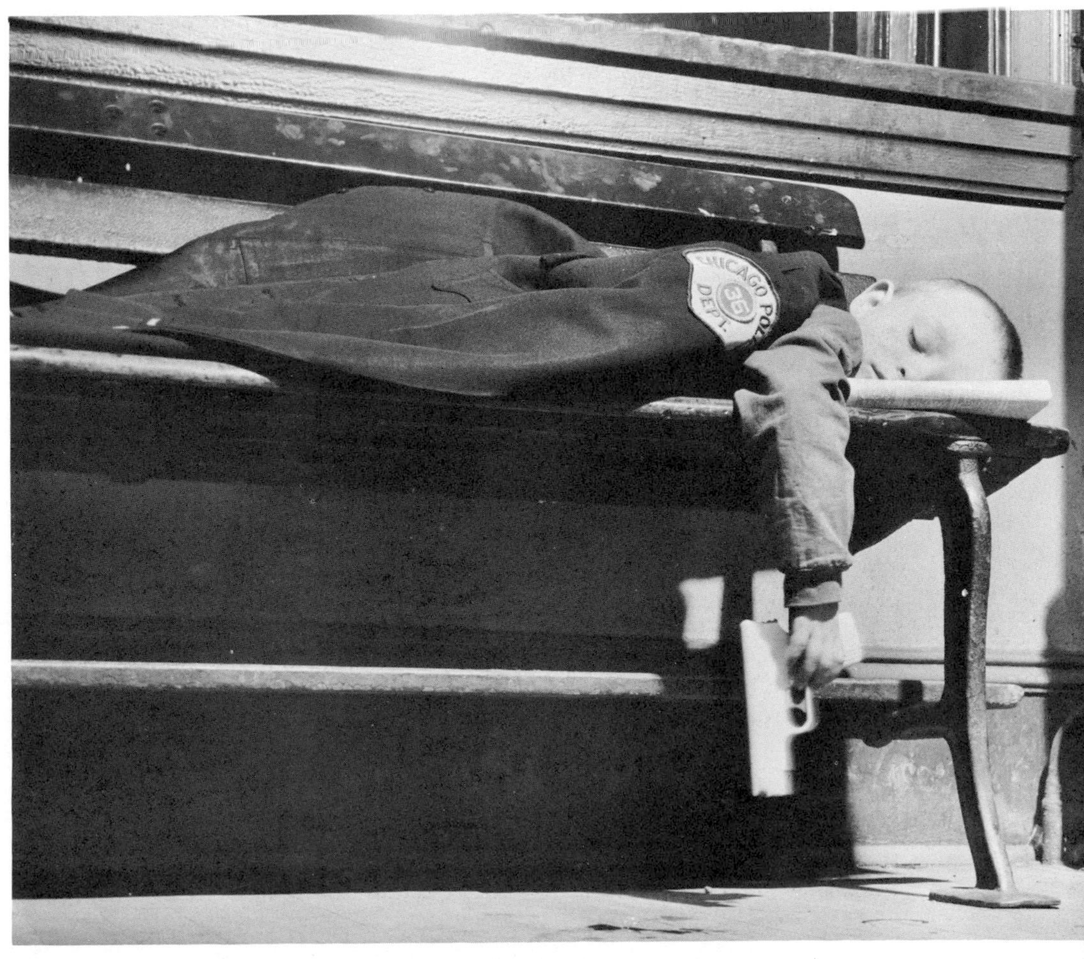

A variety of folders are available to hold favorite photographs for a holiday greeting. Some folders are designed so that the picture slips into a front opening (top); *others hold the picture inside* (bottom).

GRAY SCALE

A gray scale is a paper print or a transparency which consists of a number of square or rectangular areas, each increasing in density by a constant amount from the preceding one, to produce an evenly graded scale of grays between white and black. In the case of a transparent scale, the range is from nearly transparent to a fairly high density (usually about 3.0).

The gray scale has a number of functions in photography. It is used as a test object in sensitometry to produce a graded series of known exposures on a plate or film. In color photography, it is used as a reference object which, being neutral in color, must appear at the same density in all steps in all three color-separation negatives for accurate color balance. In a color transparency, it must reproduce as a neutral gray on all steps.

A specially devised gray scale is the basis of the Zone System of Previsualization in photography, first used on a practical basis by Ansel Adams. In this system, the scale is made in an annular shape, rather than rectangular, so that it can be pasted to the dial of a Weston exposure meter. By using the meter with this scale, it is possible to determine in advance the relative shade of gray an object will reproduce in a photograph.

Also see: Exposure with the Zone System; Gamma.

GREETING CARDS, PHOTOGRAPHIC

[Photographic greeting cards give the warm, personal touch welcomed by everyone. Greeting card kits make easy-to-do projects for the photographer.]

• *Also see: Bookplates, Photographic.*

THE FIRST AND MOST IMPORTANT step in making a photographic greeting card is choosing the original picture. In general, the subject to be used depends on the relationship between the sender and the receiver. Greetings between families and close friends or neighbors tend toward family groups, personal portraits, interior and exterior views of the decorated home. The more impersonal greeting may be a scenic, an action sport, a fantasy tabletop, or an abstraction. In any case, the original negative or transparency must be properly exposed and well composed or it will not be worth the time or expense of making cards.

METHODS OF MAKING CARDS

Cards may be printed from a single negative, from a composite copy negative, or from several negatives. With the single-negative method, the essential message may be contained in the subject matter, which makes it easier to print, since most of the work goes into the planning. For instance, a person may be photographed reading a newspaper or letter, or looking at a book title on which a special message has been printed.

Another method is to photograph the message spelled out with building blocks, cut-out letters, snow, or sand. There are an infinite number of ways to make letters which spell out a short greeting; choice of a method appropriate to the message makes a successful card. Once the set-up has been photographed and you have a good negative, making the cards is simply a matter of printing by contact or enlargement.

If the prints are enlargements, it is possible to write a message with a very soft, blunt, lead pencil directly on the printing paper. Project the image onto the paper to make sure you will be writing in a strong-black area. Place a red filter over the enlarger lens and write the message. Remove the filter, expose the paper normally, wipe off the writing (being careful not to damage the emulsion), and develop normally. The writing will appear white on a black area.

Making a single negative from a paste-up is a slightly longer process, but it does provide maximum flexibility in styles of layout and lettering. It is the method used in the manufacture of commercial greeting cards. After deciding on the picture and lettering style you which to use, mark out on a piece of illustration board a square or rectangle of the same proportions as the negative you will make. If you are using a 2¼ × 2¼ camera, the marking should be square; if you will make a 4 × 5 negative, the rectangle should be drawn to those proportions. Remember that the paste-up should be large enough to be worked on conveniently and to be copied without using close-up accessories.

Plan the layout, enlarge or trim the picture you wish to use, draw or letter the message (alphabet kits can be bought at most art or stationery stores) and paste the components down on the board according to the layout. The completed paste-up is then copied and the negative is used for printing.

Multiple-negative printing is not difficult. The usual method is to select the picture negative and combine it with a second negative containing an appropriate message. Both Ansco and Eastman Kodak have a variety of greeting-card-message negatives to fit any size print you wish to make, and unless you are exceptionally good at lettering, the best and easiest method is to purchase one of these greeting card kits. There are types for every taste, from simple black-and-white cards, to elaborate folders for color snapshots, to the Slimline cards which are lithographed in color.

FOLDER-TYPE CARDS

Folder cards are made so that the sensitized side of the paper is used for the print and the back for the message. They are almost as simple to make as single-sheet cards and provide more room for messages. These cards can be handled by a printer if you want your name imprinted on them.

They can be made in any size, but one of the most popular is the 4 × 5-inch, made on either a 4 × 10- or 5 × 8-inch sheet. They can be made with an enlarger, by

Tabletop pictures can be set up at any time of the year. They may strive for a realistic effect or be in a humorous or fantasy mood. Variety stores offer a wealth of material in plastic figures and machines, so your greeting-card photograph can illustrate almost any holiday, anniversary, or announcement. (Photo: Edna Bennett—Set design: Franklin Bennett)

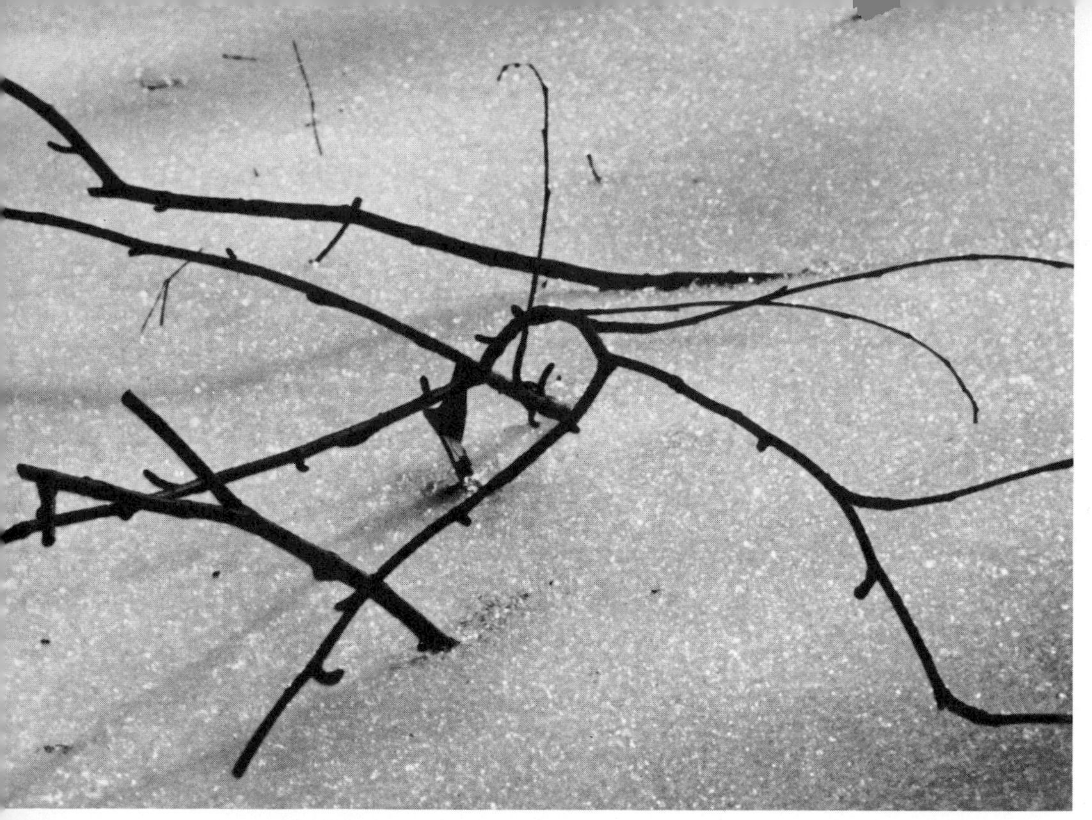

The range of subject matter for holiday greeting cards has no limit—it may be a complicated set-up or a simple nature study, as long as it carries the flavor of the season. Mounted on lightweight board, this ones carries its greeting on the reverse side. (Photo: Edna Bennett)

reduction, or on a contact printer. Be sure that the area of sensitized paper that is not being printed upon is protected from the white light. It is easy to forget that the paper is twice as long as the picture.

A long narrow picture, perhaps a scenic, can be printed on the full sheet to form the outer covers of the folder. The message is inside.

Another popular style of folder card is the slip-in, where a print is inserted under a cut-out opening. Slip-ins can be made by hand, but those offered by the photographic companies save time and effort and have the greeting already printed. An average folder measures 4¼ × 5½ inches with a masked opening inside which accepts any standard contact or jumbo square, vertical, or horizontal print. There is also the French-fold greeting design which accepts a print in a masked opening on the front or inside the card. Folders also are available with a 2 × 3-inch horizontal or vertical opening for insertion of color prints.

The French-fold card can also be made without the masked opening. An 8 × 10 sheet of paper, folded once horizontally and once vertically will make a 4 × 5-inch card. The layout for this type of card must be carefully planned so that the card will open with the print and the greeting in their proper places. Sensitized paper designed for folding is available.

BE CONVENTIONAL

Use your imagination on the subject matter, but be conventional in deciding the size of the card so you will be able to use standard-size envelopes and printing papers. Most greeting cards should be printed either on a textured finish or on glossy paper (matte dried).

The whole family may be grouped around a natural focal point such as a piano, a fireplace, a doorway, a staircase—or pursuing a hobby or profession. A self-timer makes it possible to include the photographer in the scene.

Double-weight paper is good for the single card or prints which will be used in the slip-in folders. Ad-Type paper, a thin flexible stock, is used for French-fold cards. Blue toning is sometimes effective for snow scenes on Christmas cards. Investigate the greeting-card home-production outfits manufactured for either single print or folder types. A typical outfit for single cards consists of eight negative masks, each including a holiday sentiment, an opening for the negative, and a guide on each mask for placing the paper. Two masks are offered for horizontal and two for vertical negatives of various sizes. One of each of these masks prints the picture with a top and side bleed. The other two print with white margins all around, permitting the cards to be embossed with the embossing guide included in the kit.

If you are not a darkroom enthusiast, the finishing of your greeting cards can be done by your local photodealer or a professional photographer's studio, especially if you want color prints.

GROUP PICTURES

[There are two major types of group pictures—the group that shows faces, and the group that tells a story and indicates action. This article covers the single- and multiple-column line-up pose, the informal circular pose, and other group arrangements. It also describes how to achieve unity in a group picture, and suggests some novel ideas for posing.]

• *Also see: Banquet Photography; Portrait Photography.*

PHOTOGRAPHY OF GROUPS CAN BE one of the most absorbing aspects of photography, or it can be the most boring. The photographer who regards group photography as a test of his imagination and ingenuity produces the most delightfully arranged photos, while the indifferent cameraman produces group pictures which bore one at first glance.

Making group photographs interesting is largely a problem of arrangement and of camera angle. Other variables, such as lighting and backgrounds are important, but the main feature that spells the difference between the common and the eye-appealing is the subjects' arrangement and the angle from which

Even in group photos, an imaginative photographer can put his point across without showing the subjects' faces. The three elderly men seem to be gazing at the road and summer countryside, a symbol of their own youth, and the distant rural church, their future. Rolleiflex with Adox R-17 film exposed at f/11 for 1/60 of a second. (Photo: Larry June)

the photo was taken. Since each type of group study presents different problems of variation, they will be considered separately.

GROUPS THAT SHOW FACES

The beginner will usually try to photograph a large number of people by arranging his subjects shoulder to shoulder in a single line. This placement wastes the largest part of the negative space and obscures facial details because of the generally greater distance needed from subjects-to-camera to get the line-up arrangement on the negative. The more people in a group, the longer the line, the greater the camera-to-subject distance, and the smaller the facial features.

But the single-column line-up frequently seems to be the only way in which a large number of people can be included in a single frame. In these cases the camera angle may be changed from the usual chest-high, front-center position. Try a wide-angle lens stopped well down with the camera at ground-, knee-, or waist-level and shoot down the row of figures. Such a camera position fills one edge of the entire negative with interesting detail and permits the pleasant composition of gradually diminishing figures. If faces are the primary concern, shoot from cheek height down the line of faces.

Another variation of the single column is to arrange the subjects chest-to-back and shoot down the line. Of the several camera positions possible, two are often very effective. One is to arrange the group in a line diagonally from the camera, thus showing each face beside the one in front of it. It is also effective in the shoulder-to-

This group photograph achieves unity through action. The audience is concentrating on the movements of the performer. The low shooting angle gives equal prominence to all faces. Tanack 35 mm camera with Plus-X film. (Photo: Michael E. Bry)

The family group is difficult to photograph because of variations in size and sex. But if they are arranged in orderly or symmetrical fashion, and an attempt is made to get something different and eye-catching by means of camera angle and props, some very unusual effects can be achieved. (Photo: Grace Rothstein)

chest column to shoot from above the level of the row of heads. Frequently this camera angle is utilized with several rows of persons. Interesting narrow compositions can result from such group arrangements.

The position above the level of a group of heads requires less depth of field than any of the procedures so far suggested, for the higher the camera, the more nearly equal the distances to individual faces.

POINT OF FOCUS

On what point in a long line of figures extending away from the camera should the photographer focus to get all the faces sharp? Proper use of the depth-of-field scale, engraved on many lens mounts or on the focusing knob, will automatically set the focus at the optimum point. Determine the distance from the camera of both the nearest and farthest figure, then rotate the focusing ring or knob until both distances are against the same aperture reading. (The aperture readings are paired, one on each side of the focus marking. One corresponds to the near limit of sharpness, the other to the far limit.)

With fixed-focus cameras, point of focus need not be determined, since everything from about six feet to infinity will be acceptably sharp. Single-lens reflexes, press, and view cameras enable the photographer to judge the sharpness of the image on groundglass or in the finder. To determine the point of focus for adjustable cameras or lenses without depth-of-field scales, consult the appropriate depth-of-field. (See: *Depth of Field and Hyperfocal Distance.*)

If it is necessary to guess at depth of field, bear in mind that sharpness is not symmetrically arranged around a point of focus; two-fifths of the in-focus distance will be in front of the point and the remaining three fifths will be behind it. Stop down as far as light conditions permit, then divide the total depth of the group by five and focus on a point two fifths behind the nearest member.

ARRANGEMENT VARIATIONS

Many photographers and subjects object to the fact that in variations of single-column line-ups, certain figures are emphasized because of their proximity to the camera. This emphasis can be eliminated by arranging the group in several rows. Many interesting and effective compositions can be worked out with double, triple, and quadruple line-ups. Because of the great variety of geometrical figures possible when photographing groups, it is inadvisable to consider triangular, square, and rectangular group arrangements individually.

Above: *This informal group portrait is meant to be slowly viewed to take in each detail of clothing, attitude, and personality. The boys appear to have stopped for only a moment for the photographer.*

Right: *Suddenly they're in motion and the entire feeling of the photo has changed, though the subjects remain the same. Being able to see the fine lines of an individual expression is less important than the over-all mood.* (Photos: Lou Bernstein)

A first principle in picturing several rows of figures is to arrange the group and place the camera so that the faces are as large as possible with the group filling the entire negative. There is a certain feeling of intimacy between the subjects and the viewer if the camera is close and faces are large. Groups at great distances from the camera, showing full-length figures, never seem to achieve this desirable feeling of intimacy.

Securing "large" faces in group studies of several rows can be accomplished in a number of ways. First, you can arrange the groups so that all heads are in the same plane by sandwiching the second row of persons so that their faces appear between the heads of the first row. The heads of the third row should appear between those of the second row. Another method of having faces appear large in the print is to elevate the camera for a down-angle shot. This angle can also be used to eliminate uninteresting details of clothing, awkward hands, and other distractions.

A second principle for photographing groups composed of several rows is: Whatever the pattern of the group—triangular, rectangular, or oval—make it a symmetrical arrangement. While this article is, in a sense, a plea for flexibility and life in group studies, there must be some orderliness in the arrangement of a group of persons.

Principle three should be: Always walk around a group at least once to find the most striking camera position. Often you can effectively combine a downward angle with a semiprofile view. Experimentation and observation will lead to many fresh viewpoints.

The fourth principle: Informality

among the persons photographed does much to make interesting group pictures. A group of girls will appear much more attractive and eye-catching if photographed during a lighthearted conversation. A glee club photograph is bound to be more interesting if the men are actually singing.

The final principle: Select a nonobtrusive background. Faces are given "the big play" by neutral shades in the background. Sketchy or blotchy flowered backgrounds detract from face studies. Simplify your props too when your primary concern is to present the faces of several persons.

GROUPS THAT TELL A STORY

Far more variation, interest, and ingenuity can be used with group photographs which tell a story. The photographer is free to employ his skill in arranging his subjects into a composition that is informative as well as dramatic.

Telling a story with the camera implies that the photographs will show a group of people who are very definitely doing something, so that the viewer of the pictures sees the action immediately and the people in the group only secondarily.

It should always be remembered that the action is paramount, and every detail, every person in the group, the background, the lighting, the camera angle should all be coordinated to emphasize and dramatize the action. This singleness of purpose makes imperative the omission of irrelevant, cluttering details.

Various courses can be followed to make the action stand out in the picture. As the most direct method, there is repetition of action—having all members of a group doing precisely the same thing. All the persons need not carry out the action in exactly the same way, but they must all unmistakably participate in the group activity. None should simply stare at the camera.

Action can also be emphasized by having one or two persons participate and the rest of the group watch the performance with evident interest. Even one person can "carry the story" provided all of the other persons included watch the action with sufficient interest.

A further variation is "cross action," in which there is a central action carried on by one or two members of the group while the rest both watch the central figures and carry on the action. As an example, consider a golf pro teaching a

beginner how to hold a club. The teacher and pupil form the center of interest, while the other members of the group, in the background, both watch the pro and also try to hold the club in the same way. This repetition of motif adds emphasis to a picture; it has always been a favorite device among painters.

UNITY IN GROUP PICTURES

Another suggestion for improved storytelling group photos is: Be certain all elements of the photograph are harmonious. The lighting, the arrangement, background, and persons should naturally all belong together in one picture.

Many photographers who take group photos make the mistake of trying to show all faces in equal prominence, even when the "story is the thing." They have everyone posed in such a way that all the faces show, even though, naturally, a group would never form in such a fashion. The effect is somewhat ludicrous, because everyone immediately recognizes that the story presented is not a natural one. The photograph is not convincing.

It should be pointed out that very few groups in formal clothes align themselves along a clapboard wall of a house. Yet every year amateurs—and occasionally professionals—take some little miss in her first formal and place her in a garden. Or they line up Dad and Mother in their Sunday best by the side of the house.

A final general suggestion for group photos to tell a story: Get your group in the smallest possible space and fill the frame with subject matter. Do not waste negative area by having wide gaps between persons in a group unless these spaces add to the story.

Once in a while the photographer likes to go to extremes and use a group at a distance in a large area.

Faces are almost obscured in this photo; the effectiveness of this group shot comes from the surroundings, a cigarette, shadows, and light. Nikon F with 50mm Auto-Nikkor f/1.4 lens. Tri-X film exposed at f/4 for 1/30 of a second. (Photo: Ross Lowell)

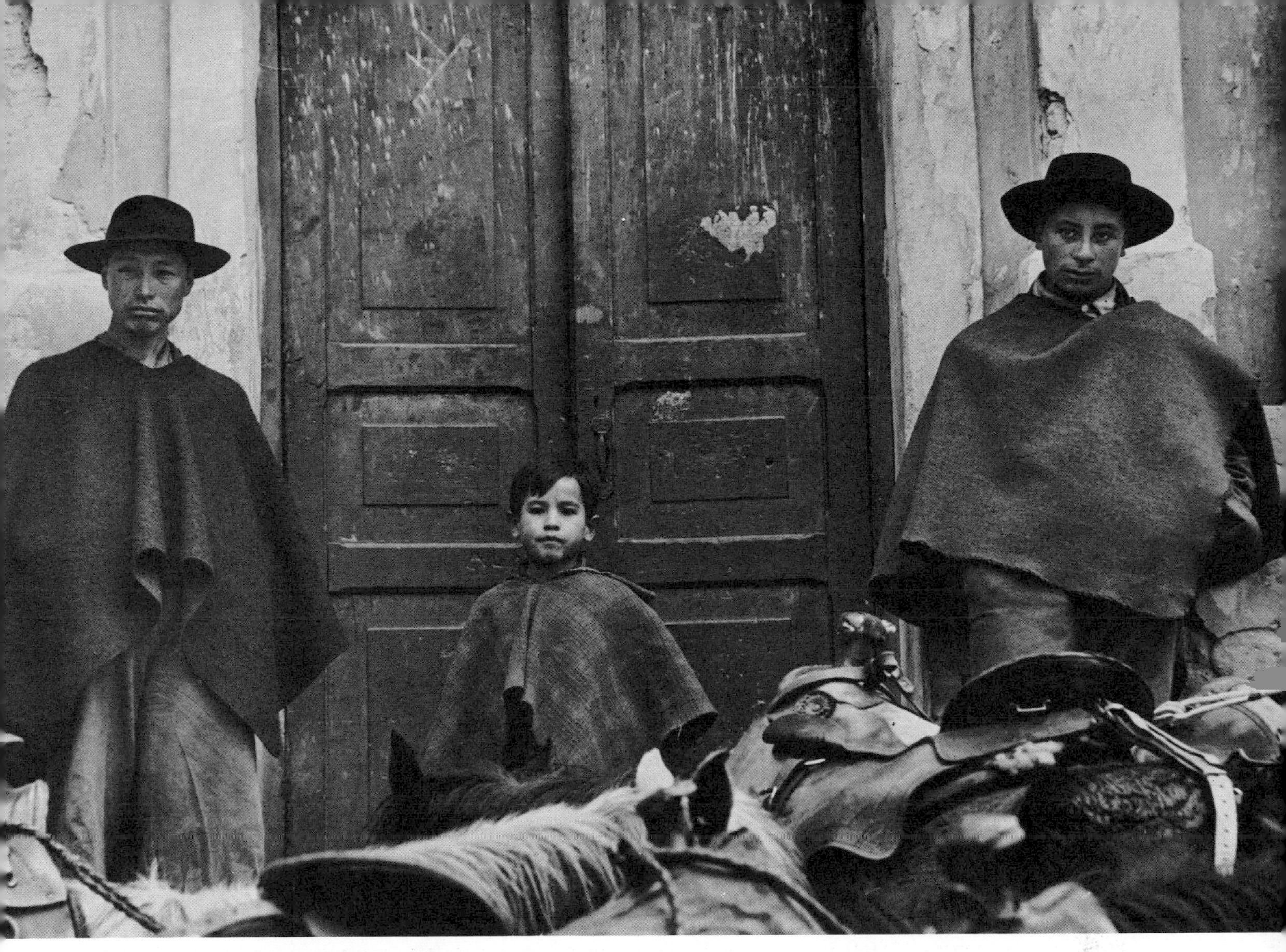

The group doesn't have to be closely spaced. The background and foreground of this photo from Columbia tells as much as the faces. Pentax with Plus-X film exposed for 1/60 of a second at f/5.6. (Photo: Ross Lowell)

It will appear relatively small and achieve the effect of loneliness or emphasize the beauty of the setting. This can be done effectively when the story is in the setting, not in the features of the individuals who make up the group.

Often group studies can be made more interesting by framing. Frames can be provided by trees, doorways, people—all of which add up to more interesting photography.

A final dressing-up procedure is dramatic expression. Although often overdone and often misused it is still the unusual and dramatic face that catches the eye. Psychologists long ago agreed that our faces were "maps of our feelings," and any picture which gives an insight into feelings is bound to catch attention.

□

GUM-BICHROMATE PRINTING

The gum-bichromate process is an almost obsolete method of making prints. Since this method is incapable of rendering fine details sharply, it is used mainly in pictorial photography where broad effects are desired. It is strictly a contact-printing process, requiring strong daylight or sunlight; if a large print is to be made, an enlarged negative has to be prepared first. Finally, only a limited range of tones is possible. To secure deeper blacks and a greater tone scale, the photographer must resort to multiple printing in which the paper is resensitized several times, with the negative being replaced on register marks for alignment, and succeeding exposures made and developed on the same print until the desired depth is reached.

The process is based on the fact that a bichromated and pigmented colloid becomes insoluble in water in proportion to the exposure received. Thus if a coating of gum arabic pigmented with any sort of water-color pigment and sensitized with a bichromate is exposed through a negative and then placed in water, the unexposed parts will wash away almost completely; the partly exposed parts will wash down to some extent; and the fully exposed areas will not wash out at all.

Unfortunately this doesn't work quite as well as it sounds. In practice, it is very difficult to get the pigment to wash out cleanly in the highlights and, for this reason, only a thin coating is applied. This in turn means that only a medium gray can be obtained in the deepest shadows. If the paper is coated heavily enough for full blacks, the highlights will not wash out completely, and the resulting image will be dull and foggy looking, with grayed-over whites.

For those who are interested in experimenting with the process, the following instructions will provide a good beginning.

PAPER

Any good grade of drawing paper with sizing can be used for gum-bichromate printing. If multiple printing is to be done, it will be necessary to use an all-rag paper, as wood-pulp papers will not stand the repeated wetting and drying without buckling and excessive shrinkage.

It is necessary to use a highly sized paper so the coating will stay on the surface and not sink in. Some all-rag bond papers and writing papers are adequately sized; most drawing papers are not and, in general, it is best to apply sizing to any paper. Even if it is already sized, the additional sizing will do no harm.

To make a sizing bath, use the following:

Gelatin	1 ounce	30.0 grams
Water	10 ounces	300.0 cc

Let the gelatin soak in the water for awhile, then warm gently until it is dissolved. Now make up the following solution:

Potassium chrome alum	45 gr.	3.0 gr.
Warm water	10 oz.	300.0 cc

When thoroughly dissolved, add this solution to the warm gelatin solution. Apply the mixture to the paper while it is still hot, rubbing it well into the pores with a small sponge. Allow the paper to dry. If the paper is very porous, it may need to be sized twice, and dried between coatings.

SENSITIZED COATING

The first thing to do in preparing the coating is to dissolve some gum arabic in water; since this takes days, it should be done well in advance of use. The best way to dissolve gum arabic is to suspend it in a cheesecloth bag in a jar of water and let it hang there until all the gum is dissolved; the impurities remain in the bag.

Use about three times the volume of water as gum, that is, for every ounce of gum use three ounces of water. It will take two to three days to dissolve. When finally dissolved, add a few drops of formaldehyde, carbolic acid, or thymol, to prevent bacterial decomposition and souring of the gum.

The pigment can be any grade of watercolor; the best kind is the usual watercolor sold in tubes for artists' use. Blacks or dark browns are most common, but any other color can be used.

The sensitizer is a saturated solution of potassium bichromate. Mix about two ounces of bichromate and about ten ounces of water. After they have stood for some days in a bottle, there will be a residue of undissolved bichromate in the bottom of the bottle, proving that the solution is saturated.

The coating for the paper is made by mixing the proper proportions of gum solution, pigment, and sensitizer. The proportions will vary according to the purpose, the type of negative being printed, and a number of factors which cannot be specified. Only experiment can tell, but for a starting point, see the table for suggested proportions.

	Heavy Coating	
Pigment *(measure ribbon from tube)*	4 in.	10.0 cm
Gum	½ oz.	15.0 cc
Bichromate	1 oz.	30.0 cc
	Medium Coating	
Pigment	2 in.	5.0 cm
Gum	½ oz.	15.0 cc
Bichromate	1 oz.	30.0 cc
	Light Coating	
Pigment	1 in.	2.5 cm
Gum	½ oz.	15.0 cc
Bichromate	1 oz.	30.0 cc

Depending on the tube which contains the watercolor pigment, the amounts given may have to be modified. The quantities above will make enough to coat several sheets of 11 × 14 paper, but the mixture costs little and it is best to prepare ample quantities.

The paper may be tacked to a small drawing board; the coating is then brushed on smoothly, using a wide camel's-hair brush. As soon as the paper is covered, a narrower, fitch-hair "blender" similar to a bromoil brush is used to smooth the coating. This is continued until the coating begins to dry and stick to the brush, at which point the paper should be placed in the dark to dry, while still tacked to the board. The paper is not sensitive until it is dry, so the coating may be done in a dimly lit room.

PRINTING

Printing is done by contact. The paper is exposed either to a carbon arc, daylight, or bright sunlight. No time can be specified; it is necessary to find out the required exposure by experiment. A sheet of printing-out proof paper may be used as a guide, but even then it is necessary to find the ratio between the exposure required for a proof and the exposure necessary for the gum paper.

To develop the latent image, the print is placed in a tray of water at 65 to 75 F. It is left face up until it flattens, then is turned face down and left floating on the water. The print will develop out by itself in about an hour. If the image shows completely in a shorter time, the print is underexposed; if it refuses to develop out clearly in an hour or so, it is overprinted. Sometimes an overexposed print can be developed out by using warmer water or by adding a few drops of ammonia to the water.

When development is complete, the print is laid face up on a tilted sheet of glass to drain for a few minutes. Then the glass is placed horizontally for drying, with the print still face up.

If the image lacks contrast after the print is dry, it is possible to apply another coating of the pigmented gum over the present image and print it a second time, in some cases a third or fourth time. It is necessary to have some system of registering the negative exactly over the image each time; probably the best way is the use of a punch and pegs, as used in Dye Transfer printing.

PELICANS **HARALD DOERING**

The success of this photograph is achieved not because it is an interesting picture of two pelicans, but rather because the subjects have been treated as abstract forms. Even the most awkward creature has its moment of grace, and that is what the photographer has caught here.

The sensuous curves of the birds' necks are strengthened through contrast with the straight lines of the bills and wings. The over-all effect of flow and grace is intensified by the use of strong sidelighting and extremely shallow depth of field.

ERNST HAAS

Biography

One of the most celebrated and influential photographers of his generation—and one of the most individualistic—Ernst Haas today is best known for his work in color. Through the use of reflection, motion, composition, and simply by his own way of seeing, he has shown in his major color essays his belief that subject matter is secondary to treatment. Haas is not afraid of the commonplace: his most important work has often been done on familiar, almost cliché subjects like New York, Paris, Venice, bullfights, rodeos, even the debris around his New York studio.

Haas has also worked in black-and-white and photojournalism in covering, for example, the war in Indochina. Other documentary assignments for magazines have taken him all over the world. His black-and-white portraits include the widely published pictures of George Bernard Shaw, Nehru, and Alfred Einstein. Several of his pictures appear in the *Family of Man*. He has also done some work in advertising and much work as a still photographer for such film directors as Carol Reed, John Huston, and Howard Hawks. He likes to keep variety in his work, and although his emphasis today is in color, he gives himself many different photographic projects ranging from segregation in the South to a lyrical color essay on Knoxville, Tennessee, seen as the home town of writer James Agee. Haas has always preferred to work up his own assignments, presenting them in edited form, with layout suggestions.

Ernst Haas was born in Vienna in 1921. As a young man he attended medical school, his education being interrupted by the war. After the war, his strong artistic bent won out over medicine, and he eventually became interested in the possibilities of the camera. His first pictures were abstract, in anticipation of the direction he has taken in recent years. Other pictures were pictorial, atmospheric and poetic. A selection of his early work was shown at his first exhibit, given at the headquarters of the American Red Cross in Vienna in 1947 by Mr. Steve Munsing.

At about the same time he began working for the American-sponsored *Heute* magazine. It was Arnold Kubler, the editor of *Du* magazine of Zurich, who advised Haas to work "on the human scale," to abandon his inanimate subjects for a while. Accordingly, back in Vienna, he did his first notable picture story, the *Returning War Prisoners*. On seeing this story and other Haas pictures, Robert Capa invited him to join the cooperative picture agency, Magnum, in 1949, a year after it was founded. Werner Bischof, with whom Haas always felt artistically allied, joined the same day. At Magnum, Haas found a congenial working atmosphere. It was during this initial Magnum period that he did the memorable *Miracle of Greece* story.

In 1950, Haas came to the

Ernst Haas / Magnum.

Ernst Haas / Magnum.

United States for the first time and did a black-and-white story for *Life* on New Mexico, followed by his first color essay, *New York,* which ran 24 pages. The *New York* essay was a landmark for *Life* as well as for Haas. *Life* had never before run a major color story shot with only a 35 mm camera and Haas, before the essay, had shot only one roll of color film. His next major story was *Paris,* done in the same style as *New York* and including his first studies on motion.

About this time, Capa began to chide him for being "too esthetic," insisting Haas needed more "human experience." Taking this advice, Haas went to cover the war in Indochina with the French Foreign Legion. While in southeast Asia, Haas did essays on Bali, Laos, and Angkor for Paris *Match.*

During an assignment in Spain for the movie *The Pride and the Passion* in 1956, Haas used his free time to photograph bullfights, continuing his experiments with the interpretation of motion with the still camera. *Life* published a dozen pages of these pictures and gave him an allowance to continue his motion studies.

Haas' old interest in nature and abstractions was renewed while waiting for security clearance to do an assignment for General Dynamics in San Diego, California. There on the California beaches Haas began to explore the minutiae of sea life with his lens, pursuing his inclination to reduce physical objects to their essence. The results of these last few years of photographing nature in color will appear in Haas' first book, *Elements,* to be published in 1963.

A recent highlight in Ernst Haas' career was his one-man color exhibit at New York's Museum of Modern Art in 1962, the first such show to have been given there. Prior to this Haas had the honor of designing the world-traveling Magnum exhibit, "The World as Seen by Magnum Photographers." In addition, the Eastman Kodak Company is giving five exhibits of his color work world-wide showings.

Also, four half-hour television programs conceived by Haas and called the *Art of Seeing* were presented in 1962 to widespread critical acclaim. Haas enjoys lecturing and projecting his color and has done so extensively. Today he works on his own and through Magnum.

At this writing, one of Haas' fondest dreams is becoming a reality —people are becoming interested in hanging his color prints on their walls. Dye Transfers, from a selected group of Haas color negatives, can now be found in private homes and in a growing number of business offices.

Haas draws and designs constantly. The other visual arts as well as music and literature play a dominant role in his life and are reflected in his work. He has devoted much time to organizing his ideas about photography, about its place in our life and culture, and is particularly concerned that photography should not be overwhelmed by technology—that the camera remain an instrument, not an end in itself.

Haas has written: "Photography as a contemporary medium confronts us with a contemporary

Ernst Haas / Magnum.

problem. In the time of our critical struggle against the mechanization of man, photography presents us with one more instance in which we must humanize a machine on which we are dependent—the camera."

Endeavoring to put a finger on his esthetic approach, he says: "In every artist there is poetry; in every human being there is a poetic element. We know...we feel...we believe. As knowers, we are like scientists relating through logical determination. As feelers, we are like poets, relating the unrelated through intuition. As believers, we are only accepting our human limitations. The artist is born with the seed of a gift. Through it he must express the summation of his feeling, knowing, and believing in a unity of his life and work. The total expression of this gift is the secret promise he is forced to make to himself. It is his purpose for living, his responsibility for being."

HALATION

PETER KRAUSE
Manager, Phototechnology Department, Ansco

[Halation is a little-known hindrance to image sharpness. In this article the effects and causes of both reflex and diffuse halation are discussed. The anti-halation backing on films and plates is explained, in addition to other means of preventing halation.]

• *Also see: Emulsion Chemistry; Emulsion Manufacture; Films, When and How to Use Them.*

THE TERM HALATION ORIGINALLY was used to describe the ring-like phenomenon resembling a halo that was observed around point images recorded on photographic plates. After it was determined that this halo was caused by light reflected from the rear surface of the glass support, the more descriptive term "reflex halation" was adopted for this unwanted, secondary image.

Still later it was recognized that the size of the point image increased with increasing exposure, and that the boundary of most point images tended to be diffuse rather than sharply defined. This spreading of the image was caused by light scattering within the photographic emulsion layer; the term "diffuse halation" was chosen to distinguish it from reflex halation (Figure 1).

REFLEX HALATION

Reflex halation no longer is a significant problem with modern photographic films or plates, since several methods are available for protection against it. Nevertheless, a brief review of the basic aspects of reflex halation is needed, since under adverse exposure conditions it can contribute to image degradation.

Some of the light that enters an emulsion layer during exposure traverses it and passes through any support made of clear, transparent film or glass. Light rays which enter the support at right angles to its surface, or at a small angle from the normal, emerge nearly unattenuated into the air space behind the rear surface. Only a small por-

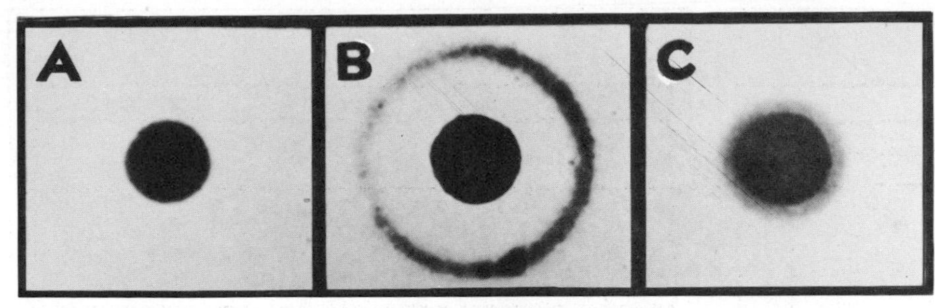

Figure 1. *When a circular spot, A, is photographed on a plate not protected against reflex halation, a halo-like image is found around the primary point image, B. Light scatter within the photographic emulsion layer causes diffuse halation, C. Here the point image has grown in size owing to excessive exposure, and the primary image is surrounded by a diffuse boundary zone.*

tion of the rays are absorbed or reflected back toward the emulsion.

However, when the entrance angle equals the so-called critical angle (which is about 40 degrees for glass and somewhat less for film base), total internal reflection occurs and all light rays are reflected back to the emulsion. Light which enters the base at an angle greater than the critical angle also is totally reflected, but the path length through the base is greater and light intensity is reduced correspondingly. Therefore the intensity of the reflected light is at its maximum at a distance from the primary image which is governed by the critical angle (τ). When the primary image is a point, a halo forms around it.

HALATION AND BASE

The distance, d, which separates the primary image point from the reflex halation image of maximum density, is dependent on two main factors: 1) the refractive index of the base, n, and 2) the base thickness, t. The relation between these factors is expressed by the following equation:

$$d = 2t \times \frac{1}{\sqrt{n^2 - 1}}$$

This means that the distance from the primary image at which the reflex halo has its maximum density increases with base thickness. For glass, n is usually 1.54; hence d equals 1.7t. The diagrams in Figure 2 illustrate these relationships.

It should be noted that most films for everyday use have thin supports. With such films, the reflex halo is so close to the primary image that it appears more like a diffuse boundary zone than a separate image. It can be mistaken for image spreading caused by light scatter within the emulsion.

ANTIHALATION METHODS

To protect photographic films and plates from reflex halation, three basic methods are used, singly or in combination.

1. A separate layer, which will absorb any actinic light that passes through the light-sensitive emulsion, can be placed between the emulsion and the support (Figure 3).

2. The support can be dyed so it will absorb unwanted light. Since light rays must traverse the support

Figure 2. *The causes and effects of reflex halation in a photographic plate having a thick-glass support, left, and in a photographic film having a relatively thin base, right. The thickness of the base is t; the critical angle at which total reflection occurs at the base-air surface is τ; and d is the distance between the primary image point and the point, A, at which the reflected light has its maximum intensity. Note that the reflex halo is separated by an appreciable distance from the primary image when the support is thick, but is separated by only a small distance when the support is thin.*

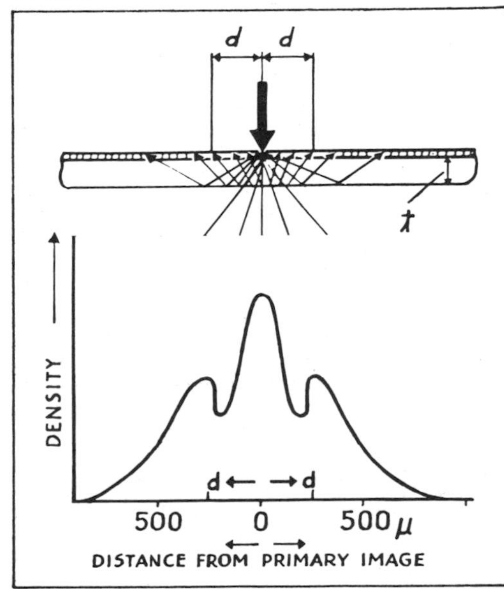

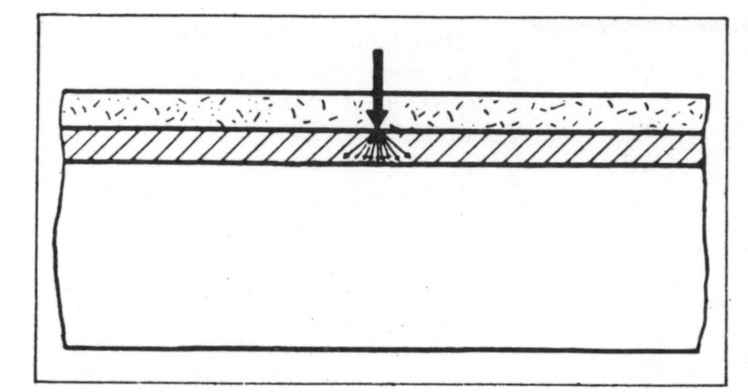

Figure 3. *Reflex halation can be eliminated by a layer coated between the light-sensitive emulsion and the support which absorbs actinic light.*

twice, the effective density of the support is doubled. A neutral gray tint is commonly used for this purpose, and films are then known as gray-base films. Common examples are black-and-white motion-picture and 35 mm still-camera films.

3. A permanent or removable antihalation layer is coated on the back side of the support. This layer contains dyes, pigments, or other light-absorbing compounds (Figure 4).

Obviously the prime requisite of an antihalation layer is to reduce to an innocuous level the intensity of all actinic light reflected from the rear surface of the photographic film or plate. This is accomplished in most instances when the effective density of the antihalation layer is above 1.5. Other requirements that must be considered are:

1. The colorant or other light-absorbing substance must be completely decolorized or removed during processing. (An exception is a dyed film base which normally retains its color.)

2. The light-absorbing substance should not discolor or otherwise affect the processing solutions adversely. (Removable antihalation layers usually are removed from the support in a prerinse before developing.)

3. The antihalation layer should not affect the photographic characteristics of the emulsion during storage or before processing.

Light-absorbing substances that are suitable for antihalation layers are organic dyes, such as indophenols and certain diamine-triphenyl methanes; colored inorganic compounds, such as manganese dioxide or colloidal silver dispersed in gelatin. The colloidal silver layers are employed with many reversal color films; the silver is removed with all other image silver during processing.

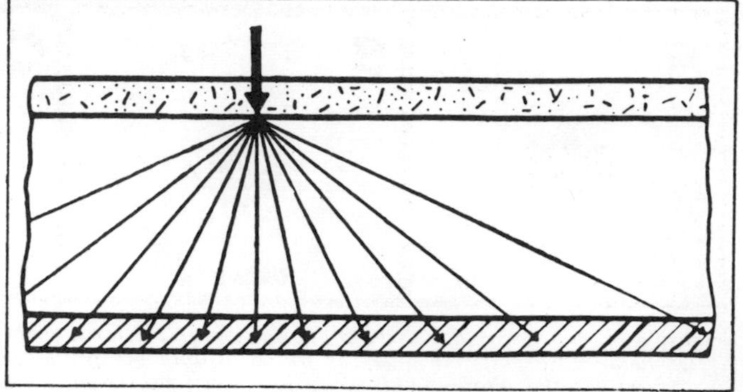

Figure 4. *Another type of antihalation layer is often used with black-and-white sheet and roll films. This layer, usually of gelatin, is coated on the back of the support and contains a light-absorbing compound. It may be removed, or the light-absorbing compound destroyed or decolorized, during processing.*

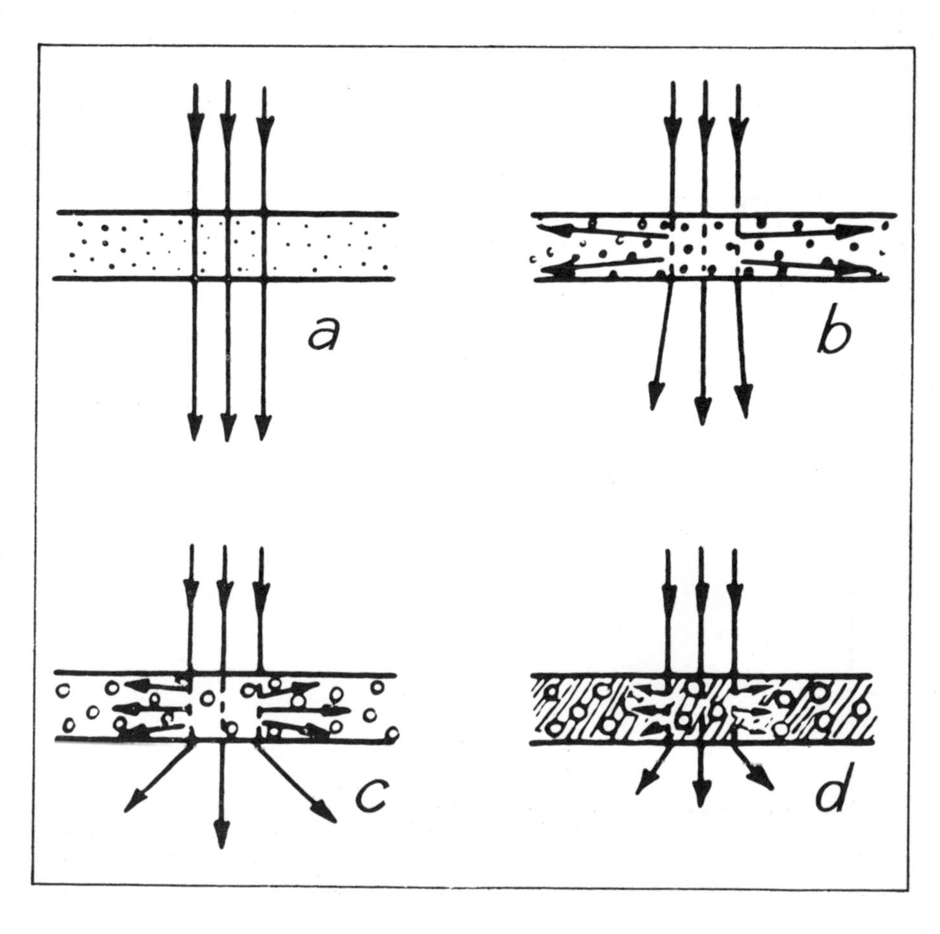

Figure 5. *These diagrams illustrate schematically how the amount of light scatter and the spreading of the scattered light are influenced by the average grain size and absorptance of an emulsion. Emulsion* a *has extremely fine grains (less than 0.1 micron in diameter) and the right-angle light rays are not scattered to any appreciable extent. Emulsion* b, *which has somewhat larger grains than* a, *scatters light much more, but light absorption is relatively low. Hence the scattered light spreads a good deal. Emulsion* c *has still coarser grains (average diameter, about 0.4 microns) and light scatter is at a maximum. Light absorption also is high, therefore the spread of the scattered light is less than in* b. *Emulsion* d *has the same grain size as* c, *but a colorant has been added to absorb scattered light, so the diffusion halo is smaller than in* c.

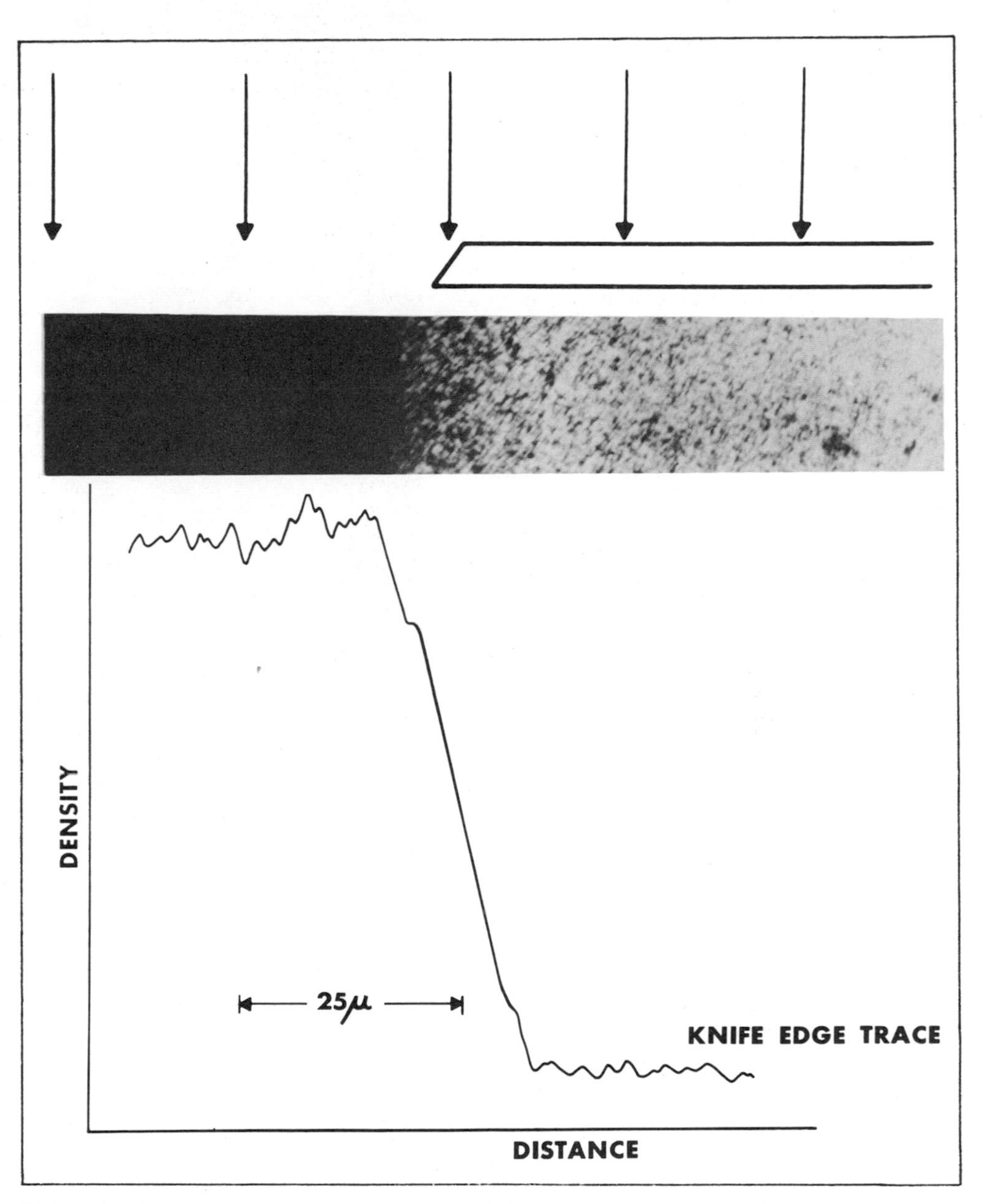

Figure 6. *When a knife-edge, or other opaque object having a sharply defined boundary, is placed in close contact with a photographic emulsion and the emulsion is exposed and processed, an image is obtained that has a more or less diffuse edge, as at top. This diffuse halation is caused by light scattering within the emulsion. When this edge image is scanned with a microphotometer, a trace is obtained, as demonstrated by the graph at bottom. The shape and slope of this trace are indicative of the acutance of the photographic emulsion. The sample shown here has rather low acutance and does not yield images of good definition. There is too much diffuse halation.*

DIFFUSE HALATION

It has been pointed out that light is scattered within the emulsion layer of photographic films and plates. The principal causes of this scattering are the refraction of light rays by the emulsion gelatin, and the reflection and refraction of rays by the silver-halide crystals imbedded in the gelatin.

The extent to which light is scattered within any emulsion depends on the amount, packing density, shape, size, and size distribution of the silver-halide crystals. It also depends upon the halide composition, the refractive index of the colloid, the nature of other emulsion additives, and the wavelength of the light.

Diffuse halation causes spreading of the primary image (Figure 1), with a degradation of small image details. The intensity of the scattered light decreases with increasing distance from the primary image, as a result of light absorption within the layer and light losses in the boundary regions. Figure 5 illustrates schematically how the degree of

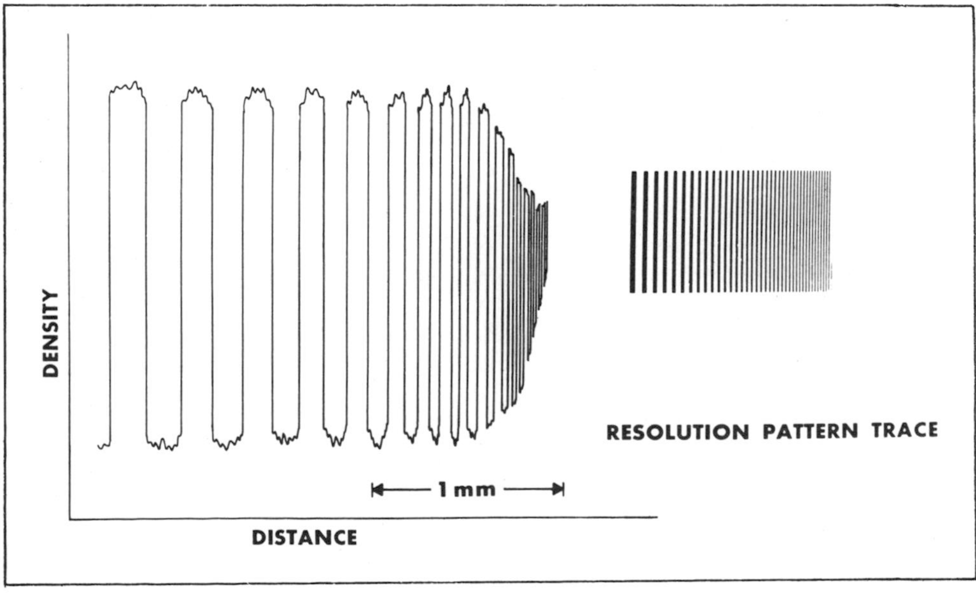

Figure 7. *Diffuse halation may also be evaluated by means of a bar pattern such as shown at the right. In the original pattern all lines have the same length but they differ in width and spacing. When such a pattern is reproduced with a photographic film and the image scanned with a microdensitometer, a trace is obtained as indicated above at the left. The spacing and amplitude decrease with line frequency and eventually no discernible difference remains between lines and spaces. This is so because light scatter within the emulsion causes the density of the clear spaces to increase and the line width to spread. A frequency-response curve derived from such a trace gives the same information about diffuse halation as a knife-edge trace, but in a different form.*

scatter and the intensity of the scattered light changes with average grain size and layer absorption.

Light scattering does not increase linearly with grain size, but reaches its maximum when the average grain diameter ranges around 0.4 micron. For example, the scattering of blue light is at a maximum in a silver-bromide emulsion having a relative refractive index of 1.47 when the average crystal size is 0.43 micron.

Spreading of light within the layer, on the other hand, decreases as scattering increases, because light-absorption characteristics of the emulsion become greater. Hence the density of the diffusion halo tends to be at its maximum when light scattering is greatest, but the size of the diffusion halo tends to be larger when light scatter is low.

ACUTANCE

In the past the resolving power of an emulsion was often used as an index of its capability to reproduce fine image details. More sophisticated recent studies of the factors which influence the subjective judgment of image definition have shown that resolving power is an inadequate physical measure of this aspect of image quality. These studies also have shown that so-called acutance or frequency response of an emulsion correlate well with value judgments of image definition.

Acutance values can be obtained from microdensitometer traces of knife-edge exposures (Figure 6). The spread function of the layer can be computed from such a trace by the formula:

$$\text{Acutance} = \frac{\overline{G}^2 x}{DS}$$

where $\overline{G}$ is the average gradient of the curve at equal increments of density, and DS is the density scale.

Frequency-response curves can be obtained by determining how the amplitude of a graded test pattern varies with respect to the spatial frequency of the pattern (Figure 7). The numerical values of acutance that can be derived by the method outlined above, and those derived from frequency-response curves, are related to each other—one can be computed from the other. In other words, both measure the spread function of the emulsion or, as it used to be called, its diffuse halation.

It is evident that the definition of a photographic image, hence its quality, is greatly dependent upon its susceptibility to diffuse halation. Individual factors that contribute to this type of halation have been identified and their importance evaluated. But it is not always possible to minimize all the adverse factors, since other requirements such as speed, gradation, and graininess must also be considered, and these often react adversely to the same controls that minimize halation.

Nevertheless, great progress has been made in the past decade in reducing diffuse halation through reductions in emulsion-layer thickness; proper control of size, shape, and distribution of the silver-halide grains; and use of light-absorbing compounds in the emulsion.

PHILIPPE HALSMAN

Biography

Philippe Halsman has built his reputation as a portraitist on his ability to capture the personality of the sitter. He believes that the primary aim of photography, unlike the aim of the fine arts, is not the reflection in every picture of the artist's own self, but the attempt to penetrate the subject's essence and to capture the truth.

Photography was the furthest thing from Halsman's mind when he left his native Riga in Latvia to continue his studies in electrical engineering in Germany and Paris. However, while in Paris in 1931 he became a professional photographer, married a French girl, and made the City of Light his home. The fall of Paris at the beginning of World War II found Halsman's wife, Yvonne, with their baby in New York, and Philippe with one million Parisians on the roads of France.

Philippe Halsman / Albert Einstein.

Through the intervention of Albert Einstein, an emergency visa was granted, and in November 1940, Halsman arrived in New York with a small suitcase in one hand and a box containing a large twin-lens reflex of his own design in the other.

The Halsmans embarked on very difficult times: they had almost no money, could barely speak English, and knew no one in New York. But Halsman steadily made his way as a free lance photographer and in 23 months he had his first *Life* cover. Nine years later he was the first photographer to reach a total of 50 *Life* covers, and today he is still the champion with 93 to his credit.

Halsman has had a widely varied and exciting career. In the winter of 1960 he and his wife spent two months and two days in Soviet Russia where Halsman was given permission to photograph a number of outstanding Russian personalities. Sixteen of these photographs were published in *Life* under the title, "The Russian Elite." The story was a major journalistic *coup,* a feat compared by one long-time Moscow resident with that of photographing "gun-shy tropical fauna in their native habitat."

Fifty of these same photographs have subsequently been reproduced as Dye Transfer prints by the Color Corporation of America and have been shown in Pittsburgh at the Gallery of Fine Arts of the Carnegie Institute. Halsman hopes to move the show to the Soviet Union "so that the masses may get a good look at the elite they themselves scarcely know."

An earlier *Life* assignment came in 1956 when Halsman traveled extensively to search out and photograph the most beautiful women in the world. In 1962 he made a second world tour, for *Time* magazine, which published his color essay on the world's reigning beauties.

In addition to these activities, Halsman has published a number of books. These include: a picture book *The Frenchman* (1949); a fairy tale *Piccoli* (1952) which has since been translated into three languages; *Dali's Mustache* (1953) in collaboration with the surrealist artist Salvador Dali; *Philippe Halsman's Jumpbook* (1959) which features an assortment of famous people jumping before the camera; and in 1961, *Halsman on the Creation of Photographic Ideas.*

Philippe Halsman / Dali Atomicus.

Halsman's work is almost evenly divided into three parts: magazine stories, advertising pictures, and private portraits of men and children who can afford his fees. (Halsman himself cannot afford them and has, therefore, no portraits of his own family.) Although he continuously photographs women for magazines and advertising, he has for the past ten years refused to accept private commissions from female sitters. The reason given is that he believes women cannot avoid being prejudiced when judging their own likeness.

Halsman is a strong exponent of studio work where the basic elements that make up a photograph—lights, subject, background, angle, and arrangement—can be brought under strict control. He feels that photojournalism and related fields of photography are not truly creative since absolute control is not possible. This, of course, is a minority opinion, but it points out how methodically Halsman works to achieve his results; he does not rely on any successful accidents.

Halsman has also pointed out that it is not only technique which creates a successful portrait. In an article for *Popular Photography* (December 1958) he observes that it is the photographer's duty "to influence and stimulate the subject's expressions, and to capture them at moments of his own choice. Very often it is not the good photographer who makes the good portrait, but the good psychologist. In many sittings I have felt that what I said to the client was more important than what I did with my camera and my lights."

Again in the same article Halsman explains his approach: "In a portrait sitting, we have to try to capture the essence of a human being. When we think we have achieved it, we must be sure not to leave it diluted and lost in our picture. We have to show it with utmost clarity and force, and each technical step must contribute to this end. This is the meaning of the interrelation of technique and emotion. An uncut diamond has only a potential value. Only after it is cut and polished does it shine in the dark."

HANDS, HOW TO PHOTOGRAPH THEM

Norris Harkness
Photography Writer

[Hands may be photographed alone or made to play a major part in a figure pose. Here various techniques are analyzed and methods of working discussed.]

• *Also see: Model Posing for the Amateur; Models and Directing for the Professional.*

One immediate answer to the photographer's frequent question of what to do with all the equipment he has so carefully collected is, "Why not try hands?" They are all around him, they need fewer props than almost any other type of subject, and they make first-rank pictures for either camera exercise or exhibition work.

But the photography of hands is likely to lead the amateur into treacherous paths. He attempts poses that he hopes are artistic but which end up being nothing more than "arty." He may make a number of hand shots in familiar attitudes. If the palms are upward, those shots often receive names like "Supplication" or "Hunger." If the palms are turned away from their owner, the name may be "Horror" or "Fright." The illustration of such sentimental abstractions may be all right for the artist who sees things that way, but the results are never deeply satisfying.

HANDS AT WORK

From the Latin *manus,* meaning "hand" are derived "manufacturing," "manipulate," and the other active words which imply doing something. Why not stick to the feeling that most of us have about hands and make pictures of them actually at work? We shall be relieved of the need for the abstract title and of the necessity for compositions that are just compositions rather than storytelling, interesting pictures. At the same time, our posing problems become tremendously simplified.

With the "at work" picture, we have only to set the hands at their task and then select the moment for the exposure. Fortunately, hands do not freeze in self-consciousness as do faces when the photographer says "Hold that!" We can let the action continue until we have the

The beauty of a quiet, simple act is expressed in this picture. The dark background emphasizes the subject and the lighting helps to give just the right amount of detail. **(Photo: Minor White)**

Top: *Posed hand pictures are easily possible because hands do not freeze in self-consciousness, as facial expressions do. A more natural action was achieved here by using a fast exposure. Notice that a good deal of the area is kept to explain what is happening.*

Bottom: *The child's game of Cat's Cradle is the subject here. Note how gracefully and expressively the hands and fingers fit in with the abstract design of the string.* (Photo: Vernon L. Smith / Popular Photography)

effect we want, and then ask the subject to hold the pose until the exposure is made. Lighting and the other technical parts of the work can be done at leisure, and there is comparatively small chance of failure.

LIGHTING TECHNIQUE

The technique of lighting hand pictures is quite similar to that of portraiture. Usually two lights are enough, though some effects are best obtained with only one. In some cases, it may be found that an added spotlight or additional back-lighting will help.

With the standard two-light plan, the fill light should usually be near the camera and below the lens, while the modeling light is positioned to provide the desired play of light and shadow. The modeling light, as its name suggests, is the light that brings out the texture and form of the subject matter, while the fill light simply supplies the fundamental light which illuminates the shadows. It is good to begin with the regular 45-degree lighting with the weaker fill light placed at the camera and the modeling light approximately 45 degrees above and to one side of the subject.

The fill light may well be diffused, but the skin tones and tiny catchlights which make for skin quality are best held with a bare, unfrosted bulb in the modeling light. This light can be placed anywhere —its position is the main factor in successful pictures after the pose has been selected. If the light is behind the hands it will illuminate their edges; if it is nearer the line of the lens, the light will be flatter, will yield less depth, and minimize any three-dimensional effect. The 45-degree lighting is usually the most successful, with a straight sidelight-

Photographs of hands need not be serious studies. In this photo the mind is led to laughter and possibly to deeper considerations. Nikon F with Plus X exposed 1/125 of a second at f/2. (Photo: Lou Bernstein)

ing next in favor.

When working with a negative material, such as black-and-white or negative color film, always take your main meter reading from the shadow areas. This method assures the recording of details in the shadows. However, do not disregard the highlight areas which, if too bright, will be overexposed. Keep the lighting ratio within the confines of the film's brightness range by adjusting the lights' distance from the subject.

FLASH

Flash can also be utilized for taking photographs of hands and, as with floods, two bulbs work better than one. The flashbulb used as the modeling light should either be closer than the fill light, or the fill should be diffused and reduced in intensity by being covered with a white handkerchief.

To determine the positioning of the flashbulbs, it is best to first use floods in reflectors. Once the lighting arrangement has been established, replace the floods with flashbulbs and calculate the exposure by dividing the subject-to-modeling-light distance into the particular flashbulb's guide number.

PROPS

Simplicity of composition and in the use of props is of vital importance. Everything in the picture must fit the thought behind it, and no unrelated objects should be present in the scene. Seldom do pictures suffer from too few elements; but many contain more objects than are necessary to get the story across. If there is any doubt as to whether a certain prop is necessary, leave it out and let the observer concentrate on the more important things.

The most frequent criticism in hand shots is that rings and jewelry attract too much interest. It is always better to eliminate the more elaborate pieces. Plainer rings and bracelets will add to the realism and usually should be retained.

COMPOSITION

The cropping of hand pictures often raises problems. In one case the hands alone may be shown, with the print trimmed away until nothing else is left; in another case the wrists and even the elbows may be needed to give a meaningful composition. The texture of the skin and the importance of the arms in the explanation of what the hands are doing can dictate the cropping, as can the shadows.

The main factor is more likely to be the center of interest—the task the hands are accomplishing. A good method of determining the best composition is to make a print of more of the negative than you think will finally be used, and then mask off the edges until you have the most effective picture.

Don't fail to make use of shadows. Objects in natural lighting cast shadows, and the angle of light that best shows texture must put shadows in the picture. In some cases they are not important and can safely be cut by the edge of the print, but more often the picture is stronger if the whole shadow, or most of it, is made a definite part of the composition. Sometimes, too, a well-planned shadow can be used to suggest objects which do not actually show, but which add to the story by their implied presence.

The same principles apply to outdoor hand shots to those in which the hands tell the story while occupying only a comparatively small part of the picture area. The extended fingers carry the story which the remainder of the picture explains. When a picture is strong enough to need no title, little more can be asked of the photographer.

MOVING HANDS

Often the interesting subjects you have selected cannot be stopped in the performance of their task. The work they are doing or the action with which their movement is associated may demand that the stopping be done by the camera rather than by the hands themselves. Here the difficulty increases. The thinking that goes into the choice of the best pose is the same, but the photographer must be ready to make the shot when the perfect moment arrives, and his equipment

The hands of a homesteader's wife in Woodbury County, Iowa reveal a lifetime of toil and exposure in one of the famous F.S.A. photographs. **(Photo: Russell Lee)**

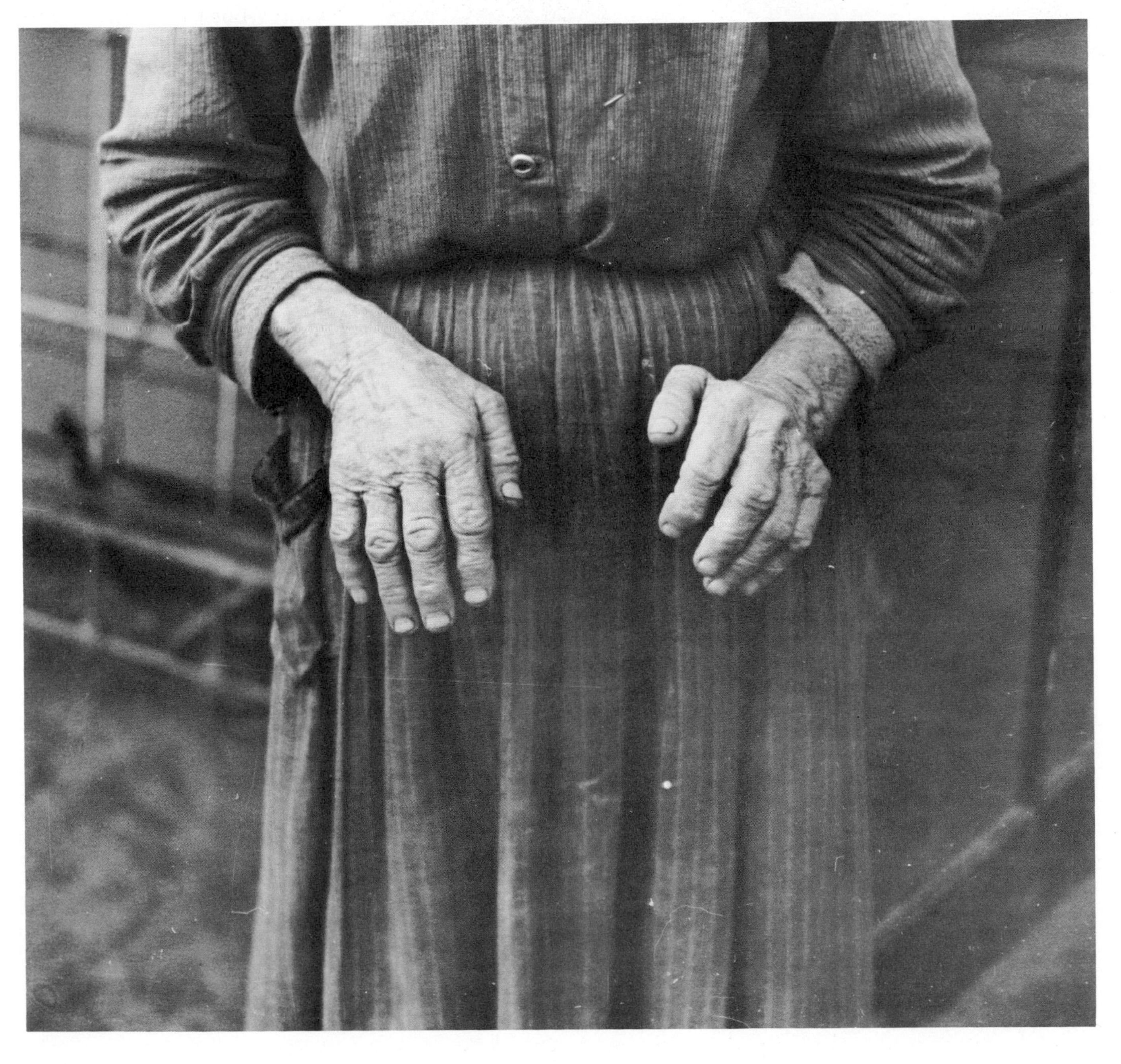

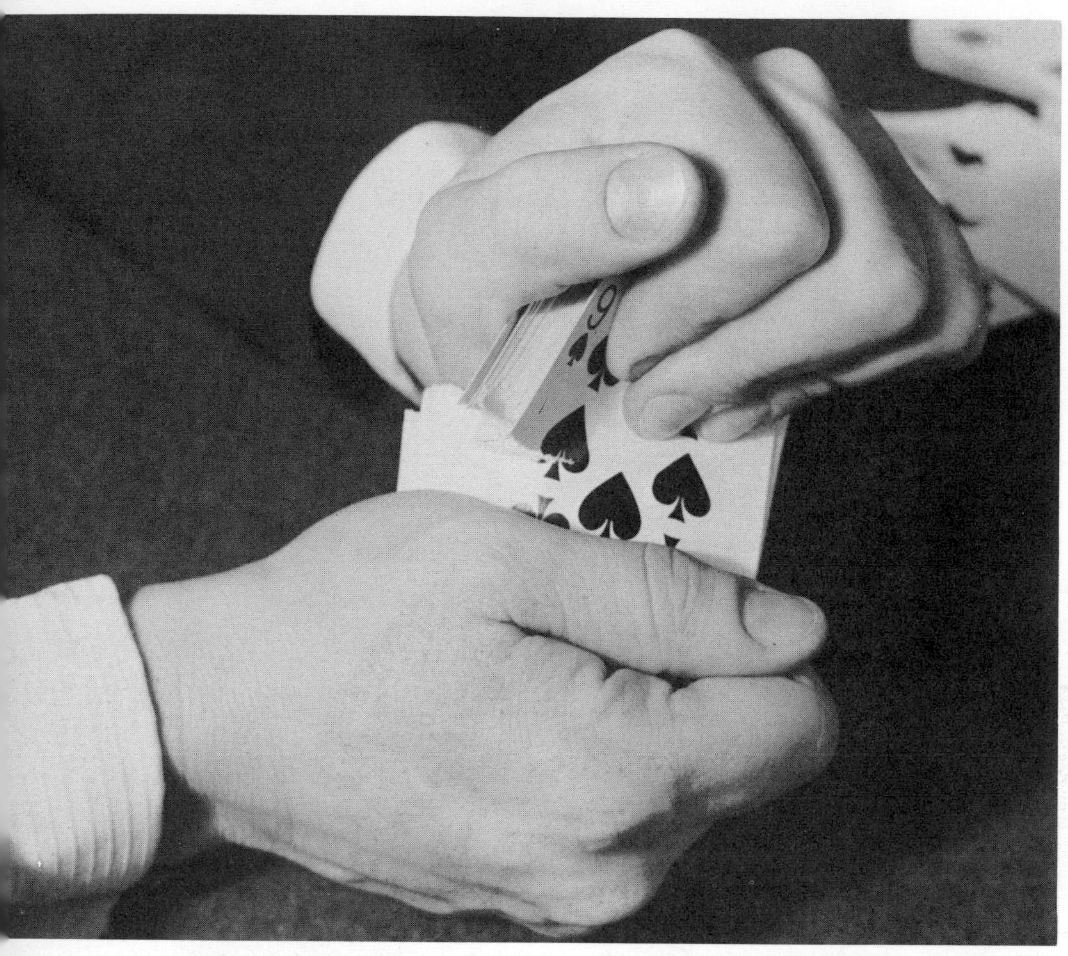

With modern fast film and the use of electronic flash or fast shutter speeds, hands may be photographed in action. This photograph was made on fast pan film with two reflector floods used close-up with the shutter stopped down to **f/22.** **(Photo: Norris Harkness)**

—both mental and photographic—must be fast enough to stop the motion satisfactorily.

This almost always calls for synchronized flash with shutter speeds of at least $^{1}/_{100}$ of a second, and much faster for close, rapidly moving subjects. The bulbs should be placed approximately as they would for longer exposures with floods, and the shadows must be sufficiently illuminated to keep them from creating empty, uninteresting blanks. One bulb near the lens and another in the 45-degree position will often work well, though putting the second or modeling light above and somewhat behind the subject leads to attractive results in many cases.

The vital element, however, is the releasing of the shutter at exactly the right instant. There is one most effective pose and position and, if that is missed, the shot cannot be as successful as one perfectly timed. Often the movement can be repeated several times for the photographer's study and selection of just when the best moment occurs. If that can be done, watch the entire action carefully and pick out two or three possibilities; then have the performer work in a given spot so that there is no trouble with focusing, and wait for the moment. A few rehearsals will add greatly to the chances of a good pictures. Keep in mind that an "almost right" picture is little better than just anyone at all, and that it is far easier to make a few more exposures the first time than to come back for a retake. Sheer luck may give you what you want the first time, but careful watching and preparation for what will happen almost always assures striking results.

ERICH HARTMANN

Biography

Born and educated in Germany, Erich Hartmann immigrated to the United States in 1938, working for four years in a textile mill. After three years' service in the U. S. Army in Europe during World War II, he began photography in 1946 with portraiture. Gradually entering magazine photography, he joined Magnum in 1951.

Hartman has done major editorial projects in industry for *Fortune* magazine and for such organizations as the Ford Motor Company, IBM, Bristol Aeroplane Company, The Pillsbury Company, and others. Other assignments have been published by *Redbook, Life, Newsweek, The Johns Hopkins Magazine, Queen, twen,* and many others.

Hartmann has had a one-man show at the Museum of the City of New York ("Brooklyn Bridge"), and his story, "Our Daily Bread," is now traveling in the United States under the sponsorship of The Pillsbury Company. His work is also represented in the collection of the Museum of Modern Art and in "The World of Magnum" exhibition.

Erich Hartmann describes his aims and his work, as follows:

"What brought me to photography is the opportunity and the obligation to use resources derived as much from outside the photograpic realm as from within it. Photography is an individual—often a solitary—endeavor and this pleases me, especially in a time when work in increasingly many fields is done by groups rather than by individuals.

"My professional and personal aims are virtually the same: I want to experience and to communicate with photographs what I find moving and deserving of comment in the world and in the time in which I find myself. I have several interests not connected with photography and they have contributed strongly to the kind of photographic work I do and to my photographic expression.

"We are constantly being bom-

Erich Hartmann / Magnum.

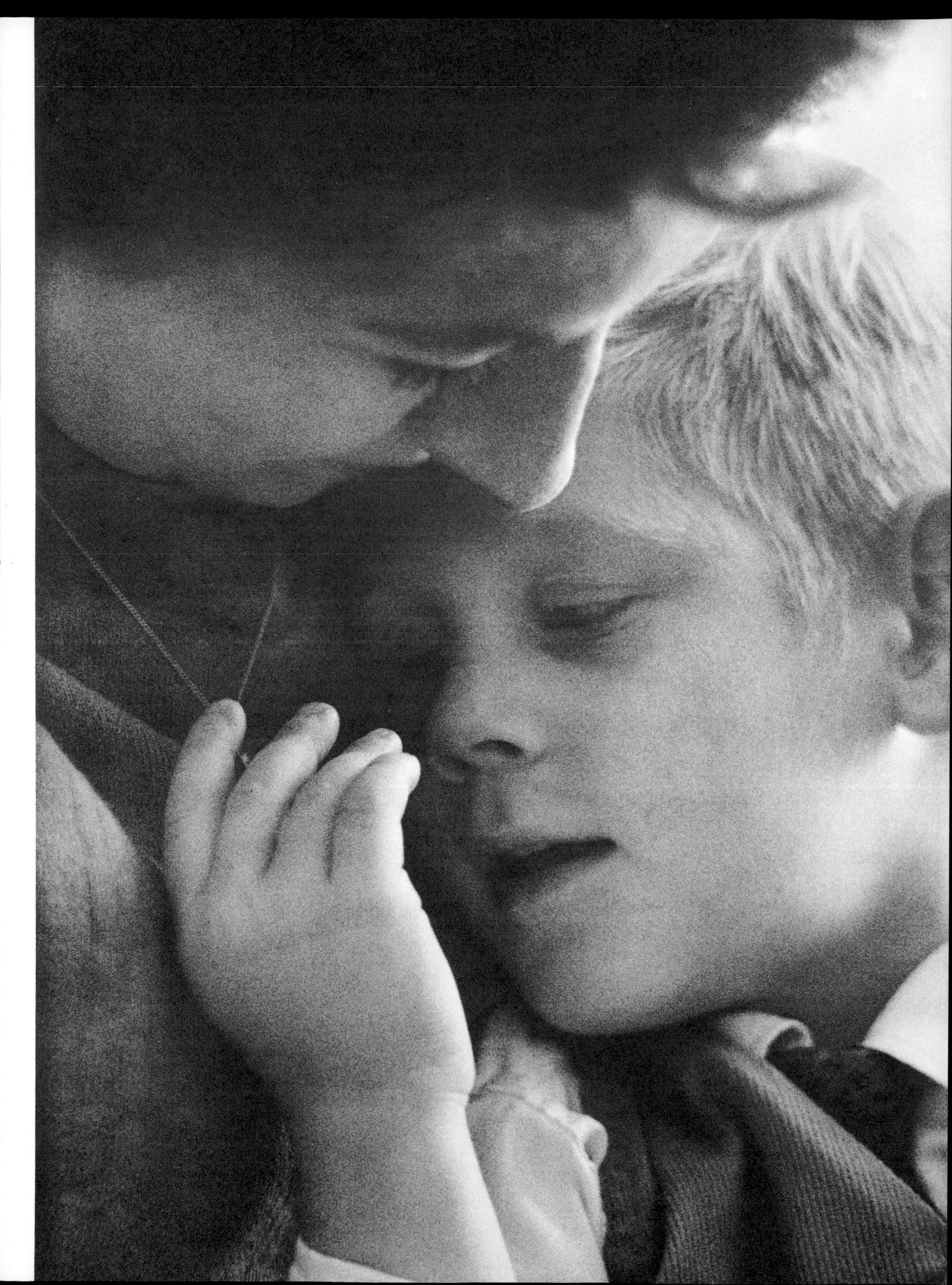

barded by every available form of communication and I have no illusions that my work will be able to contribute significantly to change men or events *en masse,* in a direction which I would consider beneficial. Based on this belief and based equally on the subject matter which interests me as a photographer—not necessarily the dramatic or the currently interesting—I cannot claim the mass audience for my work which is the objective of most photographers. On the other hand, I believe implicitly that the eloquent communication of a deeply felt experience, regardless of subject matter, will reach an audience of importance and will thus fulfill the aim of any photographer not only to produce pictures, but to have them seen towards a desired effect.

"A large portion of my work is concerned with people because people are the most inventive and newsmaking part of our lives. But very often I am as much attracted to the evidence of their presence and efforts—whether good or evil—as I am to the people themselves. Often also I work with "things"—with scientific or artistic or technical creations capable of revealing the nature and accomplishments of people—and sometimes I am happiest to work with the utmost concentration in a totally unpopulated place—a forest or a few rocks by the sea—where the encounter between inanimate object and my perception can be utterly free and direct and where I can work the greatest liberty of personal expression of which I am capable.

"Photography continues to be increasingly exciting and worthwhile as a way of life for me because of its rigorous demands for discipline, for courage, and for the effort which it invites and demands to understand and to speak persuasively in the visual language. My rewards have already been great and lasting: I have been able to witness wonderful and frightening people and events at close range; I have traveled wide and often, mostly alone but sometimes in the company of people whom I love and admire; best of all, being a photographer has trained my eyes and my spirit towards an awareness of my world and what it contains which makes my life full and rich."

Married and the father of two children, Erich Hartmann presently lives in New York City.

Erich Hartmann / Magnum.

Erich Hartmann / Magnum.

SIR JOHN F. W. HERSCHEL

Beaumont Newhall
Director, George Eastman House, Rochester, New York; Author of "The History of Photography," "The Daguerreotype in America"

[The work of Sir John Herschel was important in early photography. His research in the use of hypo, his development of the cyanotype, and other findings are discussed by a recognized photographic historian.]

• *Also see: History of Photography.*

The astronomical researches of Sir John F. W. Herschel (1792-1871) have so overshadowed his contributions to other fields that he has been almost forgotten as the inventor of a photographic process which preceded the publication of the independent processes of Louis Jacques Mandé Daguerre and William Henry Fox Talbot. He proposed the words *photography, negative,* and *positive,* invented several types of printing papers, and laid the basis of photochemistry (which he named "the newly created science of actinochemistry") by his observations on the reaction of light-sensitive material to invisible as well as visible radiation.

Herschel first heard of "Daguerre's concealed photographic process" on January 22, 1839, after his return to England from a four-year stay at the Cape of Good Hope where he had studied the stars of the Southern Hemisphere. He at once began experimenting in the hope of duplicating Daguerre's re-

The earliest extant photograph on glass, by Sir J.F.W. Herschel, showing the scaffolding erected for dismantling his father's telescope at Slough. Taken September 9, 1839. Copy of print made by Herschel by projection from the original negative, 3½-inch circle. Science Museum, London.

sults. Nine days later Fox Talbot published his "photogenic drawing" process, specifying a strong solution of table salt for the fixing bath. Herschel suggested that a solution of the salt $NA_2S_2O_3$, which he first described in 1819 as hyposulfite of soda (hence "hypo"—the subsequent discovery of another group of sulfur compounds made it necessary to change the nomenclature to sodium thiosulfate), was more appropriate for this purpose, noting that it has the property of dissolving silver chloride "almost as readily as sugar in water."

In a letter dated February 28, 1839, he gave Talbot permission to announce to the French Academy of Sciences the use of hypo as a fixing bath, enclosing several experimental prints with full notes on the method used to fix them. The announcement was made by Talbot on March 1. In the light of this clear-cut evidence of Herschel's priority in the use of hypo, it seems strange that Talbot should have claimed it as an original invention in the calotype patent he filed in 1841.

PUBLISHED FINDINGS

Herschel's first publication of his photographic work was not made until March 14, 1839 when he read a paper to the Royal Society of London, and exhibited to them twenty three specimens which the secretary of the Society described as consisting of "...a sketch of his telescope at Slough, fixed from its image in a lens, and the rest copies of engravings and drawings, some reverse, or first transfers; and others second, or reversed pictures." He noted that sensitive paper reacted in varying degree to the different colors of the spectrum.

At about this time, Herschel visited the French scientist Arago, who had backed Daguerre and was responsible for the government's purchase of the daguerreotype process. There he saw Daguerre's results for the first time. He is reported to have said to Arago: "In comparision with these daguerreotype masterpieces, Mr. Talbot produces nothing but mist. There is as much difference between the two products as between the moon and the sun." He concluded that even Talbot would have had to agree with him.

A second publication dated February 20, 1840 recapitulates the 1839 paper. In it he proposed the words *negative* and *positive* for the "first transfer" and "second transfer" of his previous article. He described the following experiment using a glass plate as a support for the sensitive salt (the first indication of what later became common practice). A weak solution of silver chloride was poured over a plate placed horizontally in a glass vessel. After it had stood for some time, the liquid was carefully decanted and syphoned away, leaving a thin film on the glass surface. This was further sensitized by a bath in silver nitrate. He noted that negatives made on these plates appeared positive when laid on a dark ground, and thus pointed the way to the ambrotype.

But perhaps the most important part of this paper dealt with the reaction of light-sensitive material to various colors. One curious phenomenon has since been named the Herschel effect: if a fully exposed print-out paper is further exposed to red light, before fixing, the image will *fade* rather than darken and eventually disappear, leaving blank paper.

In 1842 he described light-sensitive paper which employed the salts of iron. One of these, which he called the cyanotype, has survived as blueprint paper. It is surely the simplest photographic process; paper is sensitized by washing with solutions of ferric ammonium citrate and potassium ferricyanide, respectively. After exposure, the yellow-green image becomes a permanent deep-blue one simply by immersing the paper in cold water. The chrysotype was somewhat similar. Paper washed with the ferric-ammonium-citrate solution was exposed and the weak image resulting was brought up to a rich brown onc by washing with a solution of gold chloride, rendered neutral with sodium carbonate. It was fixed in alternate baths of weak sulfuric acid and hydrobromate of potash.

For these papers on photography Herschel received the coveted medal of the Royal Society. It was the third which the Society had bestowed on him.

A man of science, Herschel was apparently more interested in the theory of the photographic process than in its practical application. Yet he was not insensitive to its pictorial qualities. Sir William Newton read a paper on pictorial photography to the Photographic Society in 1853, in which he complained about the great discrepancy then existing between the brightness reaction of the human eye, and that of the photographic negative, to colors. Herschel recommended the liberal use of bromine to increase the red sensitivity, and a yellow filter to remove many of the blue rays to which silver salts are overly sensitive. This suggestion was probably impractical, but in theory he anticipated the discovery by Vogel in 1873 of orthochromatic emulsions.

Herschel also proposed a system of motion-picture photography in 1860: "I take for granted nothing more than... the possibility of taking a photograph, as it were, by a snapshot—of securing a picture in a tenth of a second of time; and... that a mechanism is possible...by which a prepared plate may be presented, focused, impressed, displaced, numbered, secured in the dark, and replaced by another within two or three tenths of a second."

Herschel died in 1871, the very year of the invention of the gelatin dry plate which made his dream of "snapshots" a reality.

□

KEN HEYMAN

Biography

Few young photographers can be said to show both promise and fulfillment to the extent that Ken Heyman does. He has the promise of a brilliant career (it began about 1957), and at the same time he has already attracted a following, not only among editors and art directors but among other photographers—including the half generation just now grasping the bottom of the ladder.

Pervading all of Heyman's work is a deeply felt concern for the human condition. His pictures are nearly always of people: people in misery or contentment, in doubt or in joy. Along with this dedication to his human subjects is a sure eye for design and form; usually his picture's natural impact is strengthened by an angle, curve, or other graphic device—not imposed or intrusive, but perfectly natural.

Ken Heyman was born in New York City in 1930. His academic beginnings at Columbia University would have destined him to become a lawyer, but he lacked the necessary enthusiasm, and took the opportunity to leave school for the Army. After military service, he returned to Columbia, this time to concentrate on the humanistic studies that interested him most: sociology and anthropology. Under the tutelage of the distinguished writer-teacher Margaret Mead, he discovered that photography could help him learn about people, and then communicate what he learned.

A close friendship was formed between Heyman and Dr. Mead,

Ken Heyman.

and developed into a working collaboration which still continues. They worked together in Bali and in Mexico, and have planned several more joint projects.

Heyman's first publication of pictures was in 1956, in *Photography Annual* and then in *Vogue*. He had his first one-man show the same year at the Limelight Gallery, and another two years later in the same place. He worked for *Life* briefly in 1957. In 1958 he became the New York photographer for the Rapho-Guillumette agency. There followed a rapid rise in his status, accompanied by a broadening of his human horizons. His pictures have appeared in most major U. S. magazines, and in many abroad.

In 1962, he was sent to Latin America by the United States Information Agency to photograph the planning of the Alliance for Progress. In 1963 Heyman participated in a five-man show at the Museum of Modern Art.

His first book, *Willie,* published in 1963, is an endearing and moving look at the world of a four-year-old city boy, within the compass of his own home block. Two other books are being readied for publication by the end of 1964, and still other book projects are in preparation. Heyman, like many another photographer today, finds that books reach a select and attentive audience.

Ken Heyman places particular importance on the relationship between photographer and subject, refusing to permit the camera to come between them. Likewise, popular photographic values come in for careful scrutiny. He has written, "Seeing surface values such as height, shape, and texture is not so important as seeing the meaning and the content. Without the latter, you do not have a picture."

His concern with people is emphasized in a further quotation: "If you think about your subject only as a finished photograph, you can preconceive the picture and then cram your subject into it. But if photography is a matter of seeing and of genuine human involvement, then you must allow the subject to be something more than a prop. This is a two-sided thing. If one uses photography as a creative outlet, he may ignore the important fact that in the photography of people he should be taking pictures of other people's self-expression."

Heyman makes clear his feeling about the intrusion of cameras and equipment (in a statement which, like the preceding, was written for *Popular Photography*): "What really happens when a good photographer starts shooting? He is in such control of his camera and equipment that they become invisible in dealing with the subject. The correct lenses, cameras, and related gear should be automatically selected—the photographer should never have to stop and think about them as he deals with the subject. They should not be a handicap in performing his job or

Ken Heyman.

Ken Heyman.

his art. Unfortunately, many photographers become obsessed with cameras and gadgets so that they can't do the best job that is possible."

One notices generally that in a Heyman picture there is no direct relationship between camera and subject; the photographer has kept himself out of the situation. As Heyman puts it, "When I shoot, I lose myself—I don't exist. The subject exists. The camera does not. The lighting and the mechanics of shooting are automatic. I may move closer. I like to get as close to a subject as I can. If I make a statement, I have to make it so that people can see what I'm trying to say. Distance breeds obscurity."

Ken Heyman lives in a brownstone house in midtown New York City. He is married and has two children; his brother-in-law is the photographer Bert Stern.

— H.M.J. Kinzer

HIGH-SPEED PHOTOGRAPHY

JOHN H. WADDELL, Fellow, Royal Photographic Society
Executive Adviser, Douglas Aircraft Co., Santa Monica, California

[Photography at speeds ranging from a few thousand to several million pictures per second is a comparatively recent development. In this article the various techniques of high-speed work are explained with special attention given to light sources, shutters, optical equipment, and the various special cameras involved.]

• *Also see: Ballistic Photography; Electronic-Flash Lighting and Exposure.*

HIGH-SPEED PHOTOGRAPHY IS GENERally understood to mean the making of pictures at speeds faster than the usual operating range of conventional shutters. High-speed photographs may be still pictures made at exposures of less than $^1/_{1000}$ of a second, multiple-image still pictures, motion pictures made at a rate of more than 128 frames per second, streak pictures, or short-exposure sequence pictures made at a high repetitive rate.

Perhaps the simplest "high-speed" system to understand is the adaptation of a simple camera for making sequential stills—that is, a sequence of images of various stages of one action photographed on a single piece of film. With the camera on a firm support, a fixed slotted disk is placed in front of the lens. A rotating slotted disk, driven by a synchronous motor, is placed in front of the fixed disk. Light reaches the film only when the two slots are lined up. Picture frequency is governed by the revolutions per second of the slotted disk. For example, if there are 20 equal slots in the disk, and it rotates at 10 rps, the picture-taking frequency is 200 per second.

Tungsten spots or floods can be used to illuminate the subject, and a dark background—black velvet is best—to prevent the multiple image from being obliterated, since the exposure of the background will be the sum of the exposures of the individual pictures.

The picture-making procedure is simple: the lights are turned on, the disk motor is started, the shutter is opened to B, the subject action takes place, and the shutter is closed.

In a variation of this system, an ordinary unmodified camera is used with the shutter open to B, while the light is interrupted. The most common light source for this technique is repetitive electronic flash; continuous light sources can be used if they are fitted with a blinker or "light chopper." Advertising and feature photographs are often made by this method, and it has also been used in studies of projectiles in flight and in other experiments in motion analysis.

SHUTTERS

The mechanical shutter, whether of the leaf or focal-plane type, is a relatively cumbersome device. To date it has been limited in reliable operation to a top speed of about $^1/_{2000}$ of a second. Even at this unspectacular speed there is likely to be uneven operation because of the inertia and momentum of the moving metal parts. In order to overcome this, inertia-free shutters of two principal types, magneto-optic and electro-optic, have been developed. These depend for their light-stopping effect upon the ability of polarizing filters to stop the passage of polarized light. There are no moving parts in the shutter itself. Basic to the operation of the magneto-optic shutter is the Faraday Effect, which can be described briefly as the rotation of direction of plane-polarized light when passed through a double-refractive substance in a magnetic field.

A strong electrical field will also "excite" a substance possessing properties of double refraction, so that polarized light can be transmitted or stopped by an electrical pulse as well as a magnetic field. This is the Kerr Effect, and the electro-optic shutter is generally called a Kerr cell.

The Kerr shutter is faster than the magneto-optic shutter, due to the absence of magnetic "resistance" (hysteresis). The magneto-optic shutter is good only to about 10^{-6} of a second, while the Kerr cell can be used to 10^{-8} of a second.

Both of these shutters employ

This is the first photographic motion analysis, made in 1877 by Eadweard Muybridge in California.

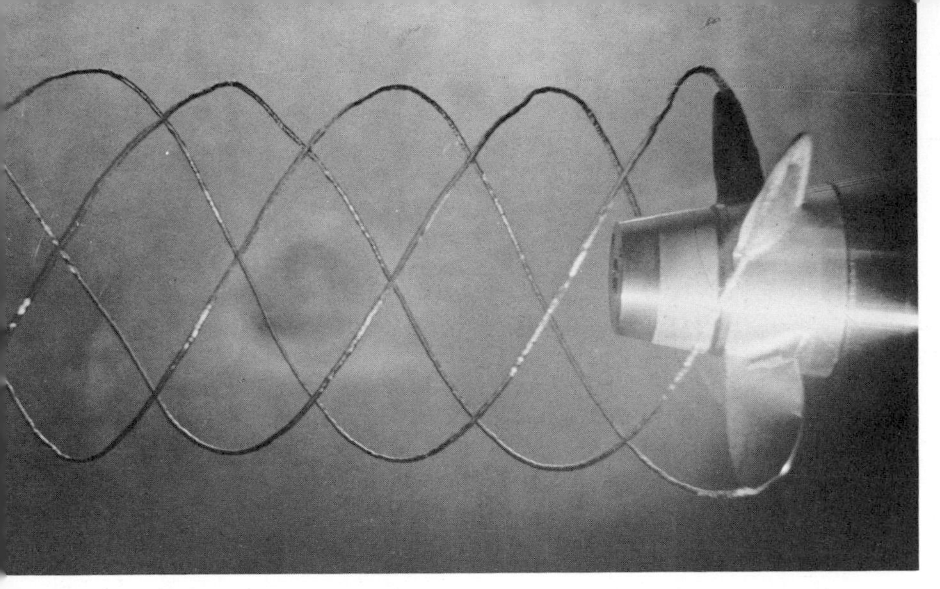

Tip vortex cavitation photographed by electronic flash. Propeller speed, 2070 rpm. (Photo: Naval Ordnance Laboratory)

polarizing filters, one in front of and one behind the cell. Their planes of polarization are crossed. In the magneto-optic shutter the cell is generally of flint glass or quartz; purified nitrobenzine is the most common double-refractive substance used in the Kerr cell, though other liquids possessing this property have been used.

Both of these shutters require extremely high-voltage circuits, so the power required to operate them to a certain extent limits their size. Moreover, the polarizing filters employed usually reduce light transmission to about 25 percent of that entering the optical system. Due to these practical considerations the maximum effective aperture available when using either of these systems is about *f*/16.

LIGHT SOURCES

High-speed still pictures are usually made by using a light source which is activated for less than a millisecond ($^1/_{1000}$ of a second).

The classic light source is the electric spark, which has been used since the beginning of artificial-light high-speed experiments made in England more than 100 years ago. Today, while the spark itself still performs varied and useful work, the electrical-discharge principle which made it possible has been further refined to create two new sources: the electronic flash and the wink light.

A capacitor, an induction coil, a gap or filament, and a switch are the primary components of the circuit. In practice a transformer and rectifier are used to furnish the direct current necessary to charge the capacitor. The lower the voltage and the lower the capacity of the condenser the faster the reaction of discharge, and the less light.

When used as high-speed light sources, the spark gap, or its deviations, such as the guided or Liebessart spark gap, have their electrodes so positioned that there is no simple voltage discharge of the capacitor. The electronic flashlamp, too, is so designed that it will not fire with only capacitor voltage across the electrodes at its rated voltage. Firing is controlled by a third electrode inserted very near the spark gap or tube electrodes, and connected to the induction coil. The second lead (grounded side) of the induction coil is connected to the ground side of either the gap or the charging capacitor. When the switch, which may be in either the primary or secondary circuit of the induction coil, is closed, the very high voltage of the coil ionizes the gas between the electrodes, and only then is the capacitor instantly discharged between them.

Any one of a number of devices may be used as the firing switch: a manual normally open switch, a relay, a hydrogen thyratron tube, or other types.

WINK LIGHT

Simpler circuitry activates the wink light, which is a low-voltage tungsten-filament bulb momentarily overloaded by the discharge of a capacitor. Only the closure of a switch is required for firing. Capacity and firing voltage are comparatively low, yet the light output from even a small aircraft panel light (Type 324) is amazingly bright. Since little information is available from lamp manufacturers on this application, it is necessary for the user to acquire the data on the lamp type and its operating characteristics through experimentation.

Light sources of these types are used for both reflected- and transmitted-light subjects The spark, because of its short duration (submicrosecond, or under $^1/_{1,000,000}$ of a second) is used primarily for ballistic and wind-tunnel studies. It can "stop" a bullet in flight: a 3000 feet-per-second projectile will travel only .003 inches during a $^1/_{10}$ microsecond exposure time, and a sharp picture will result.

SILHOUETTES

The index of refraction of air will vary with pressure and temperature changes. Therefore if a shadowgraph or Schlieren system is used, in which the subject is between the light source and the camera, the shock waves become visible. This phenomenon is utilized in wind-tunnel studies.

Experimental electronic flashlamps

Schlieren pictures (spark source) with submicrosecond of projectiles in flight. (Photo: Schardin)

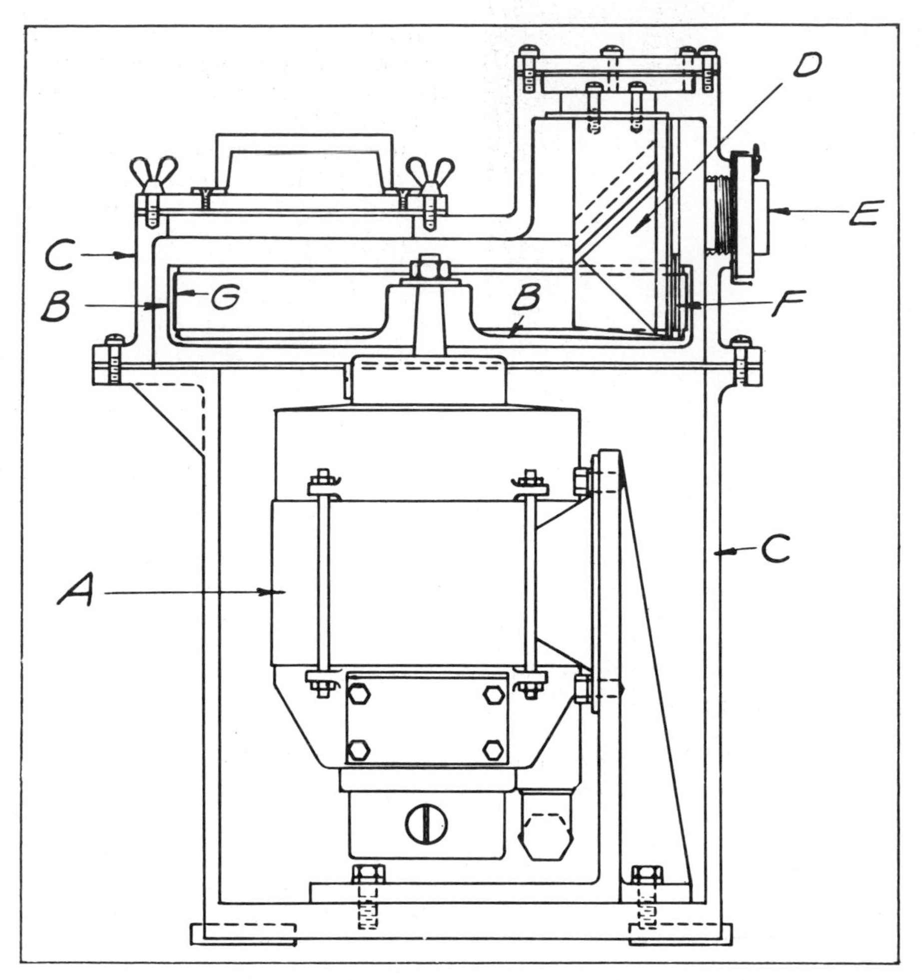

Sectional drawing of rotating-drum camera. A, 180-cycle a-c synchronous motor; B, aluminum-alloy drum; C, bronze housing; D, glass prism; E, photographic lens; F, slit and aperture; G, recessed groove for film. (Hercules Powder Company)

and circuits have been designed which have worked in the sub-microsecond range, but for usual applications the exposure times range from 10 to 300 microseconds. The electronic flash has been used to photograph projectiles in flight, the moving wings of insects and hummingbirds, and even cities at night from high-speed reconnaissance aircraft. This light source has a very high infrared output, which is opening up many new fields of application.

MOTION PICTURES

The basic work of securing pictures at very high taking rates preceded the popular motion pictures developed by Edison and the Lumière brothers.

In these 19th-century experiments film was placed on a drum and rotation speed set at a very high rate. A rotating (interrupted) spark gap, similar to those used in radio-telegraph transmitters, was used for a light source. After the drum was started and brought up to speed, the spark circuit was set off, the shutter opened, and the subject photographed. Picture-taking rates of up to 200,000 per second were achieved by this method. Later the spark was synchronized to the film by using a commutator on the drum.

When perforated motion-picture film came into being, these "still" pictures were optically printed and shown as a motion picture. This basic work, used in a film released by Pathé of France in 1915, provided the foundation of later work by Edgerton in which the electronic flash was utilized with continuously moving film to produce 35 mm motion pictures (see *Harold Edgerton*).

A commutator on the sprocket triggered the electronic flash. The precision of the commutator was a limiting factor, so that these negatives had to be optically printed to secure good registration for projection. When the film went through the camera at 100 feet per second, the picture-taking rates shown in Table 1 could be obtained.

At these speeds it was necessary to reduce the flash time to one microsecond in order to reduce smearing of the image to .001 inch. To get frequencies of 3000 and above, multiple-flash units were used, the lights being fired in sequence. The capacitors could not be charged fast enough, and enough heat was generated to melt a glass electronic-flash tube. Use of a quartz tube minimized the fusion problem.

Pictures of cavitation studies have been made at rates up to 20,000 per second at California Institute of Technology by the moving-film and multiple-electronic-flash method. Prince and Rankin of the General Electric Company mounted film on the inside of a drum, employed a pinhole instead of a lens as a photographic objective, and used a similar light source. The pinhole pattern on the drum was laid out so that 120,000 pictures per second could be obtained.

OPTICAL-COMPENSATION EQUIPMENT

To prevent streaking in electronic-flash image formation, cameras employing optical compensation are employed. The three basic image-compensation methods are: the rotating-lens, the rotating-mirror, and the rotating-prism cameras. Two of these methods depend on synchronizing the velocity of a moving image and a moving film; in the third a rotating mirror is used to make discrete pictures on a stationary film.

The rotating-lens camera uses a continuously moving film. When a lens is moved in the same direction as the film, the image will also travel in the same direction. A complete lens may be used, or the lens may be divided into two parts—a fixed front element and a series of rear elements mounted on a rotating disk.

When the full lens is used, a series of them are mounted on the

Table 1

Film size	*Picture height*	*Pictures per foot*	*Pictures/sec at 100 ft/sec*	*Image smear in 10 microsec. per flash*
35 mm	.75 inch	16	1600	.012 inch
16 mm	.30 inch	40	4000	.012 inch
8 mm	.15 inch	80	8000	.012 inch

rotating disk, with a fixed aperture between the rear element and the film plane to control the picture size and the angle of exposure. A large number of lenses are used; the Jenkins camera employed 20. There is a serious optical problem in obtaining lenses matched for focal length. If the lenses are not matched, each picture will have a different magnification, and when the picture is projected it will seem to be out of focus, due to the constant change in image size. The necessity for matched lenses makes the cost of such rotating-lens cameras very high.

The rotating-mirror camera uses a multifaced mirror between the lens and the film plane. When using moving film, the "double-angle" effect occurs, so that the film must travel at twice the rate of the rotational speed of the mirror. Furthermore, a right-angle optical path is required between the lens and the film plane to prevent the image from coming back on itself.

The stationary film-rotating mirror system is being extensively used for picture-taking rates up to 4,000,000 per second. The image is brought in with a long focal-length objective to the rotating mirror through a diamond-shaped aperture (this eliminates image smear), then through a re-imaging lens to the film plane. The stationary drum is slightly less than 90 degrees in length; the film is on the inside of the drum. Cameras of this type are in commercial production and are used for very high-speed events, such as shock tube, high-velocity wind-tunnel, and detonation and plasma-jet studies.

ROTATING-PRISM CAMERAS

The last of the optical-compensation cameras are of the rotating-prism class. These cameras are used in the laboratory and field for analysis of practically any motion which occurs too fast for the eye to see, whether it be a chemical, mechanical, electrical, or astronomical phenomenon. Their weight has been reduced to the point where an eight-pound camera will make 12,000 pictures per second on a 100-foot roll of 16 mm film.

The rotating-prism camera was first used in the United States, but various types are currently being made in the USSR, East and West Germany, Japan, and Sweden. It has become the "work horse" of photographic motion analysis because of its ease of use, reliability, and portability.

In the rotating-prism camera, a parallel-faced prism is interposed between the lens and the film plane. Any even number of faces may be used; prism design is contingent on the index of refraction of the glass,

Diagrams of methods of photographing explosives. (Hercules Powder Company)

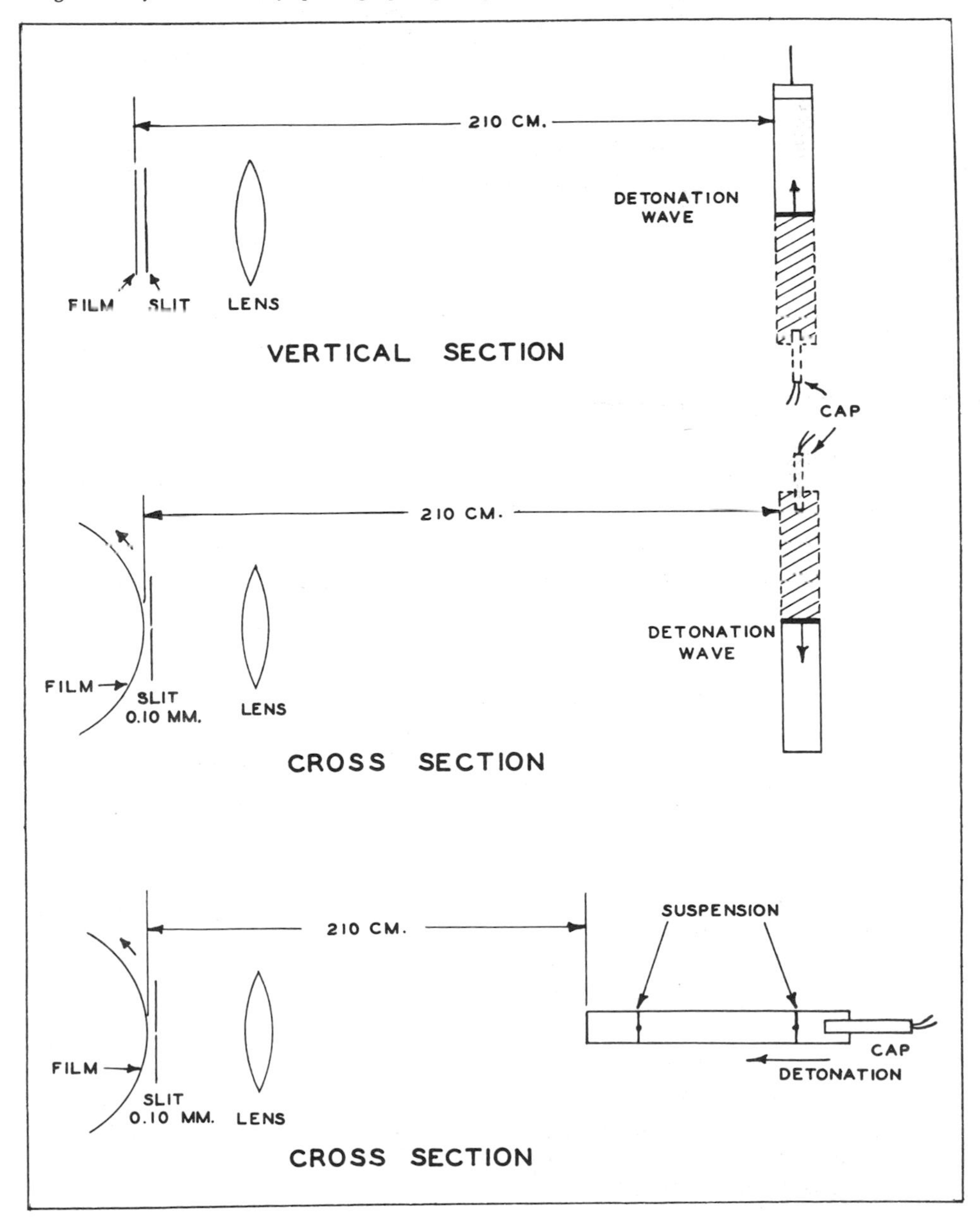

Rotating mirror re-imaging fixed-film camera capable of a picture-taking rate of more than one million pictures per second. (Photo: Beckman & Whitley)

the number of faces required in the work, the picture height, and the rotational angle on the one side of the optical axis through which the picture is exposed. At the film plane can be either the fan of a sprocket or a gate. The prism is coupled by a gear train to the sprocket to maintain registration of the frame line to the perforations of the film.

Earlier cameras employed two electric motors, or one electric motor with a belt drive to the sprocket. Later, synchronous or governor-controlled motors were used on the sprocket itself, making more accurate constant-speed cameras. The latest cameras have a single motor on the take-up, with the film itself acting as a belt to drive the sprocket. Timing lights (glow lamps) are used on the side of the film to record time and picture-taking rate.

Time resolution can be improved by adding a pick-up (magnetic or electrical) on the sprocket and using the pulse to fire an electronic flash-lamp. Picture-taking rates up to 6000 per second can be obtained with a 1½ microsecond exposure. Exceedingly sharp pictures are obtained, since the lamp is fired with the faces of the prism perpendicular to the optical axis and with the prism's rotation eliminating picture smear. Rotating-prism cameras have the picture formats and maximum speeds outlined in Table 2.

STREAK CAMERAS

Three basic types of streak cameras are currently in use: the continuously-moving-film camera, the rotating-drum camera, and the fixed-drum camera.

Continuously-moving-film camera. In the continuously-moving-film camera, the film is moved past a slit at the film plane which faces the event being photographed. In its simplest form, this camera is a rotating-prism camera with the prism shaft removed and compensation made for the resulting longer back focus of the system. By adding a half diopter lens to the ordinary objective, correction is usually obtained. Film velocities up to 300 feet per second can be obtained.

Operating on the same principle that makes possible the panoramic-view camera and the Sonne continuous-aerial-mapping camera (the "similar-triangle" principle) single pictures of subjects moving at very high speeds can be obtained.

For example, in photographing a projectile moving at 3000 feet per second with a camera whose film moves at 100 feet per second, the camera is placed at a distance from the subject which result in a 30× optical reduction at the film plane. The camera is placed so that the direction of film movement will be opposite to the direction of subject movement. Correction of the speed distortion is achieved by knowing certain lengthwise dimensions of the subject and making appropriate allowances.

The continuously-moving-film camera has been called a "ballistic-synchro camera." It is widely used in the study of flame, detonation, and electrical arcing, as well as for oscillograph-trace recording.

When used as a continuous oscillographic recorder, frequencies up to four megacycles can be recorded. Only the ± "x" axis is used on the scope tube. A total amplitude of about one inch on the scope tube reduces the writing speed for good images.

Rotating-drum camera. In the rotating-drum camera, the film is mounted on the inside of a drum which is rotated at high speed. Centrifugal force holds the film in place; if it were mounted on the outside of the drum it would have a tendency to fly off.

The lens, with a capping shutter, is on the axis of the drum's rotation. A 45-degree mirror, also centered on the axis, places the image on the inside sensitized surface of the film. This camera also uses a slit at the film plane. Time markings can be placed on the film with either a superimposed oscillator output on a cathode ray oscilloscope or with a timing light (glow lamp or cold cathode lamp). There are commercial versions of this type available. They are used extensively for flame and plasma-jet studies.

Fixed-drum camera. In the last major class of cameras, the film is fixed on a stationary drum and the image is swept over the film. As in the previous set-up, the film is on the inside of the drum. The lens is on the center of the drum, and the rotating mirror (45-degree) reflects the bundle of rays to the film. In one revolution of the mirror, the picture axis will rotate 360 degrees. In order to overcome this, a dove prism (usually a double dove for balance) is placed between the lens and the mirror. It is rotated at half the speed of the mirror, since complete rotation of the image occurs every 180 degrees.

The drums are quite large, so that the image sweep will be as high as possible. The capping shutter is electronically controlled to prevent superimposition of the image. Image sweeps of up to one cm per microsecond are possible with these cameras.

SPECIAL-USE CAMERAS

A number of high-speed cameras, such as the Prince and Rankin pinhole camera previously mentioned, have been designed for specific uses.

Four others which deserve note are the McEachron camera for studying lighting, the Suttanoff camera for detonation studies, the Tuttle and Newcomb grid camera, the Courtney-Pratt lenticular-grid camera, and the Russian 32,000,000-picture-per-second camera. The last three are image "scanning."

The history of image-scanning cameras began with Ives at Bell

Table 2

Pictures per second

	HIGHEST RATE NOW	HIGHEST POSSIBLE (ANTICIPATED)
8 mm or ½-height 16 mm	24,000	120,000
16 mm	12,000	60,000
35 mm (half frame)	6,000	—
35 mm	3,000	5,000
70 mm (grandeur size)	—	2,500
70 mm (2¼ × 2¼)	600	1,250

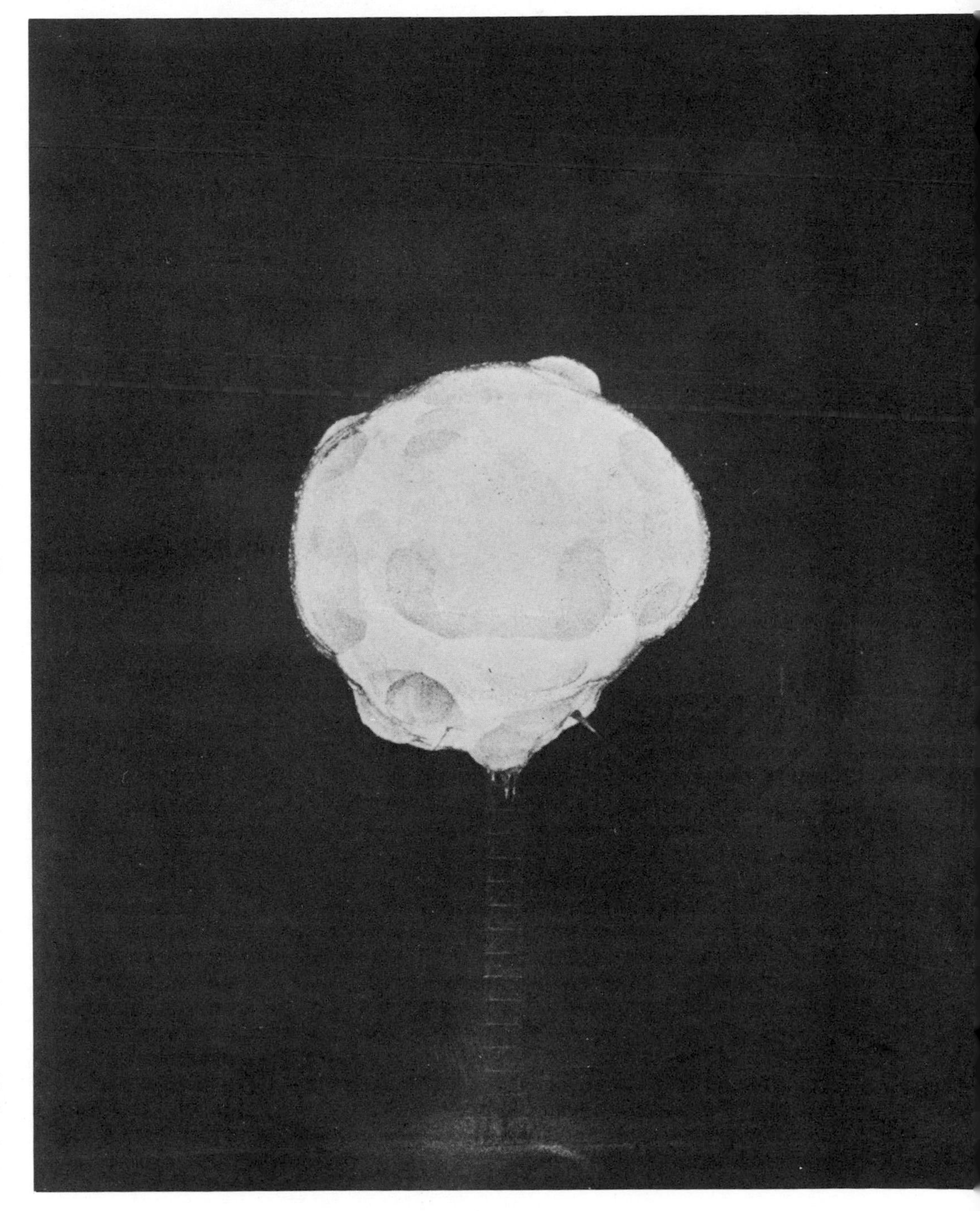

Magneto-optic photograph of atomic detonation at Nevada Proving Grounds. (Photo: E. G. & G.)

Telephone Laboratories who conceived the principle of the parallax-panoramagram camera, wherein a camera was rotated in an arc while taking 17 equally spaced pictures on a single plate. A vertical grid was positioned so that the pictures could be made on the single film. When the grid was placed in front of a transparency, the picture viewed would be completely stereoscopic in appearance. (This is the same principle used in advertising pictures where the model winks or smiles; in this case only two pictures are made.)

Using this grid basis, a mirror rotating at high speed swept across the gridded path. When a transparency was made of this negative and viewed in the same way in which the picture was made (the mirror was rotated at slow speed and the eye took the place of the camera), the action was slowed down in direct ratio to the rotational speeds of the mirror.

The Tuttle and Newcomb method consisted of printing these images onto motion-picture film to secure high-speed motion pictures; it is very similar in principle to the Suttanoff camera.

The Courtney-Pratt camera consists of a lenticular grid placed in front of the film plane. A movable lenticular grid is moved across the other plane as the shutter is opened, and a series of pictures at rates up to 200,000 per second can be obtained. These discrete pictures are very small. With small subjects a view camera can be the basic camera, making this method comparatively inexpensive.

Sequential stills have been made by using a multilens camera with the shutters opening in sequence, one after another. Muybridge established this technique, and Schardin, Naslin and Fayolle, and Naval Ordnance Test Stations have used it extensively.

The Russian camera uses a series of rotating mirrors taking advantage of the doubling of speed thus provided. The first mirror is good for 2,000,000 pictures per second, the second mirror 4,000,000, the third mirror 8,000,000, the fourth mirror 16,000,000, and the last mirror 32,000,000.

John Henning (left) *was a sculptor known for his reduced copies of the Parthenon frieze; Alexander Handyside Ritchie, also a sculptor, was an Associate of the Royal Scottish Academy. Photography by Hill and Adamson.* (Collection of Heinrich Schwartz)

DAVID OCTAVIUS HILL (1802—1870)

Biography

Shortly after the introduction of the calotype process in 1839, David Octavius Hill, like many other artists and engravers of his time, turned his attention to photography. The new process immediately stirred his imagination, but his intensive photographic activity did not start until the Spring of 1843. It was at this time that he decided to commemorate in one epic painting the founding of the Free Church of Scotland.

In order to paint the numerous participants in this ecclesiastical meeting, many of whom were in Edinburgh for only a short time, (some 470 members are shown on the final canvas) Hill decided to enlist the aid of photography. He did not, however, feel equal to this huge task, and so it was that Robert Adamson became his assistant.

Hill and Adamson collaborated on several hundred photographic portraits. A great number of these were preliminary "portrait studies" for the Free Church painting; others were portraits and group portraits of members of the aristocratic and fashionable Scottish society and of outstanding visitors to Edinburgh—a unique portrait gallery of the early Victorian period.

Hill and Adamson also did genre pictures and landscapes in Edinburgh and other Scottish cities, notably Newhaven and St. Andrews. In 1846, one year after Fox Talbot had published his album of calotypes, *Sun Pictures in Scotland,* Hill and Adamson edited *A Series of Calotype Views of St. Andrews* (21 calotype plates, plus one calotype vignette).

The calotypes by Hill and Adamson surpass in quality all other pictures produced by this process. (The calotype was soon to be displaced by the collodion process, invented in 1851.) The character of these pictures is described in the following quotation: "There is the same broad freedom of touch; no nice miniature stripplings, as if laid in by the point of a needle—no sharp-edged strokes; all is solid, massy, broad; more distinct at a distance than when viewed near at hand. The arrangement of the lights and shadows seems rather the result of a happy haste, in which half the effect was produced by design, half by accident, than of great labor and care; and yet how exquisite the general aspect."

For this work Hill and Adamson used a specially constructed camera. Their lens, an ordinary Petzval portrait combination possessing no particular aberration, is now in the Science Museum, London. It is likely that they also used a short-focus landscape lens, particularly during the beginning of their photographic activity.

The calotype process as well as the equipment used by Hill and Adamson required very long exposures (three to six minutes) and was limited in the main to outdoor photography. Most of their "interior photographs" were taken outdoors

Above: ***Lord Cockburn, family, and friends. Here is an example of Hill and Adamson's group photography.*** **(Collection of Heinrich Schwartz)**

Besides doing studies for the group of the Scottish Church Assembly, Hill and Adamson took many portraits of friends and famous visitors to Edinburgh. This is a photograph of the author, Mrs. Anna Brownell Jameson.

Newhaven fishwives. From a calotype print made by Hill and Adamson about 1844. It is an excellent example of their genre work. "They used the grain of the paper like painters," writes L. Moholy in A Hundred Years of Photography, *"to build up the tone values, avoiding hard lines and sharp contrasts. Unimportant details are absorbed partly by the grain, partly by the shadows."*

with the illusion of an interior being created with the aid of a curtain, a table, and a few books or other objects carefully arranged around their models.

It is not possible to distinguish Hill's and Adamson's individual contributions to their unique photographic work. However, the assumption is gaining ground that Adamson, too, had a very decisive part in the artistic merits of their work and that he was far more than merely the technical adviser and collaborator of his older friend. At any rate, after Adamson's departure from Edinburgh and his subsequent early death, Hill quit photography and devoted himself exclusively to painting.

Around 1860 Hill's interest in photography, apparently dormant since Adamson's death, was again awakened. In 1861 at Manchester and Edinburgh and in 1862 in London, Hill, in collaboration with the Scottish photographer, McGlashon, exhibited a number of photographic portraits and genre pictures as "contributions towards the further development of fine art in photography." One of these photographs ("Dr. John Brown and his cousin") was adjudged the best portrait shown at the Sixth Annual Exhibition of The Photographic Society of Scotland (1861). These late pictures of Hill and McGlashon were made by the collodion process. They were the last of Hill's photographic work.

After his death, Hill's photographs were recalled to public attention at the great exhibition of the Royal Photographic Society in 1898. His work was introduced in America in 1905 in the pages of the periodical, *Camera Work,* founded and edited by Alfred Stieglitz. Later his pictures were shown in exhibitions at the Albright Art Gallery in Buffalo.

A considerable number of Hill's waxed-paper negatives have been preserved, some of which will still yield prints of acceptable quality.

—Dr. Heinrich Schwartz

□

LEWIS W. HINE
(1874—1940)

Biography

When Lewis W. Hine started photographing, he did so with a purpose; he was a reporter in pictures, a visual educator awakening people to life. The human drama of immigrants at Ellis Island was his first theme, and from this beginning he went on to photograph the social-welfare and reform movements of the early 20th century. His work was published in social-work magazines, where photographs and text were combined for the first time to tell a story.

Hine's pioneer photostories were carefully planned. In January, 1909, came the first, "Child Labor in the Carolinas" by A. J. McKelway with "some human documents" (photographs) by Lewis W. Hine. A little

Lewis W. Hine / Ellis Island, 1905.

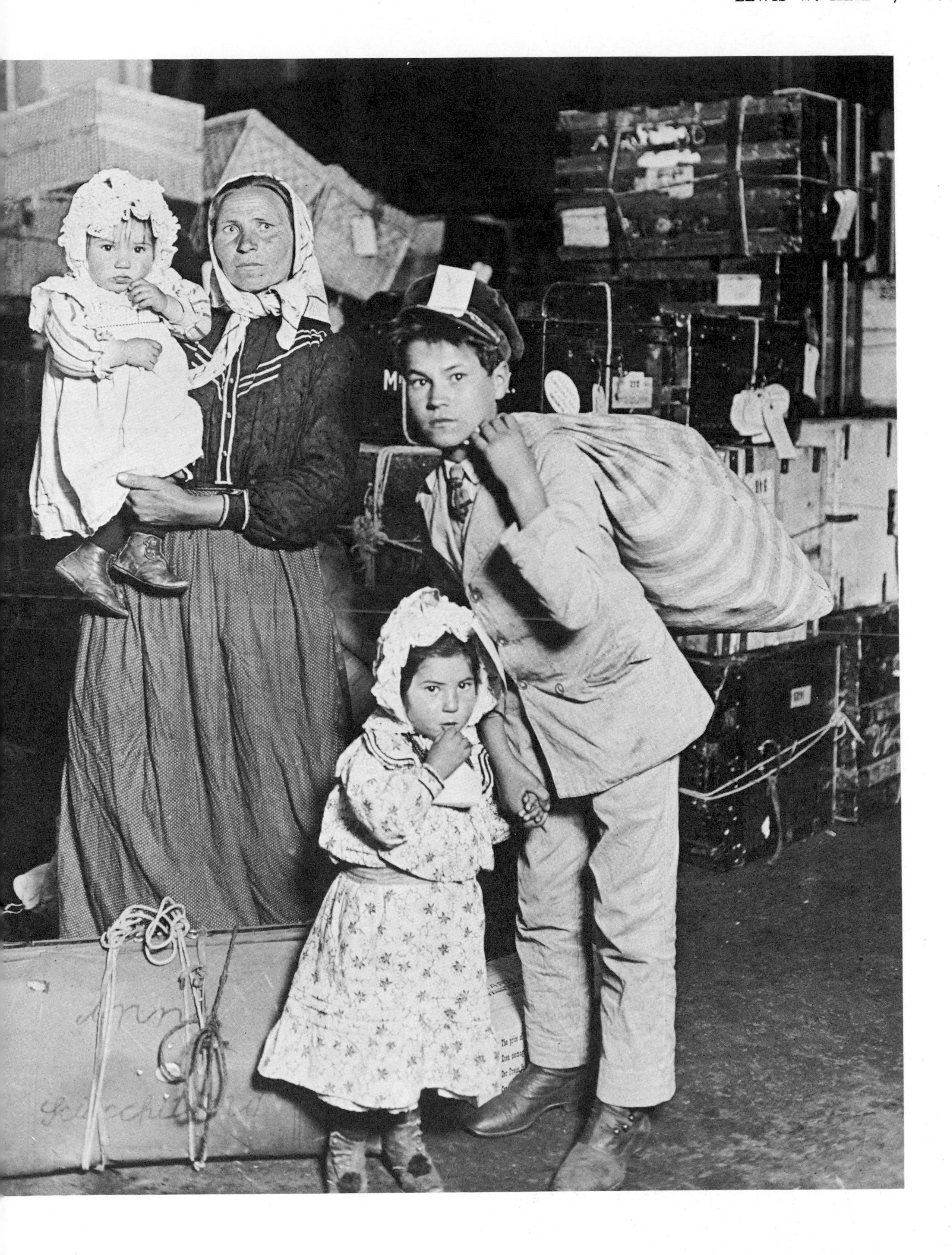

later the *Survey* printed a special eight-page insert on coated stock, "Southerners of Tomorrow," with photographs and captions by Hine. The same month the *Outlook* published "Day Laborers Before Their Time: A Story in Pictures by Lewis W. Hine," comprising eight pages and 14 illustrations.

By 1910, the picture story was well established as a means of pressing home significant sociological truths. In that year, *McClure's* published "Toilers of the Tenements: Where the Beautiful Things of the Great Shops are Made" by Elizabeth Shepley Sergeant, with photographs by Hine—16 in all, ten of them half-page cuts in a special insert with explanatory captions—and 18 pages of text.

Some years later, in 1914, the phrase "photostory" was used for the first time in the title of a *Survey* article "Children of Cotton: Photo-Story by Lewis W. Hine." Five years later the phrase appeared again, in the *Survey* of September 6, 1919, in "The Children's Burden in the Balkans: A Photo-Story by Lewis W. Hine and Homer Folks."

Hine worked closely with his editors and writers; he knew how to get the type of pictures required. For example, he would talk to the children in the mills, making surreptitious notes with his hand concealed in his coat pocket. Later he managed to photograph the entries of their birth in family Bibles on the pretext of gathering data for child life insurance. Such data was often indispensable for the purposes of the photostory.

Diplomacy was Hine's great asset in entering the forbidden zones where child labor flourished, whether in Southern cotton mills, New Jersey cranberry bogs and canneries, or New York City sweatshops. Today the problem of the camera reporter has to an extent been simplified by the 35 mm and smaller cameras, but Hine had to persuade first before he could blaze away with hazardous magnesium powder. Somehow he did persuade his subjects to forget their condition, to allow themselves to be photographed naturally.

An intuitive pictorial sense may be observed in all of Lewis Hine's work. Control of lighting and composition focus attention on his central theme, and heighten the emotional power of his photographs. Fortunately Hine's negatives have been preserved. They are now in the George Eastman House, Rochester, New York.

Lewis W. Hine / Child Labor, 1908.

HISTORIC ARCHITECTURE AND MONUMENT PHOTOGRAPHY

Laura Gilpin
Writer, Photographer, Santa Fe, New Mexico

[Throughout the world there are many structures which have survived the passage of time, either because of their architectural merit or historical significance. Here are ways and means of preserving these historical treasures through photography.]

• *Also see: House and Home Photography.*

Ever since photography became a practical means of securing an adequate image, historic architecture has held a prominent place in the choice of subject matter among photographers. Unfortunately many hundreds of these photographs are made without creative insight or historic knowledge and are therefore useful only as records.

During my travels to many parts of this continent, I have watched tourists quickly snapping shutters without giving any real thought to what was before the lens. Perhaps the very ease of operating today's perfected small cameras is dulling the perceptive qualities of the users.

The importance of understanding architecture—its function, its character, its general mass, its ornamentation, or lack of it—cannot be overemphasized. The importance of the setting—be it a city street, a mountainous landscape, a flat plane—has been considered by the architect, and should be equally considered by the photographer. Finally, the more the photographer knows of the historic background

This photo tells a good deal about Great Britain's past and present. Big Ben, the 13½-ton bell whose sound signifies "London" is behind the giant clock face of the tower of the Palace of Westminster where the British Parliament sits. The statue is of Queen Boadicea, who led the ancient Britons against the invading Romans. Leica M2 with Ilford Pan F film exposed at f/16 for ½ of a second. (The British Travel and Holidays Association) of the subject, the better he can interpret what lies before his camera.

EQUIPMENT

It is taken for granted that the photographer has a working knowledge of the technique of his craft before embarking upon such a specialized field. As a general rule, it is well to keep equipment as simple as possible, and, when traveling, as light as possible. Adequate tools, however, should be included since there are definite requirements for good work.

Cameras. View cameras with swing adjustments are best for the most serious work. Reflex and 35 mm cameras, particularly the interchangeable-lens type, are also capable of fine work.

Tripod. A tripod is a must, whether the camera is large or small. Slow speeds are often necessary, and a tripod assures a steady camera.

Lenses. Lenses of several focal lengths will always be needed. A normal focal length, a wide angle, and one or two lenses of long focal length should be part of the equipment.

Filters. A K2, a G, and an A filter will do most of the work required by any job. A polarizing filter should be included when windows and glass are to be photographed.

Meters. Many fine meters are available today. There may be occasions when an elaborate meter such as the S.E.I. Photometer can be very helpful in reading specific values at a distance.

Holders. Good sheet-film holders for large cameras and extra backs for roll-film cameras such as the Hasselblad provide the photographer with the choice of a variety of film material. A changing bag may sometimes save the day.

DESIGN

In any medium of expression, design is the foundation from which the message springs. Through design, the character and form of the object portrayed are expressed. The utilization of space is the concern of the artist, whether he is an architect, sculptor, painter, draughtsman, or photographer. The filling of an empty space, or an area of a given size and shape, with line, form, planes, tones, and color is a challenge.

The photographer must approach the problem in a manner different from other artists. He must learn to dissociate reality from the interpretation of it if he wishes to be creative. The groundglass, or finder, must be considered as a drawing board on which the elements of design are arranged and harmonized. This may be accomplished in a number of ways: by changing one's point of view; by choosing a different light so that a shadow may fall in a certain area; by utilizing different lenses; by changing the tone values with different filters. Too few photographers work to create a design by completely filling the size of the negative area. Far too many rely on cropping—one of the deadly sins for a photographer. Sometimes cropping is necessary, but the effort should always be made to fill the allotted space.

The photographer's pencils are rays of light, controlled not by hand, but through the lens, giving the user the power to speak. One may well compare photography to music. Photography uses waves of light composed and harmonized to express an idea; music uses waves of sound for the same purpose. Unless sound waves are arranged to fit a design containing a basic idea and are expressed through pattern, line harmony, and tonal values, they have no meaning and are merely a confusion of sound. One may say the same of photography.

Left: *Figure 1. The aspects of any building must be studied constantly under a variety of light conditions. This scene was made with morning light. Palace of the Governors, Uxmal, Yucatan.*

Below: *Figure 2. The same scene in afternoon light focuses the viewers attention on the fully lit background area.*

SCALE

Scale is a relative dimension and is often very difficult to obtain. The inclusion of an easily recognizable object, such as a human figure, is one solution, but special care must be used to maintain the relative proportion to the whole.

One of the most difficult architectural pictures to make is the "whole" view. Here the setting becomes important, and the structure must have relation to its surroundings. Care must be taken to have the subject remain the dominant feature, with the surroundings contributing to the over-all effect.

DETAIL

Architectural detail gives the photographer great scope for his imagination and creativeness. The use of texture, the play of light and shadow become elements to be arranged into design. Structures containing ornamentation may produce many fine pictures. Those containing only flat planes present an entirely different problem which must be solved satisfactorily. The aspects of any building or monument must be studied constantly under a variety of light conditions. Which is the most interpretative? Which will provide the mood of the structure? Often gathering clouds or a passing storm may enhance this quality of mood.

Figures 1 and 2 demonstrate the effect of the time of day on the relationship of two buildings. One was made in the morning light, the other in the late afternoon.

LINE AND TONE

A black-and-white photograph is composed of continuous tones, from

Figure 4. *There are times when an aerial photograph can give the best interpretation of the historic setting. Here Fort Union, New Mexico and the incoming Santa Fe Trail are shown.*

pure white to black. Within this scale lies a wealth of intermediary tonal values which the photographer may use to the advantage of his idea. Line is created by the reflected light from the edges of the object being photographed; tone, through the reflection of solid masses. Form is created through light and shade, for without shadow there can be no form, but only a flat plane. Thus, to express pure line, there should be no shadows; to express great bulk or form, there must be deep shadows —not necessarily deep in tonal value, but deep in drawing, thereby giving the impression of three dimensions.

Figure 3. *The Maya motif is emphasized in this view of the cornice of El Castillo, Chichen Itza, Yucatan.*

PROPORTION

Perfect proportion is a rare achievement in any art. The dictionary defines proportion as the harmonious relation of parts. It is only those structures most nearly approaching this ideal which remain in the world as great monuments of architecture.

A structure of fine proportions must be interpreted by a photograph of equally fine proportions. A structure stands before us, made of stone, wood, clay, or metal, assembled into areas of form, planes, and line, existing in three dimensions. The photograph interpreting this subject is made of tones and line assembled on a flat surface in such a way as to give the illusion of three dimensions. It can never be a copy, nor should it ever be, but the interpretation must convey the impression of the original to the highest degree possible.

HISTORIC BACKGROUND

Throughout the world there are areas of great buildings, monuments, and landmarks. Some foreknowledge of the history of any chosen site can really help any photographer as he fulfills his mission. There are the

Figure 5. *Abandoned house in the ghost town of Rosita, Colorado. The strong lines and deep tones in this photograph give strength of design to a scene that might have been much less interesting with all frontlighting.*

great temples of Greece, Egypt, Italy, Assyria, India, and of Central and South America, as well as those of our own and other countries.

With structures which are related to one another, the photographer must find a logical way to show this relationship. He must seek out the characteristic elements of the architecture, the motifs often repeated with variations. Illustrated here is such a motif on the cornice of the great temple at Chichen Itza, Yucatan (Figure 3). This is essentially characteristic of Maya architecture. Similar elements may be found in all regions, elements at once denoting a special region or culture.

Occasionally an aerial photograph can best reveal a group of buildings, such as the picture of Fort Union, New Mexico with the incoming Santa Fe Trail (Figure 4). The fort stands in ruins now, but from the air the stark walls seem more impressive. And beyond, the remnants of the Santa Fe Trail are clearly visible.

DOMESTIC ARCHITECTURE

Throughout the United States there are many houses that have survived the passage of time, either because of their architectural merit or their historical significance. The principles already discussed apply equally here. In the West one phase of American history is the story of the ghost towns of the now defunct mining days—buildings falling into decay, abandoned, left to time and the weather. Here are countless subjects for any photographer (Figure 5).

CONCLUSION

Wherever man has lived on earth he has left his mark, be it a humble hut or magnificent temple. He has erected his dwelling and his shrine to suit a particular need. From the differences of his needs and beliefs, due to location and to race, has come a vast procession of buildings and monuments. Photography, because of its ability to record unusual and fleeting effects, is more capable than any other medium of interpreting for us much of this structural procession. It remains for photographers of the present to complete what has been begun; and for photographers of the future to use this wonderful medium with the utmost skill and keen vision.

HISTORY OF MOTION PICTURES

JAMES CARD
Vice-Director and Curator of Motion Pictures, George Eastman House, Rochester, New York

[The history of cinematography is closely related to the history of photography in general. Presented here is the development of motion-picture technique from early animated drawings to the inception of television. The work of Muybridge, Marey, and Edison is discussed, as well as early movies like *The Great Train Robbery, Intolerance,* and the Mack Sennett comedies.]

• *Also see: Chronology of Photographic Inventions; Cinematography, Professional; History of Photography.*

THE ESSENTIAL ELEMENTS OF MOTION pictures are the same as those of still photography: a camera, a lens, a vehicle for the retention of images, and a projector for reconstituting the images in arbitrarily controlled situations. The history of motion pictures has been, like that of photography, dependent on the development of optics, chemistry, mechanics, and electronics, except for one important difference. This difference lies in the recognition of the phenomenon of persistence of vision.

It is well known that the effect of motion on the screen is the result of an illusion growing out of a split-second lag in our optico-nervous reactions. This retinal retention of images (persistence of vision) is the single physiological fact that enables us to experience the illusion of motion in watching an interrupted series of images which space out the successive phases of actual movement. It is an arresting thought that the entire art and science of both television and motion pictures is wholly dependent on this one basic illusory perception.

EARLY HISTORY

The history of motion pictures parallels that of photography, taking a specialized course of its own only at points where the phenomenon of the eye's "afterimage" is exploited in order to convey the illusion of images in movement. The most decisive of these turning points developed out of the work of the British photographer Eadweard Muybridge, when, in 1872, he

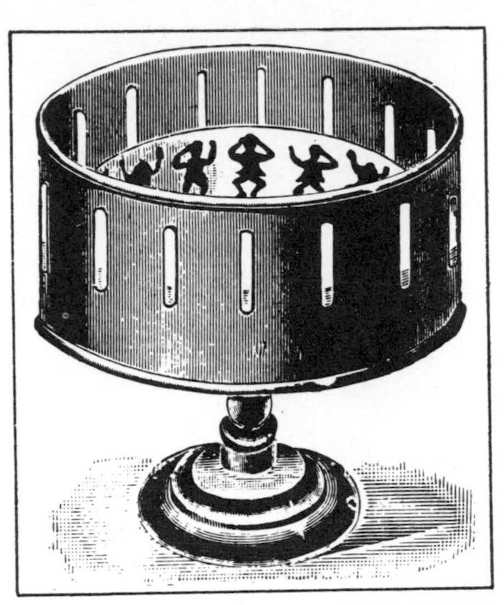

Right: *The Zoetrope was an early and simple device for viewing animated drawings.* (Museum of Modern Art Film Library)

Below: *The Kinetoscope peep-show viewing machine, perfected by Edison in 1891. The series of images passed over* R *and* S, *beneath the viewing cone,* E, *and above the electric illumination,* L.

Top: *The Kinetoscope Arcade in San Francisco, when the motion picture was comparatively new.* (Museum of Modern Art Film Library)

Bottom: *Lumière comedy. This is a single frame from the outdoor moving-picture story by Lumière. Notice the large perforations.* (Museum of Modern Art Film Library)

accepted an assignment from California's Governor Leland Stanford to photograph Stanford's horses in action at his Palo Alto track. Muybridge at that time had to work with the slow wet-collodion plates. His best efforts from 1877 to 1879 produced little more than silhouettes of horses trotting and galloping past a line-up of cameras.

Nevertheless his studies of animal locomotion were widely circulated and created a considerable stir in the world of art. Artists found it impossible to believe that some of the—to them—grotesque postures assumed by the animals in the Muybridge photographs could be genuine phases of normal movement.

Muybridge countered by adapting two common parlor toys to provide a primitive projector. One, the zoetrope, was a device for viewing painted or drawn images through slits in a revolving drum. As early as 1853 the zoetrope had been combined with a magic-lantern projector to achieve projection of moving images—but only painted images.

Muybridge succeeded in adapting his animal photographs to a combination zoetrope-magic lantern, which he named the Zoopraxiscope. When he demonstrated this machine in 1879 for his patron, Governor Stanford, Muybridge had really created motion pictures. His presentation for members of the San Francisco Art Society in May of 1880 became a truly historic occasion. It was the earliest publicly recorded showing of projected images of moving objects which had been photographed instantaneously. One newspaper reporter did not exaggerate when he wrote of this event in the *San Francisco Alta* of May 5, 1880: "Mr. Muybridge has laid the foundation of a new method of entertaining the people."

Etienne-Jules Marey, a French physiologist specializing in the study of the circulation of the blood, became keenly interested in the photographic analysis of movement; he was familiar with the work of Muybridge but wished to improve on it. In 1882 he began experimenting with a photographic gun, shooting the images of birds in flight and recording them on glass plates. In Germany, Ottomar Anschuetz, also stimulated by the discoveries of Muybridge, began experiments in 1883 which would lead to important results. The availability of Kodak roll film, which had arrived in Europe by 1887, widened the possibilities for Marey and the many other experimenters who were rapidly joining the lists of pioneers in motion photography.

THOMAS EDISON

Thomas Edison, aware of the progress made by Marey and Muybridge, saw the possibility of adding moving-picture images to the sound records he had succeeded in reproducing with his phonograph. He assigned an assistant, W. K. Laurie Dickson, to work on the project.

Two basic problems vexed inventors attempting to devise a practical motion-picture system. The first was to find a means of conveying the vast number of separate images needed to synthesize movement. Glass plates, the most obvious vehicle, could transport dozens of images spirally arranged, but the size and consequent weight of the plate became an immediate limiting factor. Edison's "sound images" had been engraved on wax cylinders for his phonograph; he tried to place photo images in the same way on a rotating cylinder.

The second basic problem was to build a camera that would transport the light-sensitive material past the lens, intermittently, in unequal time intervals. For satisfactory results, the image-receiving material had to remain before the lens for a longer period of time than it took to replace it with material ready to receive the next successive impression. What was required was a light-sensitive material of such flexible nature and hardy structure that it could sustain the stress of being moved intermittently before the camera lens. Further, the material had to be transported by a mechanical device that could accomplish this action steadily and with a minimum of violence.

In 1889 the availability of 35 mm Eastman Kodak celluloid film solved the first part of the problem for Edison and Dickson. Edison perforated it so that the sprocket teeth of gears would engage and transport the flexible film without difficulty.

EARLY MOTION CAMERAS

With the problem of a suitable vehicle for the images solved, the need for an effective intermittent action became acute. Some inventors, like Le Prince and Jenkins, built machines with intermittently

The Great Train Robbery. *A still from the 1903 motion picture directed and photographed by Edwin S. Porter for the Edison Company. Several new techniques were used in this picture, including the masking technique.* (Museum of Modern Art Film Library)

revolving lenses which were brought before continuously moving film. Marey's assistant, Georges Demeny, evolved a camera with the "beater" or dog movement which was adapted by the American inventor Thomas Armat in his Vitascope projector. A French pioneer, Léon Bouly, in 1892 patented a Cinématographe that passed unperforated film between two gripping rollers with portions of their surfaces indented so that as the recessed surfaces of the rollers met, the film would momentarily be arrested in its forward movement.

At the end of 1893 Edison decided that his motion-picture camera, the Kinetograph, was successful enough for him to begin manufacturing pictures commercially, and he built the celebrated Black Maria in West Orange. This first Edison studio was little more than a large *camera obscura* itself: a shed built on a turntable so that the whole building could be rotated to catch sunlight through an opening in its roof.

Edison's patent applications and existing records are vague about the actual mechanism of his first camera, the Kinetograph. His choice of a practical intermittent mechanism must have been a good one but, curiously, he did not use it in his Kinetoscope viewing device, the peep-box machine he developed to display the little films being produced in the Black Maria. There was some delay in manufacturing the Kinetoscope, so that at the Chicago World's Fair of 1893, it was Ottomar Anschuetz's Tachyscope and Muybridge's Zoopraxiscope that represented motion pictures to the visitors. (The Tachyscope presented images that were arranged on a whirling disc, intermittently illuminated by a spark.)

In April of 1894 the Edison Kinetoscopes were placed on exhibition in New York City. The film used in the Kinetoscope was 35 mm wide, with the perforations that were to become a world standard for a half a century. Film was loaded in the Kinetoscope on a spool bank and passed continuously in an endless ribbon before the single viewing lens; it was illuminated by a single electric bulb. The spectator's view of the film was intermittently interrupted, by a revolving blade, at the rate of approximately forty times per second, the rate per image at which the Kinetograph had exposed the film.

The Kinetoscope, with its continuously moving film, was obviously no solution to the problem of projection. Much greater illumination was required; greater clarity and steadiness was needed for the great enlargement, which only a momentarily, completely immobilized image could provide. But Edison was positively against the idea of projection and later declared under oath in court that his films had not been projected in his laboratory. This testimony was contradicted by Dickson who insisted that he had demonstrated to his employer not only projected images, but images projected in conjunction with synchronized words.

While Edison resisted projection, countless mechanics in all parts of the world were striving to achieve it. More than the Kinetoscope itself, it was the appearance of the Edison Kinetoscope films with their brilliant, well-defined images on tough nitrate of cellulose that provided the breakthrough needed to bring

Birth Of A Nation. *A long shot from D. W. Griffith's motion picture showing Sherman's march to the sea.* (Museum of Modern Art Film Library)

A close-up scene from Birth Of A Nation *showing Henry B. Walthall and Lillian Gish in the famous D. W. Griffith motion picture, filmed in 1915 for Epoch Producing Corporation.*

Movable stage. Set on complicated tracks, the stage could be kept facing the sun and the camera in the house at left could be moved up for a semi close-up. This elaborate available-light equipment was used for photographing scenes with the Mutograph camera in 1895. (Scientific American)

motion pictures to enthusiastic spectators throughout the world.

DEVELOPMENT OF PROJECTORS

Louis Lumière who, with his brother Auguste, was already in the photographic business in Lyons, France, needed only a brief examination of Edison's films and Kinetoscope in the late summer of 1894 to launch him into his work on a machine that would not only expose motion-picture-film negatives, but would print positives and project them as well. The versatile and practical Lumière Cinématographe was in successful operation at the end of 1894. It used pull-down claws, activated by a triangular cam intermittent, to advance the film. The film was 35 mm and differed from Edison's only in its perforations.

The year 1895 was the year of multiple premieres of various motion-picture systems in most of the world capitals. Ingenious inventors needed, it seemed, only to get their hands on a roll of Edison's Kinetoscope film to devise some kind of a machine that would put the images on a screen. In 1895 Robert Paul projected a film in London and the Latham brothers presented their Panoptikon in New York. Jenkins and Armat demonstrated their Phantascope in Georgia, while the German pioneer Max Skladonowsky booked his Bioscope at the Wintergarten in Berlin. Casimir Sivan produced films in Switzerland, and the Lumières proudly began their first public showings at the Grand Café in Paris.

Moving-camera technique. Filming one of the final scenes of Intolerance, *D. W. Griffith is shown crouched behind the Pathé camera and G. W. (Billy) Bitzer is standing. The moving camera was one of the many novel techniques of film making introduced or adopted by Griffith.*

During this crucial first year, Edison stubbornly refused to produce a projector. By March of 1896, with both cameras and projectors appearing in profusion around the world, many with startling improvements, Edison still did not have a projector of his own. He finally yielded to economic pressures and arranged with Thomas Armat to market the Armat Vitascope, a relatively crude device with the Demeny-type beater movement, as an Edison projector. In April of 1896 the Edison films were finally projected, with their maker's blessing, at the Koster and Bial Music Hall in New York City. Edison then lost no time in perfecting a Projecting Kinetoscope of his own which featured an extremely sophisticated and highly satisfactory geneva-cross intermittent movement.

EARLY MOVIES

The year 1895 saw the arrival of motion pictures; 1896 became the year of rapid exploitation of their potentialities. The films of 1895, made predominately by Edison and Lumière, were, with just one notable exception, simple records of movement. Trains arriving, waves crashing against rocky shores, traffic in the streets, *cuirassiers* galloping and pigeons flying provided marvels enough.

The one exception was, in 1895, Lumière's *L'Arroseur Arrosé* (*The Sprinkler Sprinkled*). Not only was this short film slapstick comedy, it told a story. Most important of all, it told a made-up story. It was a controlled directed film made to provoke a definite emotion and as such quite different from all the others that were simple records of events.

No one was more aware of the possibilities opened up by the Lumière films than France's Georges Méliès, professional conjurer. Failing in his attempt to buy an apparatus from the Lumières, Méliès bought a camera from Robert Paul of London and, by April 1896, had made his own first film. In May of that year, Lumière sent two cameramen to Russia to film the coronation of Czar Nicholas II, and the documentary was born. By October, Méliès had pushed the cinema into its other domain: he made his first stop-motion trick film. Within the next two years Georges Méliès had independently brought to the medium such commonplaces of today as stop-motion, multiple exposures, fade-ins and fade-outs, rudimentary cartoons, backdrops and sets, and the use of artificial lighting.

In the final years of the 19th century, inventions and refinements in motion-picture systems arrived in such profusion that by the time of the Paris Exposition of 1900 a truly astounding array of devices was ready for public inspection. There were dialogue films at the exposition with the voices of Sarah Bernhardt and Coquelin. The Lumière's showed hand-colored films on a screen 48 feet high by 69 feet wide to 25,000 viewers at a single session. Raoul Grimoin-Sanson's Cinéorama featured 10 radially mounted, synchronized projectors showing color films on a screen 30 feet high that totally surrounded the spectators. "Substandard," compact systems for home and school use were exhibited. Except for refinements in emulsions, color systems and acoustical devices, the cinema had arrived technologically by 1900.

PIONEER PRODUCERS

For the next 50 years, the history and development of motion pictures was principally influenced by the creative efforts of gifted artists; by their enthusiastic, often fanatical acceptance by an international audience; and by the sometimes countering effects of economic ambitions inspired by the motion picture's rapidly assumed status as a major industry. The battling tycoons and the wars of rival combinations were spectacular, and their effects often deadly, but of only transistory meaning. The contributions of the film artists, on the other hand, have become part of our cultural heritage.

From 1901 to 1906 the pioneer producers, Robert Paul, James Williamson, and Cecil Hepworth in England, Skladonowsky and Messter in Germany, Georges Méliès, Ferdinand Zecca and Emil Cohl in France, Edwin Porter, Sigmund Lubin, and J. Stuart Blackton in this country, maintained a lively competition in the output of trick films and "chase" films that seemed to have exhausted all the possibilities of camera magic and rudimentary editing.

It remained for an American film to become the earliest undisputed international success: Edwin Porter's *The Great Train Robbery,* made in 1903 for the Edison Company. *The Great Train Robbery* was neither the first story film nor the first Western, nor the first full one-reeler, but it was undoubtedly the most successful combination of all those attributes. When three years later Porter followed his masterpiece with *The Dream of a Rarebit Fiend* (1906), leadership seemed to have passed to the Edison Company.

But in 1908 the American Biograph and Mutoscope Company, Edison's earliest and most prolific rival, employed the first great film director, D. W. Griffith. The next year Griffith hired Mary Pickford, who was destined to become the first truly international star, and the eclipse of Edison as a film producer was complete.

Griffith and his agreeable cameraman, Billy Bitzer, shared enthusiasm and special talent for the new medium. With a sure eye for personalities that would register in the Victorian approach he used, Griffith had by 1912 brought to the film public such enduring players as Blanche Sweet, Lillian Gish, Mae Marsh, Henry B. Walthall, and Lionel Barrymore, who, with Mary Pickford, ensured that the star system would forever dominate the entertainment film.

Meanwhile the exported images of other players were crystallizing the world-wide acceptance of movies. The comedian Max Linder from France and the tragedienne Asta Nielsen of Denmark influenced the acting styles of films in all countries; they were acknowledged, with Mary Pickford and our first cowboy hero, Broncho Billy Anderson (Max Aronson), as superior and eminently imitable beings.

MOVIES MATURE

In 1915 Griffith capped the era of the growing seriousness of film content with his still controversial *Birth of A Nation.* An epic and partisan treatment of the Civil War and the reconstruction period, this film provided an encyclopedic demonstration of all Griffith had learned about the peculiarities of the film medium, fused and focused to a burning point of emotional effectiveness.

It is true that by 1912 Italian directors had achieved massive scope in spectacles like *Quo Vadis*; and by 1913 the French director Jasset in *A Child of Paris* and August Blom, a Dane, in *Atlantis* had proved themselves more mature and even smoother technicians than Griffith. But if doubts remained regarding the sheer virtuosity of Griffith's genius for film making, they were to be resolved in his favor by his next film, *Intolerance* (1916), which has still not been surpassed in sheer size or audacity of conception and execution.

In Sweden the director Mauritz Stiller and the actor-director Victor Seastrom were developing an approach to the film that was more imaginative and was expressed in acting more natural than the prevailing styles in this country. World War I prevented American directors and audiences from seeing much of the rapidly maturing cinema of northern Europe.

For the most part, American films had taken on a deceptive glow, thanks to a standardized excellence of cinematography that placed all emphasis on well-lighted, luxurious sets and on flattering lighting for players whose personalities so beguiled the fans that audiences could not be distracted by the arrival of an occasional masterpiece from Sweden. It was the era of the langorously backlighted female star; Gloria Swanson and Norma Talmadge shared the adulation of the faithful, along with Wallace Reid and

Charlie Chaplin and Jackie Coogan in The Kid, *1921, one of the great comedy pictures of the time.* (George Eastman House)

Thomas Meighan. Only in the action films of William S. Hart, the rollicking comedies of Douglas Fairbanks, the rough and tumble of Mack Sennett's farces did there seem to be preserved a feeling for essentially American cinema.

GERMAN FILM MAKERS

While World War I was still being fought, a group of Reinhardt-trained German players formed around a cadre of extremely imaginative designers and directors. The actors, led by Werner Krauss, Emil Jannings, Pola Negri, Conrad Veidt, and Lil Dagover responded to the understanding direction of F. W. Murnau, Fritz Lang, and Artur Robison. The directors persuaded noble work from designers Hans

Vilma Banky and Rudolph Valentino in The Son Of The Sheik, *1926.* (George Eastman House)

Poelsig, Robert Herlth, and Paul Leni, and cameramen Karl Freund, Carl Hoffmann, and Fritz Wagner to produce a long series of splendid films that carried their momentum through to 1926.

Wiene's *The Cabinet of Dr. Caligari* (1919) stirred artists the world over with its expressionistic reminder that the cinema was not required to deal exclusively in photographic realism. After the war Lang's *Nibelungen* (1923), *Metropolis* (1926); Murnau's *Last Laugh* (1924), *Faust* (1926); Lubitsch's *Madame DuBarry* (1919); and G. W. Pabst's *Joyless Street* (1925) and *The Love of Jeanne Ney* (1927) placed German films in a position of preeminence that they never again attained.

While Hollywood attracted most of the German artists responsible for what appeared to be a summit of artistry in the silent era, Russian directors startled the whole cinema world with their dynamic techniques of film editing which bore more resemblance to theories of music than to previous concepts of theater and cinema. Sergei Eisenstein with *Potemkin* (1925) and Pudovkin with *Storm over Asia* (1928) contributed these and other enduring masterpieces.

DEVELOPMENT OF COMEDY

Mack Sennett had evolved a comedy technique that was to mark a high point in the progress of American films. A frustrated comedian, Sennett had left Griffith and the Biograph Company to form his own comedy-making factory. Admitting his debt to the French primitives, Sennett developed chase and frenetic slapstick along lines as carefully planned and tellingly cut as the later films of the great Russian directors. When Chaplin arrived to take his place with Sennett's Keystone group in 1913, the system was prepared to receive his genius.

Under the tutelage of Sennett, Harold Lloyd, Roscoe Arbuckle, Ben Turpin, and Harry Langdon developed their specialties. Later, working with Arbuckle, Buster Keaton evolved his own style. The great films of these comedians, Keaton's *The General* (1926) and *The Navigator* (1924), Lloyd's *The Freshman* (1925) and *Safety Last* (1923), the films of Chaplin, and the best comedies of Mack Sennett remain today among the most unique and finest offerings of the American cinema.

In serious films, Greta Garbo and Lillian Gish sometimes brought the art of cinematic pantomime to memorable heights. The influx of foreign directors was propitious for the American film: Seastrom directed Lillian Gish in one of her greatest performances, in *The Wind* (1928), and Murnau produced a fine film when he made *Sunrise* (1927) in this country. But native directors Henry King with *Tol'able David* (1921) and King Vidor in *The Big Parade* (1925) produced authentic American masterpieces.

ARRIVAL OF SOUND

The arrival of the dialogue film was gradual, but its final and total overthrow of the silent drama was accomplished in a single year: 1929.

From 1900 to 1926 synchronized sound systems had made sporadic appearances but inadequate amplification doomed these early efforts. The "talkies" awaited the development of the vacuum tube. The popular success of the Vitaphone when it appeared as a synchronized phonographic disk system in 1926 was climaxed by the excitement over *The Jazz Singer* (1927). Sound on film eliminated the practical defects of the Vitaphone and by 1930 the silent era had ended.

Color too made its approach to the cinema tentatively over the years. Hand-colored, stenciled, and multitoned films were common throughout motion-picture history. Kinemacolor, Prizmacolor, Kelley Color, Dunning Color, and Cinecolor were among the various processes briefly attempted and soon discarded. *The Toll of the Sea* (1922) was an early two-color Technicolor feature; not until the process was refined as a multilayer system was Technicolor adequate to produce the reasonably effective *Becky Sharp* in 1935. From that time on, the all-color feature became a frequent attraction.

In the United States, the directors who made the most graceful adaptation to the techniques of dialogue films were such veterans of the silent era as King Vidor, John Ford, and Henry King, rather than stage directors hurriedly brought in to cope with speech. One exception recruited from the theater was Orson Welles, whose *Citizen Kane* (1941) continues to enjoy the admiration of a wide international audience. European directors in Hollywood contributed much to a maturing cinema: Ernst Lubitsch, Billy Wilder, Anatole Litvak, and Fred Zinnemann were among the most successful.

THE COMING OF TELEVISION

After World War II television helped deprive the cinema in this country of more than half its regular weekly audience, which had numbered at its peak as high as 90 million persons. In panic attempts to produce a "novelty" as effective as the dialogue film had proved to be in 1929, the industry in the 1950's turned back to the beginning of the century for wide-screen presentations, Cinerama, and to Professor Henri Chrétien's anamorphic lenses of 1928 to establish Cinemascope and its multiple variations.

Profound economic upheavals in

A scene from Cineguild's production of Charles Dickens' Great Expectations *as Young Pip stands before the grave of his mother and father. Directed by David Lean, 1946.* (George Eastman House)

the American film industry brought more essential changes in the pattern of production. The majority of Hollywood studios devoted themselves almost entirely to making films for television, while enormous financial resources were marshalled to sustain American production of multimillion dollar films overseas. Though American films have managed to maintain an international popularity, their prestige has suffered over the years from critical competition in world film festivals, headed by those of Cannes, Venice, and Berlin.

Heralded by festival prizes, among the great films by Italian directors that have enjoyed wide success and admiration were Vittorio De Sica's *Bicycle Thief* (1948) and Federico Fellini's *La Dolce Vita* (1960). Michelangelo Antonioni's *L'Avventura* (1960) seemed to many critics to sum up the era's trend toward a nontraditional film of completely inconclusive content.

The French cinema had, with the coming of dialogue, assumed an extraordinary level of brilliance paced by such artists as René Clair, Jean Renoir, and Marcel Carné. The 1950's found young film critics becoming directors, and Alain Resnais, François Truffaut, Claude Chabrol, and Jean-Luc Godard challenged the skill of aging masters.

The eminent British directors, David Lean and Laurence Olivier, had their literary successes like *Great Expectations* (1946) and *Henry V* (1944), only to see a new school of brash "realists" come into vogue with crisp films by Karel Reisz and Tony Richardson.

In Sweden, Alf Sjöberg *(Miss Julie,* 1950) and Ingmar Bergman are both men of the theatre, as were Seastrom and Stiller; like their predecessors they admirably hold up the best traditions of a great Swedish cinema.

The film festivals also brought to world attention films from countries never before having enjoyed wide notice outside their own language areas. *Rashomon* (1951) opened to the world the skill of director Akira Kurosawa and paved the way to thousands of foreign screens for other fascinating Japanese films. Argentina was found to have a sensitive cinema, especially in the work of Leopoldo Torre-Nilsson. And in the hands of its untiring irrepressibles, Luis Bunuel (*Los Olvidados,* 1951) and Jean Cocteau (*Orphée,* 1950), and above all in the genius of Denmark's Carl-Th Dreyer (*Day of Wrath,* 1943), the world cinema has found the means to establish pinnacles of achievement in the art of motion pictures that will remain as formidable challenges for the future.

The Cabinet of Dr. Caligari. *This German expressionist film, made in 1919, was directed by Robert Wiene.* (George Eastman House)